THREE ACTS

A reader's guide to Plato's Theaetetus. This Socratic companion serves as an introduction to philosophy through an exploration of ethics, epistemology, psychology, and metaphysics.

A Commentary
on Plato's
Theaetetus
By
Brandon Spun

En Route Books and Media
St. Louis, MO

En Route Books and Media, LLC
5705 Rhodes Avenue
St. Louis, MO 63109
Contact us at contactus@enroutebooksandmedia.com
Cover credit: Brandon Spun
© 2022 Brandon Spun

ISBN-13: 978-1-956715-73-6
Library of Congress Control Number 2022942109

All rights reserved. No part of this book may be reproduced, stored in a retrieval system, or transmitted in any form, or by any means, electronic, mechanical, photocopying, or otherwise, without the prior written permission of the author.

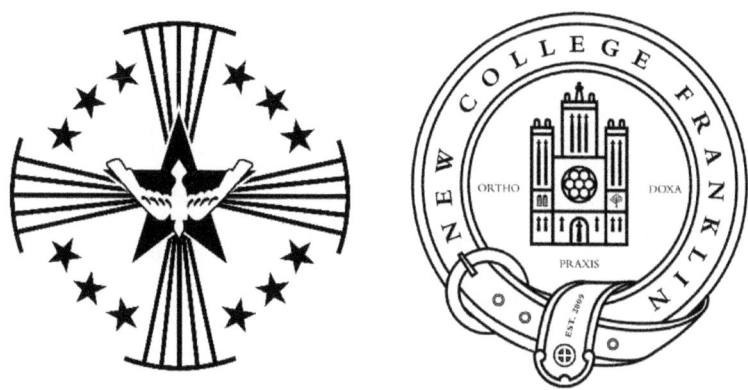

I dedicate this Commentary to the God of friendship who has called us to be conformed to the Everlasting Image and also to my family and friends, particularly Elijah and Beatrice, as well as my mother and father, who make that Image known to me perpetually.

Acknowledgments

Years ago, I suggested to my St. John's tutor Ms. Elizabeth Blettner that I write a commentary comparing Plato's *Republic* and Aristotle's *Nicomachean Ethics*. She gently conveyed her concern that I might get lost in such an undertaking. If I have gotten lost here, I hope it has not been quite in the manner she feared. I owe much to her guidance, to her love of Plato, music, the classics, and to her faith in the Word of God, near to all those who seek him in truth. I am grateful to my cohort during the St. John's days. We were blessed in friendship and fellowship in faith. I mention their names because they continue to be signs of joy and support: Stephanie Anderson, Geoffrey Bagwell, William Hawkins, Nick Kahm, Joseph Keating, and Jared Ortiz.

The beginning of this project reaches back to my undergraduate years at SUNY Geneseo, where Bill Edgar read the *Theaetetus* with his philosophy students. I am also grateful to UPS, who funded my graduate education for a time and made it possible to attend Holy Apostles College and Seminary (HACS) in Cromwell, Connecticut, where I received an education which makes this commentary possible. Their philosophy program in Christian Wisdom is taught by true masters. Doctors Eduardo Bernot, Randall Colton, Robert Delfino, Curtis Hancock, Peter Redpath, and Timothy Smith all have a marked influence on my thinking and this commentary in particular. I am grateful for their generous and rich communication of the great tradition.

New College Franklin has been my teaching home for the last decade. Without the loving support of the Dean of the College, Gregory Wilbur, this project would be inconceivable. He has provided encouragement, friendship, and an unparalleled opportunity to remain immersed in a vibrant learning community. Nathan Johnson, our Head of Program, in sacrificial friendship proofread an early version of this text and co-taught a course on the *Theaetetus* with me. He has been invaluable as an intellectual peer and personal friend (Prov. 27:17). I would not want to forget the many students who have passed through our Arithmetic class where we have read this dialogue. Whatever clarity I have attained in the commentary could not have been achieved without learning from them.

I thank my family. Philosophy remains a human project to me because of them. And I thank God, for it has not been my diligence alone which has produced whatever fruits are found here. Beside the kind providences listed in the paragraphs above, God has often answered prayer when I have been lost. It is no failure to frame one's studies in prayer, to ask even for aid in the daily tasks. Centuries ago, Avicenna (Ibn Sina), a Muslim philosopher, found himself incapable of penetrating Aristotle's *Metaphysics*.

> In such moments of baffled inquiry he would leave his books, perform the requisite ablutions, then hie to the mosque, and continue in prayer till light broke on his difficulties. Deep into the night he would continue his studies, stimulating his senses by occasional cups of wine, and even in his dreams problems would pursue him and work out their solution. Forty times, it is said, he read through the *Metaphysics* of Aristotle, till the words were imprinted on his memory; but their meaning was hopelessly obscure, until one day they found illumination from the little commentary by Fārābī, which he bought at a bookstall for the small sum of three dirhems. So great was his joy at the discovery, thus made by help of a work from which he had

Acknowledgments

expected only mystery, that he hastened to return thanks to God, and bestowed an alms upon the poor.[1]

I hope that Christians will be no less ardent than Avicenna in their studies, particularly in surrounding and supplementing their study with prayer. I must say that I seem somewhat diffident in light of his example. It is a pleasure to reflect on a few of his countless mercies.

With Much Gratitude,
Brandon Spun
December 2021

---

[1] Britannica, Encyclopedia. (1911). Avicenna. In *Encyclopedia Britannica* (11th ed., Vol. 3, p. 62-3).

Foreword

Brandon Spun's unusually rich commentary on the *Theaetetus* is sure to provoke much thought. Intended as a reader's interactive guide, it will be especially helpful to those coming to this difficult dialogue for the first time. Most striking is Mr. Spun's deep personal engagement with the dialogue and its broad range of topics, an engagement that combines philosophic logos with the Logos of the New Testament. "We are made," Mr. Spun writes, "to know and be known." The commentary invites readers to a similar personal engagement with Plato's drama and to a reflection that transcends mere scholarship and *explication de texte*.

It is easy to get lost in the labyrinth that is the *Theaetetus*. To keep us aware of the big picture, and as a reminder that the work is above all a drama in which things *happen*, Mr. Spun neatly divides Plato's complex work into three "acts," corresponding to young Theaetetus's three attempts to answer the question What is knowledge? These answers are perception, true opinion, and true opinion with an account. The running commentary operates at many levels. At the most basic level, it gives the reader valuable help with the meaning of individual Greek words and phrases. At another, it offers a wealth of perceptive and nicely formulated observations on the dialogue and its thematic connection with other dialogues, various works by Aristotle, and Aquinas's *Summa Theologica*. At yet another level, the commentary raises many pointed "questions for discussion." These questions concern the nature and kinds of knowing, wisdom, language, and the good. To this Socratic search for eternal truth, the author adds "a sense of the historical development of these questions as epitomized by Aristotle and Thomas Aquinas, among others."

I end with one of my favorite passages in the commentary. Toward the end of Act II, Theaetetus, guided (or perhaps misguided) by Socrates's aviary image, tries one last time to save the definition of knowledge as true opinion. His effort fails. Mr. Spun, in a moment of inspired synthesis, connects this crucial elenchus with various biblical texts, Aristotle's *On the Soul*, a passage from the *Summa*, Shakespeare's *Hamlet*, and pictures of two different birds that could easily be confused. He writes:

> Man is a fallible spirit! Even as we share in some limited way in the divine light (Gen. 1:26), we remain prone to mistake and false opinion. This hunter who takes hold of knowledge must therefore be capable both of the true and the false. We are spirits, participants in the divine nature, rational creatures, and also fallible opiners (Acts 17-18).
>
> And yet, we err only because and when we know something!

The excerpt beautifully captures the *wonder at being human* that pervades and enlivens Mr. Spun's generous guide to the *Theaetetus*. It also highlights what Socrates seems most intent on doing in the dialogue: using the search for a definition of knowledge to defend the possibility of error, without which inquiry and the philosophic midwife's art would be pointless.

Peter Kalkavage
St. John's College
Annapolis

Contents

Acknowledgments i

Foreword by Peter Kalkavage v

Introduction to Commentary 1

Commentary 8
    General & Detailed Outline 8

    Dramatic-Mimetic Beginnings 10
    First Reading 10
    142a-145e   Introduction, Wisdom & Knowledge:
                        Introductions—Themes, personae, character; The first 'division'—wisdom vs. knowledge

A First Digression on Wisdom 27

    Second Reading 38
    145e-151d   Definitions & Midwifery:
                        What is knowledge; Examples—arts & sciences; Patterns of definition; Jacob Klein on division; Encouragement and midwifery; The midwife and wisdom

Act I: Sense Perception (Apprehension) 67
    Third Reading 67
    151e-160e   Sense Perception (*aisthesis*) is always true knowledge:
                        General outline of third reading; Following the clue; Perception is always true; Man as the measure of all things; Relative qual-

ities; All is in motion; Qualities as the union of active and passive (sensed and sense); Primacy of motion; Deducing consequences; Wonder and philosophy; Problem of dreams; 'Solution' through a deeper relativism

Fourth Reading.. 107
160e-177a   The Defense & True Wisdom:
Protagoras's Truth—Men and Animals; Knowing and not knowing; Protagoras's own defense: wisdom is not true but useful; The Truth of Protagoras is true to no one; Political life vs. Philosophy and true wisdom

*A Second digression on Wisdom..129

Fifth Reading... 144
177b-187a   Final Refutation:
All is motion and all is rest; Arriving at being and truth

*The First Act—Simple Apprehension (Understanding).....156
Object Awareness (Intentionality); Trusting the Senses?; Semiotic Character of Sensation; The Whole Person

Act II: True Opinion (Judgment).. 186
  Sixth Reading... 186
187b-196c   Opinion (doxa) & Wax:
True opinion; The mystery of false opinion—knowing, being; An aside on the complexity of knowledge; Other-opinion; The

Contents   xi

                     block of wax; Division (examples); Dialogue within the soul

     *The Second Act—Judgment..214
         Digression on opinion

     Seventh Reading 226
         196c-201c   True Opinion and the Aviary:
                            Shameless dialectic; Having vs. holding; The aviary; Recapturing birds; False birds and infinite regress; True opinion cannot be knowledge

Act III: True Opinion + an account (Logos) 246
     Eighth Reading.. 246
         201c-206b   True opinion with an account (logos):
                            Hearsay and a dream—logos, elements, and composites; Names and logos; Syllables and Letters; Whole, All, Parts; Reversal—letters as the most knowable

*On Elements, Parts, Wholes, and the All............................293

*The Third Act of the Mind: Reasoning (Syllogism) 303

     Ninth Reading.. 311
         206b-210d   Kinds of logos, Critique, & End:
                            Three kinds of logos; The way of difference; Example; A regress to opinion; Recapitulation

Works Cited.. 335

Introduction to the Commentary

It is the glory of God to conceal a word, but the glory of kings to search that word out.

Proverbs 25:2

Plato's dialogues are charged with a unique spirit. In them, we meet not with doctrine but with the potency of the philosophic moment. A boy for the first time holding a rifle or given the helm of a ship has perhaps a similar impression, a sense that something has been placed before him which is alive to his touch, something of power and consequence that he does not yet fathom. For those who have come to love Plato, we find ourselves, if not at the helm, then on the scene of something significant. These ancient dialogues still appeal to us and fascinate us because our imaginations, our minds, our desires are concerned with the same things. Love him or hate him, Socrates asks questions we often want (or once wanted) to answer. This is because knowing and the desire to know are fundamental to us.

We are made to know and be known. As intellectual creatures, we are cognitively open to all being. This can be demonstrated by the fact that we ask questions. Made in the image of God, through whom and for whom all things are made, we have a kinship with all things because we have a special kinship to their Source. That Source is the Logos, the divine Word. Because all that *is* exists through the Logos, all being is in some respect intelligible. To be created is to be intelligible or to have the character of a *word*.[2] A remarkable

---

[2] Josef Pieper states in the *Silence of St. Thomas* that "things can be known because they are created." He then states that "things are

corollary is that we cannot ultimately be satisfied by just knowing about the creature. We wish to know the causes of things and to know their first Cause. We find it good to know and especially good to know good things. Indeed, knowledge of the true good is needful.

The *Theaetetus*, which asks 'What is knowledge', therefore holds a special place in the platonic corpus because its subject matter is inseparable from the human question—'what are we' and 'what are we for'? The question of knowledge has enormous scope and therefore touches upon, to various degrees, questions of psychology, epistemology, ontology, logic, even ethics, and religion. This is because the question of knowledge must address not merely a definition (what it means to know) but also our knowing faculties, what constitute the proper objects of knowledge, the tools by which we make knowledge explicit and sure, as well as some of the implications consequent upon being capable of knowledge, creatures who must intentionally direct themselves to their final end.

This dialogue will probably never hold first place in the canon, either pedagogically or in readers' affections. The *Republic, Meno, Phaedo, Phaedrus, Symposium, Gorgias,* and *Euthyphro* claim priority due either to subject, style, or the order of learning. Yet, *Theaetetus* stands the test of time. Its topic is critically important. The arguments and the problems it presents are relevant: dealing with skepticism; human nature; and ethics. Further, it lays out (or anticipates) the course of philosophy for centuries. Its imagery is delightful. Its breadth is awe inspiring. Its form is a work of genius. Most importantly, we can learn much from it.

---

unfathomable because they are created" Josef Pieper, *The Silence of St. Thomas: Three Essays* (South Bend, Ind: St. Augustine's Press, 1999), 53, 110.

Introduction to the Commentary

My commentary divides Plato's dialogue into nine readings and therefore is a kind of reader's guide. I include outlines, summaries, focus-questions, some line-by-line analysis, and a number of philosophic asides. I recommend that readers of this commentary read the selected sections of the original dialogue as a whole and then see what the commentary offers. However, one may also read them simultaneously.

The commentary and analysis is chiefly informed by a close reading of the text. It remains largely Socratic in style, while giving attentive readers strong direction and suggestions. I also incorporate a sense of the historical development of these questions as epitomized in Aristotle and Thomas Aquinas, among others. I rely upon these and other thinkers and traditions because I believe they enrich our reading of the *Theaetetus* while remaining faithful to it and its problems.

At the outset, I should be clear that I do not believe we shall walk away with nothing. A philosophy which merely insists that we *know nothing* is worse than wrong. Platonic skepticism is founded on wonder, on the experience of knowing something without knowing it as we might wish. Socratic ignorance is then ironic and playful, rather than an expression of an utter lack of knowledge. Nevertheless, it is also the humble admission of a man who knows that he is, in fact, not God.

At the same time, this does not mean we will walk away with every question wrapped up with a neat bow. It is likely we will neither solve all mysteries nor walk away empty handed. We will have done much if we grasp more clearly the contours of the question and have a few promising leads we can pursue.

One might keep in mind, that a dialogue is by its very nature provisional—it is not a treatise.[3] The *Theaetetus* is the

---

[3] Jacob Klein, *A Commentary on Plato's Meno*, 2012, 3–31.

first foray of an intelligent, docile, promising young man (Theaetetus) who will go on to become a noteworthy mathematician and faithful citizen of Athens. His youth is itself a limit to the drama, but one that makes us aware of our own limits and powers.

Three Acts

Excluding its introduction, which presents the character of Theaetetus as a source of thematic unity, the dialogue can be divided into three sections. After Socrates asks Theaetetus what knowledge is, Theaetetus offers three definitions:

- Perception (sensation)
- True Opinion
- True Opinion with an account (logos)

These divisions can roughly be treated as *acts* or scenes in the drama. However, they are not merely discrete efforts to respond to the question. They represent stages of inquiry, development of an investigation as it delves into the complex problems which touch upon knowing. Further, these acts or stages of the dialogue loosely parallel what have come to be called the three acts of the mind:

- Understanding (Simple Apprehension)
- Judgment (Complex Apprehension)
- Reason (Syllogism)

These three distinct mental acts are mutually connected to one another. They are not three possible options for understanding knowledge among which we must select the true one. They are instead a summary of the complex and diverse ways in which we know. The three acts of the mind are an interconnected framework which was defined and codified over centuries. We find here in Plato one of its earliest manifestations or forerunners. Aristotle develops this model further, particularly in works such as *On the Soul, Posterior Analytics, Topics,* and *Peri Hermenias*.[4] Other ancient and medieval authors clarify and formalize this framework, St. Thomas Aquinas is conspicuous among them, but he is by no means an anomaly. An explication of this model can be found in Peter Kreeft' *Socratic Logic*, an excellent text we currently read with freshman at New College Franklin and with students at Holy Apostles College and Seminary.

The point of employing this framework (or rather unpacking it to some extent in this commentary) is not at all to suggest it is the chief or only way of reading *Theaetetus*. It is not what the dialogue is *really* about. Rather, it illustrates one way, a very important and powerful way, that questions in *Theaetetus* have been explored. It serves as a significant parallel to our reading, especially insofar as it is an authentic development of Plato's own insights. I hope readers will find its incorporation organic.

Because the three acts of the mind are not explicitly developed in the dialogue, I will not explain them systematically at the beginning of the commentary. Their discussion emerges alongside the unfolding of the drama. Precise knowledge of the three acts of the mind, while useful, is not necessary. For a more thorough treatment see Peter Kreeft's *Socratic Logic* or the introduction and first lesson in Thomas Aquinas's *Commentary on the Posterior Analytics*.

On Hope: Encouragement to Readers

Philosophy is engaged in only by those who hope. Hope is frustrated by unreasonable expectations and also by despair.

---

[4] See also the opening paragraphs of Aristotle's *Physics* and *Metaphysics*.

You know something. You read these sentences only because you have knowledge. You continue to read only because you have some measure of hope. You (just like all of us) are capable of knowing more. Nevertheless, you are also not self-sufficient; otherwise, you would not read! But you have an initial or sufficient sufficiency to make a beginning. Thus, as in all our studies, it is not unfitting that we begin with prayer for greater light:

> *Come Holy Spirit, fill the hearts of your faithful and kindle in them the fire of your love. Send forth your Spirit and they shall be created, and You shall renew the face of the earth.*
>
> *O, God, who has taught the hearts of the faithful by the light of the Holy Spirit, grant that by the gift of the same Spirit we may be always truly wise and ever rejoice in his consolation, through Christ Our Lord, Amen.*

Even by the grace of God, it is likely that you will not know everything you might wish by the time you close this book. If you keep that in mind, you have every chance of learning something. The conclusion of a book need not be the conclusion of philosophy.

Perhaps no writer has more profoundly explored the significance and limits of the dialogue form than Jacob Klein.[5] He reminds us that to read a dialogue is not to receive a set of teachings but to join in a conversation.[6] We therefore cannot demand that it answer all our questions, nor can we sit back and passively wait for understanding. Again, we do well if we learn to ask good questions and how to evaluate answers

---

[5] Klein, *A Commentary on Plato's Meno*, 3–31; Jacob Klein, Robert B. Williamson, and Elliott Zuckerman, *Lectures and Essays* (Annapolis, Md: St. John's College Press, 1985), n. essays on Ion & Phaedrus.

[6] Klein, *A Commentary on Plato's Meno*, 30.

more carefully as we move forward. If you find yourself wondering what might have happened if something different were asked, if some other solution were offered, or if something was added or altered, you have entered into the living work of philosophy. You must discover the difference between logical, dialectical, and firm or scientific conclusions. May God strengthen you in this endeavor.

Keep in mind that "not all who wander are lost."[7] It is perhaps only the pilgrim who knows that he has not yet arrived home.

---

[7] J. R. R. Tolkien, *The Fellowship of the Ring*, The Lord of the rings pt. 1 (Boston: Mariner Books/Houghton Mifflin Harcourt, 2012), 171.

Commentary

General Outline of Dialogue:
- ❖ **Introduction** (Opening Scene)
  - o Present Time:
    - ▪ Euclid and Terpsion discuss Theaetetus
  - o Recalling the past:
    - ▪ Socrates meets a promising young man at a Gymnasium
- ❖ **What is knowledge?**
  - o Wisdom and knowledge
  - o Examples
- ❖ **Three Acts:**
  - o Perception
  - o True opinion
  - o True opinion with an account (logos)
- ❖ Recapitulation & Conclusion

Detailed Outline
- ❖ **Introduction (Opening Scene)**:
- ❖ Euclid and Terpsion speak of Theaetetus coming home from war, dying
  - • They recall Theaetetus's meeting with Socrates and reread an account of their discussion
- ❖ Socrates is introduced to Theaetetus by Theodorus
  - • Theaetetus's excellence

- ❖ **The initial question**
  - • Wisdom and knowledge
  - • What is knowledge
    - • Definition by example (arts, sciences)
    - • Socrates provides a pattern of a definition

Commentary

- Theaetetus's mathematical success in defining
- Midwifery—philosophic care

❖ **First Act**: Perception (Apprehension)
  - Man as the measure of all things
  - Nothing is one (Cold wind and motion)
    - Qualities do not exist by themselves stably (but from impact/intercourse)
      - Nothing is the same for anyone
    - Everything is in motion
      - Everything is becoming in relation to something else
  - All perception is true (no one errs)
  - Sophistry, Rhetoric, & True Wisdom
    - The end of man
  - Refutation
    - All is not in flux
    - Being and Truth

❖ **Second Act**: True Opinion
  - Causes of False Opinion
  - Waxen Impressions
  - The Bird Cage

❖ **Third Act**: True opinion with a logos
  - Elements, Composites (Syllables), Logos
  - A Whole, an All, & Part
  - Logos:
    - Reflection
    - Elements
    - Logos with a difference

❖ **Recapitulation & Conclusion**

Dramatic-Mimetic Beginnings

First Reading
142a-145e   Introduction: Wisdom & Knowledge
Introductions—Themes, Personae, Character; The first 'division'—wisdom vs. knowledge

Focus Questions:
1. What is wisdom?
2. Is wisdom the same as knowledge?
3. What does *nature* or *likeness* have to do with knowledge and expectation?
4. To whom does knowledge belong: to experts or to ordinary people?
5. To whom does knowledge about knowledge belong?

Dramatic Personae (Interlocutors)
Euclid of Megara	*Disciple of Socrates, present at his death*
Terpsion of Megara	*Disciple of Socrates, present at his death*
Servant of Euclid	
Socrates	
Theodorus	*Pedagogue at local Athenian gymnasium*
Theaetetus	*Student of Theodorus; Young mathematician*
Socrates the Younger	*Friend of Theaetetus*

The bulk of this dialogue is a conversation between Socrates and Theaetetus which is to have occurred sometime in early 4th century BC. Their conversation is introduced by an exchange between two friends, Euclid and Terpsion.[8] These men find one another (after a brief search), somewhere

---

[8] This is not Euclid of Alexandria, known for the *Elements*, the great mathematical textbook which includes works of our Theaetetus.

Commentary

probably near Megara where they are from. As Euclid and Terpsion meet listen to a reading of the conversation between Theaetetus and Socrates, Theaetetus is mortally ill, being brought home from an Athenian army camp at Corinth.[9] Megara stands in between the cities with Corinth to the west and Theaetetus's home to the east.

As reported in Plato's *Phaedo*, Euclid and Terpsion are both disciples of Socrates, present at his death.[10] They themselves are philosophers associated with the Megarian school, named for Megara, Greece, about 25 miles from Athens. The school was known, among other things for ethics, logic, and metaphysics. The are also associated with the rejection of change and potency.

The structure of a nested story, also known as an *embedded* or *frame narrative*, serves a variety of purposes. First, it unifies the entire dialogue within the context of Theaetetus's character (*éthos*) and history. Second, it situates the discussion in a broader political and philosophic context. Third, it sets the stage for how we are to understand philosophic inquiry as related to human character and to the polis. Finally, it contextualizes the dialogue in an act of memory or recounting. The momentary and passing event of Theaetetus's dialogue with Socrates (as well as his death) is known only because of human memory and writing, because someone desired to take up what was held in memory and commit it to writing. It is not thereby lost within the changes of perception and time. In reading, we take up again what was first in the mind and

---

[9] Theaetetus participates in the first two dialogues of Plato's trilogy, the *Theaetetus*, *Sophist*, and *Statesman*. He is likely present at the third.

[10] *Phaedo* 59c describes these men as foreigners from Megara who are present on the day of Socrates' death. *Phaedo* is also a frame dialogue.

experience of other men.[11] The flow of time is thus preserved from being mere flux by the work of memory and conceptualization. This suggests that there is much we know only because it has been handed down to us.[12]

Euclid and Terpsion decide to listen together to a reading of Socrates's early encounter with Theaetetus, one which Euclid himself has recorded with the aid of Socrates. As Euclid's servant takes up the text and reads, the dramatic setting of the dialogue, as well as the history of these interlocutors (Euclid and Terpsion) frame what follows: in friendship, dialectic, philosophy, leisure, beauty, memory, politics, human excellence (virtue), and also human limitation (memory and mortality). These are not just themes; they are the proper framework for a consideration of knowledge, for the inquiry we find within the *Theaetetus*. Thus, the stage has been set for philosophy.

In this first reading, we will pay attention to these thematic hints which will prepare us for what will follow. We will notice the words chosen by Plato and the situation in which he sets these speeches and deeds. This is important because a dialogue is as much a drama as it is an inquiry. It matters who is asking a question and whom they are asking; the when, where, and why of things matters. This is perhaps true of all philosophy—not just Platonic dialogues!

---

[11] This is not to say the dialogue is a precise history. Almost the entirety of Scripture is itself a product of memory, the memory of God's people: a living word first stored up in the hearts and minds of men and women to whom God made himself known. For instance, we know much of the nativity because Mary treasured up in her heart and pondered over and over again the events of her life (Luke 2:19). This is precisely what it means to be a disciple, to treasure in heart, mind, and deed what one has heard.

[12] In both English and Greek, 'tradition' etymologically refers to an act of handing or giving over.

Commentary

The Platonic dialogue is a drama in terms of what it represents to the reader, but even more so, insofar as the reader critically engages what has been represented. We have before us not just arguments, but individuals in concrete situations who represent distinct ways of relating to and speaking about things. Just as with any drama, the whole (its context, staging, costume, diction, and speeches) must be attended to. Perhaps this is why Aristotle describes Plato's works as 'mimes' or mimetic: imitative in word and deed of their subject matter.[13] This means that we should pay close attention to the opening details of the dialogue. It is not enough to give a logical outline of the argument because a dialogue is not merely a syllogism. It is a representation of truly human inquiry, with all its complexity and imperfection. We must engage it as such if we are to discover and appraise what it represents. For instance, sometimes the mimetic or dramatic character of a dialogue reinforces what has been said. At other times, it may run counter to (or in keen tension with) its expressed conclusions. Ultimately, the reader will only grasp the unity and life of the drama by becoming an interlocutor. The reader will only walk away with a deeper grasp of the truth if they not only read but become a participating actor, investigator, and judge.

For this reason, we will pay careful attention to the opening, recalling Aristotle's statement that "the beginning is admittedly more than half of the whole, and throws light at once on many of the questions under investigation."[14]

It is no accident that Plato's dialogue were *staged* in various locales, within or without the city: in the country, on the road, at people's homes, at schools (as in the *Theaetetus*), or even in prison. Philosophy belongs not to a special local or to a specific kind of employment, but to the human vocation.

---

[13] See Klein (2012), p.3 & Aristotle, *Poetics* I.1
[14] Nicomachean Ethics 1098b

Wherever we find man, we find the potential for philosophy. Truth, the love of truth, is the universal vocation of all men.

These dialogues present us with problems and questions which belong not just to books and minds, but to human life. Nevertheless, it is significant that a dialogue on knowledge has been situated within the context of memory and also that the auditors to this remembered conversation are two philosophers and friends (*lovers of wisdom*). Further, they listen with us to a conversation that occurred at a gymnasium. A gymnasium for the Athenian was not just a place of physical exercise but a school, a place of education in all those basic arts which a gentleman would need. Europe still refers to some of its schools by this name. The gymnasium was a place of learning and practice, something akin to the earliest schools of liberal arts. There, one trained in arts such as wrestling, music, mathematics, and astronomy—something very much like the quadrivium.[15]

With this in mind, we can note that the context or setting of the dialogue is a place of teaching and learning. This is itself significant in light of the central question (knowledge). The very existence of a gymnasium presupposes teachers, learners, knowing, and branches of learning. The whole framework of human existence is inconceivable without these institutions, practices, and expectations.

Unlike other animals who, at most, generally direct their young to certain behaviors, human parenting presupposes and demands education. A human life apart from some manner of education is virtually unimaginable. Education is both the privilege and responsibility of parents and children. Human parenting extends from earliest childhood, into teen years, and often well beyond. No other creature has so much learning to do! No other creature *can* learn, and no other

---

[15] See also Plato's *Lysis*

creature *needs* to learn so much. Our whole life virtually hangs on what we know or believe. We alone among the creatures must seek out the good for ourselves and seek it based upon our knowledge or opinion of what is true.

We probably share with Socrates the intuition, however vague, that education has something to do, not only with learning facts, but living in a community, with friendship, politics, and all that is human. Despite this commonsense account of human life and education, despite the fact that nearly all our practices bear this out, the modern age has largely lost hope in reason and truth. Education has largely been reduced to a practical or servile affair. Even the liberal arts have been militarized, subordinated to various causes and movements of the age, or severed from their roots in proper human ends.

As we enter the gymnasium and the conversation, we can begin to wonder what it might be the significance of conceiving of ourselves chiefly as doers and not first and foremost as knowers and lovers.

Introductions—Themes, personae, character
142a
Eu. **Just now** (ἄρτι) from the country…?
- Joe Sachs suggests that 'just now' evokes the *"right-now"* of perception.[16]

Terp. I was **searching** for you…wondering that I could not **find** you
- **Searching** and **finding** (ἐζήτουν…εὑρεῖν) are used in ordinary Greek discourse; however, they are also the language of mathematics and philosophy: technical terms for a *given and sought* for, the conditions and

---

[16] Plato and Joe Sachs, *Plato's Theaetetus*, The focus philosophical library (Newburyport, MA: Focus Pub./R. Pullins Co, 2004), 16.

goals of a mathematical problem. *To seek* characterizes an intellectual and a moral disposition.[17] It is expressive of desire, and desire is expressive of the person. Significantly, it is not possible to desire something without also knowing it, at least in some manner.

Wondering that I could not find you
- Wonder (θαυμάζω) will be characterized as the source of philosophy at 155d. It takes a very special sort of creature to wonder also requires definite conditions in which it occurs. Here, Terpsion *wonders* where Euclid is. He was searching for Terpsion in his regular place or *topos*. This seems to imply that certain things can be known or expected about him. Things which seem wonderful or strange are regularly expressed in this dialogue and others as *atopos* or placeless. It is worth considering that this world is a place in which wonder is possible, in which both expectation and surprise occur.

142b
Eu. A beautiful man and good (καλόν τε καὶ ἀγαθόν)
- **καλόν τε καὶ ἀγαθόν**: This is a somewhat formulaic idiom for a worthy man, one who is noble and all that a true man should be. *Kalos* has rich moral sense and is generally associated with virtue, though it can refer merely to perception or aesthetic beauty. See Matthew 7:17 for a typical use of kalos. In the *Meno*, Socrates suggests that beauty cannot and is not to be severed from truth, that ultimately truth and beauty are the

---

[17] Ask, and it will be given to you; seek, and you will find; knock, and it will be opened to you (Matthew 7:7).

same (Meno 81a). We will see another use of *kalos* in a moment.

- Theaetetus is a historical figure. He is a mathematician whose work appears in Book X and Book XIII of Euclid. He formulated a proof concerning rational and irrational lines and also a proof that there are only five Platonic solids. He lived c.414-379 BC.[18]

E.,&T. <u>I heard people praising him...that is not strange (ἄτοπον), it would have been more wonderful (θαυμαστότερον) if he had not so conducted himself</u>
- The context is hearsay. The interchange suggest that Terpsion had a kind of knowledge which allowed him to surmise something about Theaetetus's future: Theaetetus has acted as expected. In other words, he was known to be a certain kind of man, to have a specific sort of character. But how does one know such things? It is a remarkable fact that we implicitly and explicitly rely on what we know to form expectations about the future![19]

142c-d
Eu. <u>...I thought of Socrates and **wondered** at his prophetic gift...he greatly exalted over his [Theaetetus's] **nature** (φύσις).</u>

---

[18] Uta Merzbach and Carl Boyer, *History of Mathematics*, Third. (John Wiley & Sons, Inc., 2011), 76–77.

[19] Steward Umphrey, *Is Knowledge True Opinion with a Logos?*, Cassette Tape (Annapolis, Md, 1986). Steward Umphrey notes a three part division of *Theaetetus* and the fact that, all along, knowledge has been on display throughout the whole dialogue. This is true of the Meno as well.

- Nature appears here, referring to Theaetetus's character. This is a fascinating way of describing Socrates's wonder. Perhaps knowledge, all knowledge, may hinge upon nature. Nature is a cause of knowledge and expectation because we expect only under condition of regularity or stability—within the context of a stable world or cosmos.

    o Nature has something to do with the *kinds* (genus) of things we expect will happen. It is in this sense a sort of limit. Theaetetus has himself been discussed as being recognized and indeed acting as a certain *kind* of person. Nature sets certain limits on what would otherwise be infinitely complex.

- Worthiness (ἄξιος) is also introduced here. This dialogue has an unmistakable moral tone. It is not merely speculative in character.

<u>Terp.</u>   It was **true apparently**...
- This ironic juxtaposition will be explored later in our dialogue, as well as the *Sophist*. There is a dual sense to *appear to be true*, just as there is a dual sense of a likely story (see *Timaeus*). I thing may appear true because it is indeed true or simply appear so, contrary to fact.
    o *Appearance, likeness,* and *otherness* each have both a positive and negative senses.
    o Likeness and appearance are consistent themes throughout this introduction and the dialogue as a whole.

143a-143b

Eu. ...afterwards at my **leisure**...while we are resting the boy shall read to us

- Leisure is a prerequisite for and also a result of philosophy. We derive our word 'school' from the Greek word for leisure (σχολή).[20] It is a fascinating tension that students (the zealous) are those who go to school. It is worth reflecting how eager zeal, effort, leisure, and contemplation can be corelated to one another. There is perhaps a *dialectic* between them.

- The theme of motion and rest, alluded to in the very first word of the dialogue, is nodded to here by means of 'leisure'.

143c

Eu. Take the book and read

- It is hard not to recall *'tolle lege'* from Augustine's *Confessions* 8.12.

- We now leave the frame drama and enter into the dialogue proper.

143D

Soc. ...devoting themselves to geometry or any other form of philosophy(φιλοσοφίαν)

- Philosophy is today treated as a special discipline or subject. For Plato, philosophy can be used generally, to characterize any and all science, or specially to refer to the *love of wisdom*, the disposition to pursue wisdom and thus truth to its highest ends.

---

[20] Josef Pieper, *Leisure: The Basis of Culture; The Philosophical Act* (San Francisco: Ignatius Press, 2009), 19.

- See 145c-d (**Logistics/Arithmetic, Astronomy, Geometry, Music**). This dialogue takes place at gymnasium in the context of traditional learning. Students of the classical or historic liberal arts will recognize this curriculum as the quadrivium. The quadrivium (articulated in the *Republic*) is Arithmetic, Geometry, Music, and Astronomy. The trivium is Logic, Grammar and Rhetoric. In the Christian University tradition, these have served as preparation for the higher sciences of philosophy (including ethics, physics, and metaphysics).[21] Philosophy served in the Middle Ages as the handmaid to the Queen of sciences: Sacred or Revealed Theology (Christian Theology). Today, many consider the natural (hard) sciences to be the only sciences worthy of that name (science). Knowledge is cordoned off by positivism and Lockean-empiricism, limited to empirical experimental mathematical sciences. Such science is practical and powerful but virtually cut off from the most important questions: who are we, where are we from, and where are we going?

- Theodorus's character helps clarify whether those subjects by themselves (the quadrivium) amount to philosophy, that is, true wisdom, or if they only fall under philosophy as preparatory parts. Are the liberal arts a sufficient or proper education? It perhaps depends what the liberal arts are thought to include. Socrates will clarify what true wisdom is by the middle of

---

[21] Physics which means *nature* is *natural philosophy* or natural science. Metaphysics is known also as wisdom, first philosophy, the study of being qua being, and natural theology.

the dialogue and explore the nature of true freedom and leisure.[22]

- Theodorus is said to be worthy (axios) of all his students. He in turn describes Theaetetus as worthy.

143e
Theo. <u>If he had been a **beauty**...but he is **no beauty**... he is **very like you**; for he has a snub nose and projecting eyes, although these features are less marked in him than in you.</u>
- Contrary to Euclid, Theodorus states that Theaetetus is *not* beautiful. Perhaps they are both correct.

- Theodorus compares or likens Theaetetus to Socrates. It is worth considering how they are like one another. In a sense, not only the opening but the entire dialogue will explore this—Theaetetus's character and likeness to the philosopher.

- A likeness is no simple matter. On the one hand, just about anyone can discern a likeness. Every time you identify a tree as a tree, a cat as a cat, or a house cat as akin to a lion, that is when you notice a thing as a *kind* of thing, you identify what is *like*. We live by grasping how one thing is like something else or like something same in kind. This is why we do not need to relearn what a tree or cat is every time we see one. Each cat, each tree, is in some manner like each other.

---

[22] Pope Benedict XVI argues that when reason ceases to have hope in the highest truths and when it attempts to stand without the support of religion, it easily becomes the tool of prevailing power interests (Pope Benedict XVI, La Sapienza 2008).

- Theodorus asserts a likeness **with a difference**, anticipating Act III (see 209a-c).

144a
Theo. <u>I have never met such a **wonderful** good **character** (φύω)...quick **beyond** almost anyone to learn (εὐμαθῆ)...gentle (πρᾷον)...brave (ἀνδρεῖον)....I should not have supposed such a one could come to be</u>
- Theaetetus evokes wonder in others by combining in his nature (or character) qualities which are often not found together.
    - True excellence may in fact require a kind of wonderous unification of contrary characteristics. A good father, for instance, must be both gentle and firm at the same time.

    - This is because various strengths are prone to characteristic defects without contrary virtues to temper them.

- Theodorus's account or logos again characterizes Theaetetus in a twofold way (208c-d):
    - By what is common (as a student)
    - By difference (his virtues)

144b-e
Soc. <u>I have heard the name but do not remember</u>
- Memory and forgetting, already brought up in the frame drama, is recurred to.

- Theodorus asks Socrates if he knows or recognizes (γιγνώσκω) him. Recognition is a special way of knowing based on something already known.

Soc. ...See **what sort** (ποῖόν τι) of face I have
- *What sort* can take on a technical meaning in philosophy (as in Aristotle's Categories), but here it is general.
    - Socrates states he can know one thing (himself) by looking at something **like it** (Theaetetus).

<u>...Now if we each had a lyre, and he said we had tuned them to the same key...we should refuse to take his word...but now if we are concerned about the likeness (οἶμαι,) of our faces, we must consider whether he who speaks is a painter.</u>
- It is worth reflecting how the likeness of faces might fall under the realm of common knowledge but also under the expertise of the artist. It seems such knowledge belongs both to the common power of man naturally, but perhaps also to the artist in a certain preeminent way through training or education. On expertise see Plato's dialogue *Protagoras*.

There may be overlap between a field of expertise and what ordinary people understand. Implicit in this fact is the question of whether knowledge or even the *knowledge of what knowledge is* belongs to all men, only to some. If it belongs only to some, it might belong to professionals or to philosophers. A lover of wisdom is not necessarily a professional.[23]

---

[23] A.D. Sertillanges, *The Intellectual Life: Its Spirit, Conditions, Methods* (Washington, D.C.: The Catholic University of America Press, 1998).

145a-b
Thea. It **seems to me** (δοκεῖ μοι).
- Has Theaetetus been too easily persuaded? *Opinion, seeming,* and *judgment* are all at stake in this dialogue. It seems that a non-expert can yet have a strong ground of judgment, perhaps even to judge about experts in some cases.

- We are informed here that Theodorus is proficient in the classical liberal arts of the quadrivium. The sufficiency of his education, his love of wisdom is questioned in this dialogue. Socrates claims here that Theodorus is a judge of virtue and wisdom. The middle of the dialogue does not bear this out.

Soc. ...for that one to exhibit (ἐπιδεικνύναι)
- **Exhibit:** The word is perhaps chosen because of its mathematical sense of proof, related to ἀποδεικτικός from which we get 'apodictic': the kind of proof related to scientific or demonstrative knowledge. Demonstration is a characteristic mark of knowledge (episteme) for Aristotle.

The first 'division'—wisdom vs. knowledge
145 d-e
Soc. I am at a loss (ἀπορῶ) about one little matter.
- **At a loss.** The experience of aporia is a characteristic effect of Socratic inquiry. It is in some way, the beginning of philosophy, insofar as philosophy is connected with wonder. For Plato, philosophic desire itself cannot occur without perplexity.

...Is not learning (μανθάνειν) growing wiser (σοφώτερον) about that which one learns

- This is complex statement suggests that learning and wisdom are not exactly the same thing, unless one is learning about something one already knows or has learned. It perhaps means a person already possesses some modicum of wisdom!

...the wise are wise by wisdom
- Does this mean that we call the wise 'wise' because they have wisdom, or rather that the wisdom or knowledge they possess is possessed by means of wisdom?

...and does this **differ** (διαφέρει) from knowledge?...aren't the things people know the things they are wise about?...then knowledge and wisdom are the same (ταὐτὸν ἄρα **ἐπιστήμη** καὶ **σοφία**;)...

The.   Yes
- Is Theaetetus right to agree here? Are wisdom and knowledge the same thing?

- This crucial early step in the dialogue asks Theaetetus if he recognize a *distinction* or *division*—a **difference** (**διαφέρει**). The course of many of Plato's dialogues are shaped by such an initial and essential division. To divide is itself a mental act which will be explored throughout our reading. It is a form of judgment (the second act of the mind). We can take a moment and reflect, what it takes for someone to answer this question adequately:

- Socrates has suggested that to learn is to grow wiser about what we learn and also that it is *by* wisdom that we become wise. There are two implications (which do not necessarily point in the same direction):

- o 1: Whenever we learn we become wiser about something.
- o 2: Wisdom is a power or habit *by which* learning occurs.

The second point suggests that we need a power or ability in order to learn. But how could the power by which we learn or get knowledge be itself a kind of knowledge. But if it is not knowledge, what would it be. Wisdom is offered here as:

- Knowledge
- a kind of primal or primary knowledge
- and even as a preeminent or ultimate knowledge

If all of us learn, this would mean all of us are wise, at least in some measure. Even if we accept wisdom as a kind of knowledge, we might want to distinguish it either as a specific kind or as a wholly different in order.

A First Digression on Wisdom

Socrates has asked Theaetetus whether knowledge (ἐπιστήμη) and wisdom (σοφία) are one and the same. There are various senses of 'wisdom', some which are certainly more precise or more truly wisdom. Wisdom is in this sense an analogical term: one which has various senses, some more or less true, some, perhaps, preeminent. Therefore, our knowledge of wisdom can itself be more or less perfect. Here are a few general ways the term is used.

Cleverness

Cleverness and wisdom can be confused either playfully or equivocally. Calling someone in the mafia a 'wise-guy' is perhaps the first. To call a politician wise or prudent for jettisoning their moral values is the second. Just because an argument can be expressed with words one understands does not mean it is either good or true. Just because an action can produce certain limited goods, does not make it wise. It is not the merely clever person who can tell the difference.

Real wisdom is, therefore, not mere logical horsepower; it is not just a faculty of analysis and assimilation. Nor is it the ability to get oneself out of inconvenient moral scrapes.

This very ambiguity is expressed by the term 'sophist' (*wise-one*), a name taken by men in Socrates' time who professed to teach a brand of 'wisdom' that amounted to little more than cleverness in argument. They often treated a facility with words and the power of persuasion as the sole marks of wisdom. Often conflated or overlapping with others who were considered rhetors, sophists taught young Athenians how to speak confidently and overcome all kinds of arguments in the law courts and publicly. They taught men to answer whatever questions or objections anyone might put to them.[24] The rhetors often concerned themselves with the political life only, while some sophists also considered aspects of ethics, metaphysics, and physics under their study. They partially overlap with those known as generally the presocratic philosophers. Protagoras, whom we will 'hear' from in the *Theaetetus*, is a rhetor and sophist with whom Theodorus is associated.[25]

It has been said that the very term philosophy (love of wisdom) was coined to distinguish true lovers of wisdom from the pretensions of the sophists. Philosophy in this sense is precisely a description of one who has not arrived at or comprehend wisdom—one who rather pursues her. Love of wisdom, ala *Symposium*, is in this sense a love for what one lacks. This is why Socrates states in that dialogue that none of the gods philosophize (204a). In the *Phaedo*, philosophy is characterized as a way of life, one committed in the most profound sense to the highest truths—an ongoing practice of dying to the self, spurred by the hope of seeing God.

Technical Skill

Students often define wisdom as 'being able to put knowledge into practice'. This roughly amounts to technical skill. There is something like this suggested by Socrates when he speaks of artists who are trained to recognize the likenesses between faces.

Any craftsman, anyone skilled in a field of action does precisely this. In this manner, we can say there is a wisdom of the potter, a wisdom of the lawyer, a wisdom of the banker, and a

---

[24] Both Jane Austen and George Eliot characterize a person who attempts to be equally capable in any conversation as boorish. See the discussion of Frank Churchill in *Emma* ch.18, or Captain Lydgate in *Middlemarch* Ch.58.

[25] See also Plato's *Protagoras*.

wisdom of the sailor. Wisdom means in this case either the knowledge, intuition, or power that produces right, successful, or excellent action.

This will hardly do, however, as a comprehensive description of wisdom. It virtually amounts to calling wise anyone who can successfully apply anything they know. The seamstress who knows how to sew, the surgeon who can operate well, the investor who can make money are by this definition wise. This is certainly a good beginning. But have we exhausted what we mean by wisdom in the application of these various knowledges (arts or sciences)?

Further, if this is the case, we must ask whether it is the art or science or only its right application which is wisdom. That is, is knowledge the skill or is it a kind of skill itself, a skill of application?

By what wisdom or power does one apply wisdom? It would be strange a strange thing indeed if something in us which was *not knowledge* or wisdom were to command our knowledge! This is suggestive that we might need a wisdom of wisdom. Is there in fact such a primary or supreme wisdom? It seems wisdom must be itself a form of knowing. Under this construction, would it be a knowledge that guides application or something beyond all application, even if it also can govern action?

Skillful action then cannot exhaust all that we may mean by wisdom. Without denying that wisdom may belong to a seamstress or banker, there must be a more fundamental meaning. Skill alone becomes problematic when we notice that someone can be an excellent seamstress or banker but also a scoundrel.

Yet, before wholly dismissing this usage, it is worth pointing out that there is something important expressed here. We find this reflected in the Bible, in which the first occurrences of 'wisdom' indicate something like skill (though perhaps more):

> *And thou shalt speak unto all that are wise hearted, whom I have filled with the spirit of wisdom (חָכְמָה), that they may make Aaron's garments to consecrate him, that he may minister unto me in the priest's office (Exodus 28:3:).*[26]

Our reflection thus far and even the skill of a craftsman as depicted in Exodus underscores an important insight: wisdom is not merely information! It seems to be a power of *organization* or *order*. In human life, it may be wisdom that somehow organizes one's actions or thoughts in a manner akin to how a true craftsman orders and directs a complex whole, uniting each part fittingly. Wisdom is perhaps something by which or through which one orders one's life (thoughts, actions, faculties).

Prudence—practical wisdom (phronesis)

Prudence seems to reflect just this kind of organizing and ordering power. Further, prudence turns us from mere skill of action to a decidedly intellectual power, one more properly related to the domain of knowledge, even if it is ordered to action.[27] Prudence (practical judgment/practical wisdom) is the

---

[26] The Bible by no means exclusively (or chiefly) use this sense of wisdom: Deut. 4:6, 34:9; 1 Kings 3:28; Job 12:2, 12-16, 28:28; Psalms 37:30, 51:6, 90:12;, 111:10; Proverbs 1:2-7, 2:10, 3:19, 4:5, 4:7, 7:4, 8:1-14, 9:1, 9:10, 31:26; Isa. 11:2; Jer. 9:23; Dan. 1:4; Matt. 11:19, 13:54; Luke 2:40, 21:15; Rom. 11:22; 1 Cor. 1:17-24, 2:4-7, 3:19; Eph. 1:17; Col. 1:9, 4:5; Jam. 1:5, 3:13-17; Rev. 5:12, 7:12.

[27] Prudence is formally an intellectual virtue but materially a moral virtue. It is not opposed to craft, but it is concerned with the moral excellence of the act, whether it is good or evil.

chief cardinal virtue, without which there is no virtue.[28] It is that which binds acting and knowing and makes human acts *human*. Prudence and wisdom (as *phronesis* and *sophia* in the Greek) are distinct terms, though we often interchange them in ordinary, non-technical speech.

Practical wisdom takes us beyond technical skill into a distinct arena of ethics or right and wrong. In doing so, we do not leave behind other actions, but look at them from a higher vantage point. We look not at the formal skill of the seamstress or banker, but at why they do what they do (at something which directs or should direct all their acts) The knowledge and motivation of prudence has a higher formality than that of craft.

Still, there is a sense in which we have been merely thrust back upon the same problem. We associate such wisdom with council, decision, and judgment. We seek out the wise for help and we seek wisdom for ourselves, in order that we might act well. But what is this wisdom? Is it again just knowledge of good acting, of skillful action, or a habit of intuiting the right action? Or is this kind of wisdom the knowledge of something higher. In other words, is wisdom a moral *know-how*?

We have yet to determine what it is that prudence must know if one is to act well. We have to determine what it is that even prudence looks to.

We might also wonder whether knowledge of human action is in fact the highest wisdom. If man is the most important thing in the universe, this indeed might be the case. But if there is something higher, better, greater than man, man might yet have to know something about that which is other and greater than himself.

---

[28] Josef Pieper, *The Four Cardinal Virtues: Prudence, Justice, Fortitude, Temperance* (Notre Dame, Ind.: University of Notre Dame Press, 2011).

<u>Knowledge</u>

To say much here would be to beg the question of the whole dialogue (i.e., *'What is Knowledge'*). But if all men know something and knowledge is wisdom, then all men are wise or somewhat wise! This is either contrary to fact or very imprecise.

From the vantage of the *Meno*, one might say that all men are *potentially* wise or that we possess the principle of wisdom. But what is it that would distinguish the potentially and actually wise? Would they become wise *by* wisdom? Would it be a quantity of knowledge or a particular kind of knowledge which would distinguish them? In other words, wisdom might be just another word for knowledge, it may be a certain threshold of knowledge, or it may refer to a specific kind or order of knowledge.

At 145d, Socrates suggest that wisdom (or a kind of wisdom) may function as the principles of all learning![29] Wisdom is often more readily conceived of as the end, not the beginning of knowledge; nevertheless, all knowledge perhaps begins and ends in insight. The culmination of philosophy may therefore be something like a return to that which is immediate and luminous. To become wise may be a kind of homecoming. But would it be ourselves we know, some other thing, or both?

If one considers what we have said thus far, we might think of wisdom as a kind of *ruling, ordering, or governing* knowledge. We are trying to discern here the kind of knowledge that could or should govern. Would its object be

---

[29] Socrates describes wisdom as a power by which we acquire knowledge or learn. Cf. 198a-b on the art/science of arithmetic. In this respect wisdom sounds something like Aristotelian noetic insight (the understanding of first principles). "All teaching and all reasoned learning come from previous knowledge" (Aristotle, *Posterior Analytics* 71a1-10).

higher and better or would its very mode of knowing be distinct? It seems that such knowledge would need to know all the other knowledges it ruled! It would be a preeminent kind of knowing: a knowing of knowing.

Self-Knowledge (γνῶθι σεαυτόν)

The Delphic Oracle is reported to have inscribed at its temple the phrase *'know thyself'* which Socrates is said to have best fulfilled by knowing his own ignorance.[30]

Self-knowledge is by its nature a reflective or reflexive know-ledge, grasping both what one knows and who one is. It is worth noticing that we are creatures who are somewhat capable of this remarkable task. We can reflect upon ourselves and grasp something of the self as it is, even the fact of our ignorance! Knowledge is in this case not merely a passive reception of reality, as in the case of a mirror or vessel, but a live judgment and assessment, through a true interiority and wakefulness which can critically contain even itself![31] Self-knowledge, as Socrates insists, has something to do with knowing what one is, what one is not, and also where one is going (the nature and end of man).

Knowledge of Highest Causes

Aristotle defines wisdom as knowledge of the highest causes. Its object is being as such. One might keep in mind that God declares that he is very being: *I am that I am* (Ex. 3:14). Aristotle uses somewhat interchangeable the terms natural theology, first philosophy, Philosophy, the study of being qua being, and metaphysics with wisdom.

---

[30] See *Apology* 20e-21d

[31] John Paul II, *Love and Responsibility* (Boston: Pauline Books & Media, 2013).

Wisdom is associated by him with the intellectual virtues, among which are also included knowledge (science/ἐπιστήμη) and understanding (νους). We can see here that he distinguishes science or knowledge from wisdom, though not absolutely.

Understanding or intellect (nous) is the power by which we grasp logical and experiential first principles.[32] Understanding is an active power of immediate intuition or insight. It is associated with the first act of the mind (apprehension). Also known as intelligence or intellection, it has been etymologically explained as a power by which we 'read within' things, through which we apprehend the intelligible natures and features of the world around us. The term is sometimes used generically for the whole mind, just as the term knowledge or thought is used for all kinds of knowing. When used technically, it refers to the grasp of first principles (either logical or experiential).

Aristotle distinguishes nous (the grasp of first principles) from what he comes to call science or knowledge in the strict sense (ἐπιστήμη). Knowledge or episteme, when distinct from nous, is a sure knowledge based on causes, principles, and elements. Such knowledge is demonstrative or apodictic. Knowledge in this sense can answer the question 'why'.[33] The nous (our understanding of first principles) is the basis of this kind of knowing because we can reach no conclusions, no explanation of a why without knowing something prior, something certain, something without proof. In this sense, episteme

---

[32] Logical first principles such as the law of non-contradiction are the ground of every judgment and are innately but imperfectly possessed by the rational soul from the beginning. If we did not possess (however imperfectly) such principles, we would have no means by which to judge them as true when first acquired.

[33] Aristotle distinguishes in *Posterior Analytics* knowing *that* a thing is and knowing *why* it is.

is knowledge which stands upon (*epi-steme*) a foundation of that which is prior, clearer, in some manner causal, and more certain. Understanding thus under-stands knowledge or science.

Wisdom is treated by Aristotle as something distinct, even while it is a class of intellectual activity overlapping with science. It is a special class of knowledge, which falls into the same genus only analogically. This is due to the fact that the very highest objects of wisdom are known in a very different manner than the first principles of logic or those derived from sense-experience. This implies that not all knowledge is known in the same way. For instance, a lover knows love differently than a mathematician knows that a triangle's interior angles equal two right angles. We grasp the goodness of God in a different manner than we grasp that we are sitting at a desk or that a dog is a living creature.

What would knowledge of the highest causes (or the highest Cause) be a knowledge of and why would this knowledge deserve the name wisdom? In *Metaphysics* I.1, working analogically through the knowledge of generic experience, that of the artisan, the craftsman, and the master craftsman, Aristotle argues that it belongs to the wise to give orders rather than to receive them. Therefore, the highest knowledge will be the most governing. Thomas, following this, states, **"It belongs to the wise man to order things"** (Summa Contra Gentiles, I, 1).

But how does a *wise* person order a matter? In the manner of a military general who directs his cavalry: not so much by means of the art of horseback riding, but rather by knowing the end (telos). He must see from the highest vantage of things: the first and final Cause.

Moral Knowledge

As a note, it is no accident that what follows here converges with ground we have already covered to some extent.

To know good and evil is the basis of moral knowledge. We often associate this knowledge with the conscience, which itself informs prudence. But what is it we know by the conscience? Is it a set of rules or something else? Does the conscience alone constitute wisdom?[34]

Without answering these questions, we can at least notice that moral knowledge implies more than facts or rules, but values (good and evil). Values have to do with worth, truth, love, and greatness. In this manner, we have arrived at something that can be related to action while also surpassing it. Awareness and affirmation of value would be prior to and therefore capable of governing of human action.

Further, value is not merely objective, though it can be certainly that! But to grasp a value *as a value*, one must make a subjective judgement about it—one must value or *evaluate*. For this reason, value can only be grasped in freedom![35]

Such wisdom, if it is wisdom, is necessarily closely bound up with love, knowledge, desire, freedom, and choice. It would also be bound up not merely with right or wrong acts, or even with good and evil abstractly, but with the very heart and mind of a man who grasps, affirms, knows, loves and then aligns himself with some object, value, or being. Wisdom would be a personal (a person's) relation to the good. This

---

[34] The personal character of the moral life is expressed throughout scripture. The preamble of the first commandment of the decalogue characterizes ethics and law (the life of God's people) within the context of a personal God who acts historically and relates to them personally. The law then belongs those who are God's people. They call men to be like God, to the love of God, to eternal friendship with him, and are perfective of personhood. In fact, they are fulfilled in the person of Jesus Christ who is the friendship of God and man

[35] Curtis Hancock and Eduardo Bernot, "The True, the False, the Lie, and the Fake," Course Notes (Holy Apostles College and Seminary, Cromwell, CT, spring 2021).

implies the involvement of the intellect and will (heart and mind), the engagement of the whole person (Mtt. 22:37-39).[36] It is this kind of wisdom or knowledge (inclusive of prudence) which would elevate an act beyond being merely a technical skill.

Summary

We have gone far in laying out some preliminary possibilities. The point is not to choose one sense of wisdom in such a manner that disqualifies all others. We can recall that it belongs to wisdom to order!

We might begin ordering by feeling out the relation between doing one's work well, self-knowledge, science, a knowledge of the highest cause(s), and value. We will have a chance to revisit wisdom in the fourth reading.

---

[36] Ibid.

Second Reading

145e-151d Definitions & Midwifery
What is knowledge; Examples—arts & sciences; Patterns of definition; Jacob Klein on division; Encouragement and midwifery

Focus Questions

1. What is the problem with Theaetetus first 'definition' (his examples)? In what way do they help?
2. To whom or to what craft or science would *knowledge of knowledge* belong?
3. How is Socrates's pattern of definition (clay) helpful? (147c)
    a. What kind of definition is it?
    b. What are its strengths and weaknesses?
    c. What does it assume?
    d. What does the act of defining assume?
    e. If you were to use his pattern, how would you define knowledge?
4. What is the significance of Theaetetus' work on squares and their *powers* (what we sometimes call 'roots' today)?
    a. What was his chief method?
5. What is the significance of Socrates claim about gods and men? (149c)
6. Why does Socrates describe himself as a midwife?

Instead of following up Theaetetus's response to his question about wisdom, Socrates turns his attention to knowledge. It will remain for the dialogue as a whole to clarify their relation (wisdom and knowledge).

It makes sense, however, that he shifts the focus of the discussion to knowledge. Knowledge, after all, generally seems to come before wisdom. In the ordinary sense, it seems people

Commentary

learn or know many things, long before they are considered wise. The setting of the dialogue, a gymnasium, is itself more immediately associated with knowledge in this respect. It is a place of learning. Yet, the importance of wisdom has not been wholly set aside. The significance of wisdom will be returned to. It may ultimately turn out that one will never sufficiently *know* what knowledge is without knowing what wisdom is (or without possessing some measure of wisdom). It may be that wisdom is of all knowledge that of which we are most in need.

Socrates answers Theaetetus's somewhat naïve response about wisdom by expressing his perplexity and inability to grasp what knowledge is. We should note that it is unlikely Theaetetus takes him to mean that he (Socrates) is absolutely and in every way ignorant of knowledge. If Socrates were wholly ignorant, what would it even mean for him to speak about or inquire into knowledge (*Meno* 80d-e)? Instead, Theaetetus and Socrates approach their discussion in the manner of an exercise or contest, one which is nevertheless authentic inquiry (146c, 148b-e, 151d-e).

The central question of the dialogue is now brought forward: *What is knowledge?* Precise and mathematical in his thinking, Theaetetus, in his first attempt to define it, *enumerates*; he offers a number of examples, each which he claims is knowledge. His list encompasses science (geometry) and craft (artistic production). This is a fascinating start! He enumerates examples of fields of human science and production which are acquired by effort and experience: things capable of being taught and learned.

Our use of the term 'know' can certainly encompass even more basic aspects of human life, such as the fact that we know people, colors, or shapes, whether it is day or night, how we feel, how to count, etc. But Theaetetus begins with that which often seems to particularly exemplify knowledge and knowers. Nearly all men have some share of knowledge, but most are not considered scientists or artisans.[37] Would not those men and women by knowers in the most precise sense?

Yet, Socrates claims that the answer misses the mark. To enumerate is, after all, not to define (Meno 72a-b). Theaetetus has not answered what knowledge is; he has only given examples.

Yet, we often point to examples when we begin to think about a thing. When we point out examples, we implicitly mark off the *boundaries* or designate the contours of our subject. Examples however do not of their own make a definition explicit. More importantly, it is questionable whether Theaetetus's enumeration is sufficiently precise. That is, it is unclear whether his examples comprehend the full range or a precise range of what we mean we use the word 'know'.

Theaetetus accepts that Socrates' criticism that has not defined knowledge. Socrates next provides him with a pattern or paradigm to follow, *clay is moisture and earth*. Socrates's own pattern is a model of analysis, *dividing* a thing into its elements (see 201e).

Theaetetus, quick in recognition, sees a likeness between this pattern of analysis and his own efforts in mathematics. He tells us that, earlier, he and his friend divided various lines or powers (roots) into two *kinds*. As Jacob Klein points out, it is by division alone that the *potential* infinitude of the objects we encounter become intelligible.[38]

Theaetetus shows his genius here by taking his teacher Theodorus's initial enumeration of the first seventeen squares and dividing their powers into *kinds*: commensurate and incommensurate (rational and irrational). He thus discovers a method of classification through division.

---

[37] One of the defining characteristics of a master has long been thought to be an ability to teach their craft or science.

[38] Jacob Klein, *Greek Mathematical Thought and the Origin of Algebra* (New York: Dover Publications, 1992), 56–59.

Socrates is delighted. Yet Theaetetus recognizes the greater challenge which lies before him, that he may not be up to the task of defining knowledge. Socrates encourages him, reminding him that it is no disgrace to fail to attain a prize which belongs only to the very best of competitors. He goes on to assure Theaetetus that he recognizes in him a kind of *potency,* signs of intellectual *pregnancy.* Socrates then likens himself to a midwife and states that he will help deliver these philosophic offspring, only Theaetetus must be willing to examine them after they are brought forth and determine whether they are sterile and false, or fruitful and true. With this, Theaetetus is now willing to make an attempt.

What is knowledge; Examples—arts & sciences; 145e-146a

So. I am **perplexed** (ἀπορῶ) and not **able** (δύναμαι) to **grasp sufficiently** (λαβεῖν ἱκανῶς) this by **myself** (ἐμαυτῷ)

- **Sufficiently**: What might it mean to do this with complete sufficiency? cf. *Meno* 72d.

- *Aporia* or *perplexity* means to be at 'a loss'. In aporia, one is 'without a way' or without resource to get where (or what) one wishes. The term comes from 'poros', meaning 'resource', 'way', or a 'bridge' across a river.[39] Aporia is the state of one who seems not to be able to *pass over,* to get what they desire.

---

[39] See *Symposium* 202e-204a in which Socrates mythically develops this etymology in order to explore how human beings come to possess wisdom. Erotic love, which lead us to divine truth, is personified in Eros. But eros (or erotic love) is born from the intercourse of Poverty and resource. Thus aporia is itself something

Philosophic inquiry and all theoretical science begins, in part, as a result of aporia. *Insufficient apprehension* is therefore a precise characterization of the philosophic situation. On aporia, Aristotle states in *Metaphysics* III.1:
- one cannot untie a knot of which one is ignorant
- The end is only apparent to one who has been in aporia

- Socrates' power (potential) may be insufficient because he is utterly incapable, because he the object lies beyond him in some manner, or because he cannot grasp what he has in perfect sufficiency.

- Socrates emphasizes friendship with the intensive pronoun 'myself' (ἐμαυτῷ). Philosophic inquiry is not something we do well on our own.

146b-d
Theo.   That sort of thing...
- Theodorus excuses himself from the conversation on the basis of his age and inexperience. It is somewhat ironic that Socrates refers to Theodorus as wise man (ἀνδρὶ σοφῷ). The professional teacher here lacks either the interest, intellectual power, courage, or humility for this task.

---

generative insofar as it is productive of desire or love (eros) which acts as a mediator between gods and men. Eros is therefore that desiring love which stands between lack and possession (perfection and imperfection.). Eros seeks or desires a good which is beyond or outside the self; it is an ek-static love. Desire-filled-lack becomes the mode of connecting to what is desired.

Commentary

- Socrates instructs Theaetetus to speak well and in accord with his birth (εὖ καὶ γενναίως). Theaetetus' birth and nature have been mentioned already in the frame. There is the suggestion that one's birth or nature (one's source) serves as a principle of one's action or power (potential).

So.   **What does knowledge seem to be to you (τί σοι δοκεῖ εἶναι ἐπιστήμη;)?**

- 'Ti esti' (what is...) is modified to 'what does it *seem to you* to be'. This is a sign of the dialectical nature of the conversation. Socrates asks Theaetetus to choose his own beginnings (what *seems to him*). He does not want or expect him to miraculously pass over to a well-rounded scientific conclusion. Dialectic is the practice of friends who use common words and starting places (Meno 75d).

    Aristotle describes dialectic as provisional, hypothetical inquiry, something which can lead to but is not yet properly scientific speech. Dialogue and observation, tied to our ordinary language and experience, mark off the true sources of all reflection.[40]

- Just as in English, there are a multitude of Greek words that expresses kinds of knowledge. Socrates has

---

[40] Aristotle, *Posterior analytics* 71a1-10, "All teaching and all reasoned learning come from previous knowledge...If a proposition is dialectical, it assumes either part indifferently; if it is demonstrative, it lays down one part to the definite exclusion of the other because that part is true." Hugh Tredennick, *Aristotle: in twenty-three volumes. 2: Posterior analytics. Topica*, Reprinted., The Loeb classical library 391 (Cambridge, Mass: Harvard Univ. Press [u.a.], 2004).

chosen *episteme* (ἐπιστήμη) from which we get our world epistemology. He will use many other words throughout the dialogue, but the central term around which they focus, episteme or knowledge, has come to mean scientific knowing. It is worth noting that almost nowhere in the dialogue is an explicit systematic attempt made to distinguish various kinds of knowledge, though each section makes its own contributions. They do not begin with a clear roadmap or set of divisions. Instead, they must reckon with the meaning of knowledge as a complex whole. They are not beginning with explicit and precise definitions or divisions; they are searching for them.

146c
The.   ...It is seems to me (δοκεῖ τοίνυν μοι)...the things one might learn from Theodorus...geometry, etc., .cobblery...are knowledge...

- Theaetetus, the young mathematician, gives an *enumeration* of kinds of knowledge which includes the sciences (theoretical/practical) and arts (craft).

Meno also enumerates examples, but perhaps with less precision (71e-72a). A proper division is more readily discernible in Theaetetus's account—it is accidental whether we speak of the virtue of a man or woman; it is not accidental that knowledge concerns various objects. Socrates will virtually equate definition and division.

   o There is a *division* or *definition* implicit in Theaetetus's first attempt. A good division must be both exhaustive and exclusive.[41] An exhaustive definition divides an entire genus without leaving anything out. Dividing cats into brown and black would fall short because they come in other colors. An exclusive definition should avoid overlap, such as dividing cats into small and nondomestic because there are small nondomestic cats.

Theaetetus's examples imply a division between speculative and productive knowledge. This division is well known but is it exhaustive or exclusive? It is perhaps a bit early to answer this question.

- Examples are an excellent place to begin. To *de-fine* is to set a limit or boundary; it is to *describe* the distinctive contours or internal character of a thing. In pointing at something, we have therefore our initial if imperfect definitions. This is what allows us to direct our attention to the essential *matter* for definition. This material is necessary for us because we arrive at proper definitions only by abstracting what is universal in every example. This, of course, presupposes that one's example(s) properly mark off the universal.

Knowledge is a particularly challenging topic because it requires us to explore different kinds of things known and different modes of knowing. It further

---

[41] Peter Kreeft and Trent Dougherty, *Socratic Logic: A Logic Text Using Socratic Method, Platonic Questions & Aristotelian Principles*, Ed. 3.1. (South Bend, Ind: St. Augustine's Press, 2010), 62–63.

requires us to distinguish various things which seem like knowledge.

- We can move forward noting that, useful as Theaetetus's enumeration is, it is in fact a list and not a proper definition.

146d-147c
So.   ...The art of making shoes...the art of making wooden furnishings
- In each case it seems that knowledge is *of something* (knowledge of *x*). But then, what would knowledge *of knowledge* be *about*? How could we have knowledge of that which is about something else? This is why when we try to define knowledge apart from a specific object, it might easily seem as if we are speaking about 'nothing' ("*Is there nothing in what I say?*" Theaetetus 146e; Meno 79e).
    - o Knowledge may need to be defined not only by its objects, but also by the relationship it implies one has to those objects.
    - o If different objects are known in different ways (cognized, abstracted, analyzed or induced in various ways) or if different objects are intelligible in diverse modes and degrees, we may not be able to give a single, unequivocal definition of know-ledge. Knowledge might be an analogical term instead.

Patterns of definition
147a-d
So.   Take this example...clay...or does anyone understand a name if they do not know what that thing is?

- Examples cannot define if one does not already *somehow* know how the examples express *what* one is defining. If one does not know clay *at all*, examples of the arts or artifacts which use clay are not useful.
  - An example of clay (the material itself) might be different: *This is clay.*

So. Then he does not understand knowledge of shoes if he does not know knowledge (ἐπιστήμην μὴ εἰδώς).

- This conclusion is much more questionable than the one above. In fact, this conclusion must be contrary to the fact if the sentence is taken as a whole and not as a telegraphic way of saying that 'knowledge of shoes' does not explain what 'knowledge' is. Taken as a whole, it says that one can't know about shoes if one does not know what knowledge itself is. But it seems to be precisely the case that the shoemaker knows the knowledge of shoes, even knows that he knows this, while yet not knowing precisely *what* knowledge itself is. Thus, the next conclusion is highly dubious:

So. Then he who is ignorant of knowledge does not understand cobblery or any other art

- This may mean that he who is ignorant of knowledge does not know what the word means when one uses the phrase "knowledge of x'. Or, this may mean that one who is ignorant of what knowledge is has no knowledge whatsoever.
  - Are either of these conclusions acceptable? Is it likely we should meet with a person who is ignorant in either sense?

- The artist or cobbler has a productive knowledge. Socrates is about to discuss a productive power he has. All along we have talked about *nature, power,* and *birth* as a *generative or causal*. We are about to explore a causal or generative source in mathematics: powers.

So.   ...We might have given an everyday answer...about clay...clay is earth mixed with moisture
- Socrates defines clay by means of division or analysis.

    One can divide in a variety of ways:
    - Parts
    - Elements
    - properties
    - Essence
    - Cause (matter, form, efficient, final...)

    Different divisions do not all answer the same question or answer the same way. Further, not everything is subject to the same kinds of divisions

- Socrates definition presupposes we know something about earth and moisture (*Meno* 75c-e).

- How could one use this pattern to define knowledge? An example might be found at 201c-d, where Socrates and Theaetetus propose knowledge is true opinion + an account (x +y). There they may be attempting to show its proper parts. The dialogue leads to that act of analysis or division. Whether it ends up being sufficient is yet to be seen.

Thea.   It seems easy
- Unlike Meno, Theaetetus recognizes that this only *seems* easy!

Commentary

- What does defining presuppose? It is unclear what sort of things can be defined or even how we do it well. Where do we begin? Do we begin with examples, wholes, parts, or elements? The first chapter of Aristotle's *Physics* is helpful here.

147d-148b

<u>...You are probably asking something like what came up among us...when your namesake, Socrates here, and I were talking.</u>

- We have another *kind* of likeness introduced. Theaetetus is like Socrates in looks and character. We are presented here is one who shares Socrates' *name*. This suggest we must be careful in the examination both of things and their names.

So.   What sort of thing (τὸ ποῖον)

- τὸ ποῖον—*what sort* becomes in Aristotle's *Categories* 'quality' from the Latin. Theaetetus is *categorizing* various lengths into *kinds* or *sorts*. This term appears in the geometric section of the *Meno*.

The.   Concerning the powers (δυνάμεων)...Theodorus was drawing some figures...

- Theaetetus takes what he is taught by Theodorus and attempts to give it an of organization. He attempts to classify *kinds* by division. He exemplifies the very process of science which moves from examples to analysis. He and Socrates the younger explore the first seventeen integer squares. They are attending to the *powers* (δυνάμεων) or sides of those squares, what we often call *roots*. These powers or roots are the *potential* causes or sources of the figures because in *squaring* them, one produces the *square*. For instance, a square with an area of sixteen units is produced by the power or line of four units: four *squared* (4^2). These powers are the *potential* cause of a figure's **generation**.

Theaetetus notes that:

- ...The multitude of roots (δυνάμεις) appeared (ἐφαίνοντο) to be **unbounded** (ἄπειροι).
  Glancing over a field of potentially *infinite* objects, Theaetetus notes that he formed a plan to collect them (συλλαβεῖν) into one thing (see the use of συλλαβεῖν at 201c-202c).

- Theaetetus renders the many one by collecting them with a logos.

They at first **appeared** to be unbounded or unlimited in their multitude and thus to allude comprehension. This apparently infinite multitude foreshadows the problem of appearances (the problem of perception) in Act I (151e-187a). There is perhaps a play here upon **unbounded** (ἄπειροι) and being at a loss (ἄπορος).

For a treatment of the connection between mathematics and philosophy see Jacob Klein's *Greek Mathematical Thought and the Origin of Algebra*, particularly chapter six. This section of the commentary depends on Klein's insights.

- Theaetetus **divides** the whole unlimited class of powers into two:

Commentary

        o Equilateral (ἰσόπλευρος/ τετραγωνίζουσι)—whose power is a rational number that is rational in square

        o The Oblong (ἐτερομήκη)—whose power is irrational (incommensurable with the unit measure) but whose plane figure is rational or commensurable (has a common unit measure).

The first 17 unit squares and their areas are:

| 1 | | 2 | | 3 | ... 4, 5, 6, 7, 8, 9, 10, 11, 12, 13, 14, 15, 16, 17

Their powers are:
1, $\sqrt{2}$, $\sqrt{3}$,   **2**, $\sqrt{5}$, $\sqrt{6}$, $\sqrt{7}$, $\sqrt{8}$, **3**, $\sqrt{10}$, $\sqrt{11}$, $\sqrt{12}$, $\sqrt{13}$, $\sqrt{14}$, $\sqrt{15}$, **4**, $\sqrt{17}$

Theodorus enumerated these seventeen squares. He showed which powers (represented above by lines) are commensurable with the unit measure and which are not. Theaetetus classifies those powers or 'sides' into the rational (the 'roots' of the Squares 1, 4, 9, and 16) and the irrational (the roots of squares 2, 3, 5, 6, 7, 8, 10, 11, 12, 13, 14, 15, and 17).

As a mathematical aside, notice that the rational roots progress in a pattern: 1, 2, 3, 4...What would happen if you:
- Squared each of those numbers in the pattern
- And after 1^2, subtract the squares in sequence
    (e.g., 1, 4-1... 9-4... 16-9)[42]

---

[42] Galileo made much of this progression in his study of acceleration. To paraphrase his conclusion in *Two New Sciences*: the time of a motion through x is to the time of the motion through y as the square of distance x is to the square of distance y. Thus, the distances

Theaetetus's method of division suggests that we can classify and relate things which do not fall under a single measure, even if they fall logically into the same genus. There is not one numeric logos or measure that can define rational and irrational numbers; yet we can divide and thus organize and understand the genus.

It is the goal of the scientist to bring order to multitude, unifying and organizing the many under some cause or genus.

> According to St. Thomas the whole of philosophy/science essentially involves a study of opposition between a one and a many, which, for St. Thomas is the fundamental opposition, the foundation for all other oppositions…in some way, all philosophy, every science, involves coming to know how a many is essentially one, how parts are essentially related to constitute a whole.[43]

For instance, Theaetetus derives from his division a classification of those lines which are rational and those lines which are not rational powers.

The historical Theaetetus is said to have developed a complex proof concerning irrational roots (Euclid X, def. 4 and prop. 17) as well as a proof of the quantity of Platonic or regular solids.

---

traversed from the point of departure in equal times are as the odd numbers from unity [1, 3, 5, 7…].

[43] Peter Redpath, "The One and the Many," Course Notes (Holy Apostles College and Seminary, Cromwell, CT, fall 2019).

<u>So.</u> Most Beautiful (κάλλιστα)...
- This work of Theaetetus and his friend earns Socrates's highest praise. It is paradigmatic of science (knowledge) to precisely divide a thing according to its sources and kinds. Just as important, for the dialogue, Theaetetus's effort is a model of playful inquiry, zeal, and insight.

<u>...Excellent/Preminent (ἄριστά) of men</u>
- This is high praise indeed. Sachs comments that Socrates sees an implicit proof here (that which will be found in Euclid's *Elements*, Book X).

Jacob Klein on Division

This minor digression summarizes Jacob Klein's characterization of division as the fundamental mental act by which the world can be comprehended. It is chiefly based on pages 46-60 of his *Greek Mathematical Thought and the Origin of Algebra*. In order to navigate the world, to recognize and distinguish things, we must have a way of saying *this thing* here versus *this other thing there*. But we designate something as *a this* only by having some manner of measuring it, judging it, and grasping it in its discrete unity. That might have to do with color, shape, location, behavior, or power (potency). However it is that we manage to separate one thing from another, we can note that this dividing makes the world a world. Without it, everything would be one or it would be an incomprehensible, infinite muddle of confusion.

But a thing's unity (that it is undivided in itself and thus divisible from another thing) can only be grasped by using a measure. When I scan a table, I will only see it as *one thing* if I see it as one *table*. If I do not have that measure (in this case that of 'table'), nothing prevents me from stopping a third of the way through and declaring the first third of the table to be *one*. While it is logically possible to do this, our world would be incomprehensible if we struggled to grasp the table in its unity. In other words, the various objects of the world communicate, with more or less clarity, their distinctive unity to us.

We encounter various discrete wholes and recognize them as such, even though their unity is diverse in kind. Without a *power* to know unity, the world would be *infinitely* confusing. While I can think of 1/3 of the table as a sort of whole, I only do this by some form of unity or measure. Without such a measure, nothing prevents me from subdividing the table again and again. But our common experience is not that of regressive division. We are not overwhelmed by infinite possibilities of unity. Instead, the world presents itself as full of *kinds* which we slowly learn to categorize.

Without these kinds or mental apprehension of them, we could never truly begin to know anything. We therefore depend upon a grasp of wholes properly divided from other wholes. Klein concludes not only that knowledge depends on division, but that Division itself presupposes limits, limits already grasped. Knowledge and being therefore seem to depend upon unity, kinds of unity, and that being is divided by these *kinds of unity*.

It turns out that this is Aristotle and Plato argued that matter as such, mere extensive being, is continuous and unintelligible. The world becomes intelligible not by mere extension, but first and foremost through **formal** unity: that by which being is *limited* and *definite*.

Jacob Klein discusses this ordinary mode of analysis in light of number. Arithmetic lays bare this fundamental features of our reasoning. Numbers are potentially infinite in quantity. If one did not have a way to define and specify kinds of numbers, one would not be able to speak about their properties—there could be no mathematical science. Each number would be a unique multitude of units, unrelated to prior or preceding numbers except by virtue of sequence. The number universe would be inconceivable accept as a potentially infinite sequential multitude.

Mathematicians however have a science because they divide numbers into *kinds*: by even and odd; prime and composite, etc. The mathematical universe becomes intelligible then only through such divisions or classifications. Klein explains that we classify numbers into *eidos*, which is the Greek term often translated as 'form', 'look', or 'species'. Eidos is that very 'form' which plays a central role in Plato's thought. Following Plato and later thinkers, Klein unpacks its basic function in our apprehension and reasoning. *These* kinds or species (eidos) serve as a sort of measure and unity by which to divide and understand any multitude.

> Only through membership in an *eidos* derivable from such 'sources' (ἀρχαί) does the being of a number become intelligible as determinate, i.e., as *delimited*, number, as one assemblage of just so and so many monads—whatever the mode of being of the *eide* themselves may be...While the determination of each number as 'a number of something'...can be understood only as the consequence of the special *kind* to which it belongs, i.e., by means of something *which is in itself one* and is thus capable of unifying, of making wholes—of delimiting. Precisely because the *arithmos as such is not one but many, its delimitation in a particular case can be understood only by finding the eidos which delimits its multiplicity, in other words, by means of arithmetike as a theoretical discipline.*[44]

---

[44] Klein, *Greek Mathematical Thought and the Origin of Algebra*, 56.

A definition is literally a way of delimiting, a mind of boundary or de-fining of some being or nature. It requires the separating of one kind of thing from another, whether or not they both fall into the same higher genus. If we take an example (human), we can see how division may be dialectical, that is hypothetical or experimental (two-legged featherless biped), scientific (rational animal), or proximate (self-moving thing). The tree of porphyry is a way of visualizing this process genetically.

The. But really, Socrates, I cannot answer that question of yours about knowledge, as we answered the question about length and **powers** (δυνάμεως.).
- Theaetetus recognizes that this question about knowledge lies somewhat beyond his **power**. Is it wholly out of his reach? This not only suggests a modicum of humility, but that Theaetetus has a certain degree of self-knowledge!

Encouragement and midwifery
148c-151d
Socrates encourages Theaetetus. The race is difficult but worth running even if one does not win the laurel.

The. If it is a question of **eagerness** (προθυμίας), Socrates, it will **appear** (φανεῖται).
- *Thumos* (desire, spiritedness) is a necessary quality for battle and effort. It is what characterizes the guardians in the *Republic*.
- The term 'appear' anticipates perception in Act I.

So. Well then, you lead the way excellently, take your answer about the powers as a representation (μιμούμενος)…

Commentary

- Perhaps here, 'powers' is meant in multiple senses. If it is, the hint that knowledge is a certain kind of power is not grasped by Theaetetus. He does not explore the *sort of power* knowledge might be.

  <u>...just as you embraced (περιέλαβες) them all (πολλὰς οὔσας) in one form/look (εἴδει)</u>
- Theaetetus has made one out of many by grasping some causal form. He has divided them into kinds. Socrates encourages him to do the same with the **many knowledges, to embrace them all in some one form**. Theaetetus responds (148e) that he does not know how to do this. He therefore *knows that he does not know*. Such a person cannot be wholly ignorant. It is in fact the sort of knowledge Socrates is known for (cf. *Apology* 20e-21d).

- Theaetetus states that he has often tried to answer such questions; this is not his first time reflecting on such problems (148e).

So. <u>You are in travail because you are not empty but pregnant.</u>

The. <u>I do not know (οὐκ οἶδα) [about being pregnant], Socrates...</u>
- He merely tells Socrates that he is undergoing or suffering (πέπονθα) without understanding it.

149a
So. <u>...I am the son of a nobly born (γενναίας) and virile (βλοσυρᾶς) midwife (μαίας), Phainarete?</u>
- Μαίας can mean virile, burly, hairy, or solemn!

- The etymology of 'Phainarete' is something like *virtue made manifest* or *virtue brought to light*.

  <u>...And have you also heard that I practice the same art?...other people...say that I am a most strange one (ἀτοπώτατός) and that I make men perplexed (ἀπορεῖν).</u>

149b-c
So. <u>No one of them [the midwives] attends to [those in labor] while still able to conceive, but only when unable (**ἀδύνατοι**)...they say the cause of this is Artemis, because she, a childless goddess, has had childbirth allotted to her....</u>

- It is not given to barren women to be midwifes. This should be kept in mind in terms of the analogy Socrates is setting up between their art and his own. Is Socrates ever barren or barren only now? Does the analogy break down at this point?

  <u>[Artemis]...did not give it (ἔδωκε) to barren women because **human nature is to weak** to lay hold of (ἀνθρωπίνη φύσις ἀσθενεστέρα ἢ λαβεῖν) an art of which it has **no experience** (ἄπειρος)</u>

- **Experience** (ἄπειρος) hearkens etymologically back both to *aporia* and the *unbounded* or *infinite* previously mentioned (ἄπειρος 147d). That which is *potentially intelligible* must become actually intelligible. The pun suggests this happens through experience and perhaps *travail* or aporia—the birth pangs of philosophy.

- Socrates makes a fascinating distinction between human power and divine knowledge. He claims here that man can only learn through experience. This might be worth contrasting with the argument for recollection in the *Meno*. Can these two ways of thinking be reconciled? Perhaps if one assumes that a certain kind of experience or knowledge is **given** (ἔδωκε) by nature herself. See *Posterior Analytics* Book I.1-4 & especially Book II.19. We can at least say that science and philosophy occur *through* something; they are not immediate to us. But to do philosophy, to arrive at a conclusion, we need some beginning which we do grasp immediately.

- The goddess gives this office to those *done bearing* because they are now *like* her. This has a double meaning. It may be that these women are now barren. But the account rather suggests it is also important that they *have born* children. In this sense, they have become more like her in having matured through experience and come to a certain perfection. They have been allotted their art because of a likeness to a divine being (ὁμοιότητα), one who is virginal hunter! The excellence of the mind may have something to do with its effort and purity (as the image of wax in Act III suggests). Here, it is suggested that there is something divine in knowledge, even in self-knowledge.

149e
So.   ...Is there one art for sowing, another for harvesting?
- In the agricultural world, this is not the case. The one who sows, also harvests. Certainly, Socrates is a bit playful here regarding matchmaking and bringing forth children. Nevertheless, they are closely connected in reality—the character of the child born is *related* to the pairing which produces it. Here again is

the recurring theme of birth, source, and generation. We can note that a *concept* is something *conceived* or given birth to in the mind. If the mind is the mother or womb, who or what is the father?[45]

- Socrates claims that panderers (unartful and unjust people) have given this art a bad name. Is this a veiled reference to sophists and rhetors? We are prone to affirm our own ideas and ready solutions without sufficiently examination.

150b

So.   ...Women do not, like my patients, bring forth at one time true children and at another time, images (εἴδωλα).

---

[45] Consider this poem by Gerard Manley Hopkins:
To R.B.

The fine delight that fathers thought; the strong
Spur, live and lancing like the blowpipe flame,
Breathes once and, quenchèd faster than it came,
Leaves yet the mind a mother of immortal song.
Nine months she then, nay years, nine years she long
Within her wears, bears, cares and moulds the same:
The widow of an insight lost she lives, with aim
Now known and hand at work now never wrong.
Sweet fire the sire of muse, my soul needs this;
I want the one rapture of an inspiration.
O then if in my lagging lines you miss
The roll, the rise, the carol, the creation,
My winter world, that scarcely breathes that bliss
Now, yields you, with some sighs, our explanation.

From, Gerard Manley Hopkins, *Poems and Prose of Gerard Manley Hopkins*, Repr., Penguin Classics (Harmondsworth: Penguin Books, 2000), 68.

Commentary

- The false children are described *like* the true. It is the job of someone experienced to distinguish or divide (διαφέρει) by their art the true from the false, to distinguish what is only *like* from what is authentic in its generation. Keep in mind that offspring are always *like* or *images* of what they are born from; nevertheless, this does not mean that they are always true born. The power to distinguish is one that must be acquired. Perhaps this power more than any other is exercised in *Theaetetus*.

- Socrates here describes himself as tending not to the body, as ordinary midwives, but to the soul and thinking (ψυχή and διάνοια). These are important keywords which are not returned to for some time.

150c-151d

So. <u>The god forces me to be a midwife but hinders me from generating.</u>

- This passage is slightly ambiguous, particularly in light of what he has said about the weakness of human nature.

So. <u>No god has ill will toward human beings</u>

- A remarkable claim about the divine disposition! What heights would philosophy have to reach to know such a thing with certainty! Does such knowledge belong principally to philosophy or to some other habit or tradition? Why would one need to know this?

<u>Therefore, from the beginning (ἐξ ἀρχῆς), Theaetetus, **attempt** (πειρῶ) to say what knowledge is (ἐπιστήμη). And never say that you are unable to do</u>

<u>so; for if God wills it and gives you courage, you will be able.</u>
- Socrates has exhorted and encouraged Theaetetus. He has framed this reason for courage in the context of divine goodness, aid, friendship, as well as in inner capacity.

The midwife and wisdom

This strange passage indicates much that will follow in the *Theaetetus*. It alerts us that Socrates is not just committed to an examination of arguments; he is committed to Theaetetus himself, to attend to and care for him artfully as a midwife tends to a pregnant woman. It also tells us that the outcome will also depend on Theaetetus's own attitude and cooperation.

Playfully uniting several of the dialogue's central themes, Socrates relates birth, sources, likeness, experience, and art, with virtue, character (nature), wisdom, intellectual development, and philosophy.

His account of the midwife (μαῖα) is so well-known that 'maieutics' and 'maieutic inquiry' have become virtually synonymous for dialectic and the *Socratic method*. To this day, teachers pride themselves in being midwifes to their students. We have already begun (and we will continue) to explore features of Socratic inquiry, but we should keep in mind that this *method* is not a mechanical system for constructing facts or shaping minds. Nor is it merely a means of tearing down false opinions. It is a natural, artful *road* or *way* (ὀδός...μέθοδος) of reflecting upon what we know and what we do not know. It is not a method in the modern sense but a process more like giving birth, with rhythms, variations, and conditions unique to the labor of each *mother and child*.

A midwife, Socrates explains, is one who leads a pregnant woman through the process of giving birth by means of their art. She knows when and how to induce contractions and helps deliver babies. Socrates has *experience* with this because his mother, Phaenarete (*bringing virtue to light*) was a midwife (μαῖα).⁴⁶ According to John Burnet, a μαῖα was traditionally *born* of a good family.⁴⁷ A midwife knows, best of all, who is and who is not pregnant. She can read the signs of pregnancy and labor. She is also skilled in match making, though she says little of this because the 'art' of pandering has brought this skill into disrepute.

These women, we are told, have such skill through experience and receive their art from Artemis, the virgin twin of Apollo.⁴⁸ Artemis allots this art to women past childbearing age because they are only then *like* her. Nevertheless, they are women who have *previously* born children. They are not like Artemis in perpetual virginity (having never born children), but rather in having *grown to be like the goddess*. Human nature is such that one must *grow into* a divine likeness, into wisdom and art—it has no power to do so *without experience*.

Socrates is also a kind of midwife, but of the mind rather than the body. He recognizes when young men are pregnant with thought. It is no accident that the words 'concept' and 'conceive' are associated with the act of generation.

Socrates helps these men bring forth what is in them. Their offspring, however, must be brought into the light and carefully tested after their delivery or full formation. For these men, it yet remains to be seen whether the things they have begotten are true or only false and images (ψευδῆ καὶ εἴδωλα,

---

⁴⁶ Henry George Liddell et al., *A Greek-English Lexicon* (Clarendon Press ; Oxford University Press, 1996).

⁴⁷ John Burnet and James Hastings, "Socrates," *Encyclopaedia of Religion and Ethics* (New York: Charles Scribner's Sons, 1908), 668.

⁴⁸ It is perhaps worth noting that she is also the goddess of the hunt. On the theme of hunting, see 197c-198a or Plato's *Sophist*.

150e). This is the challenging part of Socrates's art. Men are often irrationally attached to their *offspring*. Philosophy, therefore, requires a certain docility and humility, a love of truth, over and above a love for what is merely *one's own*. In this respect, the dialogue will *bring to light* Theaetetus's character.

In placing himself in this maieutic context, Socrates rejects the role of father.[49] If Socrates is a teacher, it is as a guide, not an *inseminator* of ideas. This is the distinction between training and education, between how we treat animals versus human beings. An animal is trained to a task, but a human being is led (*e-ducare*) through a process of self-development. The animal is subordinated to the task of a master while a human being is called upon to become a master himself—to realize and develop powers which he already possesses. Philosophy then is peculiar to those with an innate freedom. It is not servile either to others or to one's own desires. This all depends on what was suggested earlier, that to learn anything at all, we must already possess a principle of wisdom (145d, cf. *Meno* 81a-d).

This theme is reiterated in the *Republic* where Socrates explains that some err in thinking of education as a kind of force-feeding of the soul, a mechanical communication of knowledge to those who lack it:

> "Certain professional educators must be wrong when they boast that education is *inserting knowledge into a soul* (ψυχῇ ἐπιστήμης σφεῖς ἐντιθέναι) like sight into blind eyes…but our account (λόγος) indicates that there is already an **innate power** in the soul (τὴν

---

[49] Protagoras will be described as a father of a false argument. He has provided matter for Theaetetus, but he has not generated wisdom in him.

ἐνοῦσαν ἑκάστου **δύναμιν** ἐν τῇ ψυχῇ, *Republic* VII 518b-d).⁵⁰

He goes on in Book VII of the *Republic* to suggest there is an art (τέχνη) which facilitates the souls turning to the light, a conversion from becoming to being. He argues that the power or principle of thought in man which makes such conversion possible in the first place is something divine and unfading, but only becomes **useful and beneficent** by means of this conversion (χρήσιμόν τε καὶ ὠφέλιμον 518e, cf. *Theaetetus* 167c). The maieutic art is therefore a fitting image for the work of a teacher, for one who is a paraclete rather than simply over and above their pupil.

The maieutic art belongs to those who have experience, to those who have been in the same condition as those they help, which suggests that Socrates has been in Theaetetus's place—full of nascent ideas and ready to learn. Theaetetus and Socrates, after all, possess *essentially* the same capacity for knowledge. In this light, the teacher's role is not to make knowledge exist where there was none, but to develop and draw out the innate capacity of a student. This partly explains why philosophy is most fruitful when it attends to our ordinary modes of discourse (to the ways in which people regularly express their thoughts in speech). To exchange ordinary discourse for a purely technical jargon would be to several philosophy from its roots, from that nascent *power* or wisdom which is captured, however confusedly, in our speech.

Nevertheless, not every student is equal; not every student is ready for or desires philosophic inquiry. It belongs to a teacher to assess this, to determine the condition of the learner (disciple). A good teacher will thereby engage a fellow

---

⁵⁰ Plato and Paul Shorey, *Plato in Twelve Volumes, Vols. 5 & 6*, Reprinted., The Loeb classical library 123 (Cambridge, Mass.: Harvard Univ. Press, 2006).

human being, relying upon and calling forth natural capacities and desires. This by no means suggests a teacher merely asks questions (this is not, after all, what Socrates does). But this does mean that even as one expounds and considers various issues, ultimately, it belongs to the student to take up that material dialectically, to test and try those arguments within themselves. The *child begotten* (the logos brought forth in labor) must ultimately become the students own if they are to grow intellectually.

Finally, Socrates states that like other midwifes, he also is barren. The god compels him to help others but hinders his own begetting. This may mean that he has been barren his whole life or that he has been barren of such *generative* wisdom ever since he has taken on his maieutic role. If Socrates has never brought forth any knowledge whatsoever, he is without experience and therefore ill matched to help Theaetetus. One might, of course, argue this simply means he will reveal that both he and Theaetetus know nothing whatsoever. The dialogue will then by a total void. How would we even *know* that we do not know in such a case?

We will have to judge whether this dialogue ends up being merely a wind-egg and barren or if the truth is in some manner brought to light.[51] After all, if find that the logos of *Theaetetus* turns out to be false or to be only an image (εἴδωλα), it seems we must know something of the original if we are to judge the image as falling short of that which it *looks like*.

---

[51] In *De Veritate* q.11, Thomas Aquinas explores whether a teacher has the capacity to generate or cause knowledge. He compares the *becoming* of knowledge, virtue, and substantial-generation analogically. These three *becomings* are intertwined and explored in *Theaetetus* also.

Act I: Sense Perception (Apprehension)

Third Reading

151e-160e   Sense Perception (*aisthesis*) is always true knowledge:
General outline of third reading; Following the clue; Perception is always true; Man as the measure of all things; Relative qualities; All is in motion; Qualities as the union of active and passive (sensed and sense); Primacy of motion; Deducing consequences; Wonder and philosophy; Problem of dreams; 'Solution' through a deeper relativism;

Focus Questions

1. How well has Theaetetus followed the pattern Socrates set for him (147c)?
2. How is this definition (knowledge is perception) a better beginning than the examples (146c)? Why is perception a good starting point?
3. Why does Socrates claim this is equivalent to Protagoras's claim that man is the measure of all things?
4. What are the strengths and weaknesses of this definition?
5. Why does Socrates focus on motion and change?

General Outline of third reading

- Knowledge is nothing but Perception→Man as the measure of all things
- Perception cannot be false
    - Nothing is one; Nothing ever is but is always becoming

- - - Stillness causes destruction & decay; motion causes health and the good
    - Cannot assign a place to qualities/sensibles in themselves
      - They are the result of the impact
    - Nothings appears the same to two people
      - Nothing appears the same to the same man!
- Qualities are not things in themselves or else they would not change
  - Rather they are in the relation to other things with which they interact
    - Example of dice:
      - A half & double (a relative quality)
      - Four & six (intrinsic quantity)
        - Can Anything become great without being increased?
          - Theaetetus would like to say no, but must say yes in following the argument
- Socrates's three proposals:
  - 1. Nothing becomes more or less as long as it is equal to itself
  - 2. If nothing is added or subtracted than a thing always remains equal
  - 3. What was not previously could not now be or come to be without becoming
- The dice contend with these three assumptions
  - Theaetetus lost in wonder—Wonder & Philosophy
- Initiation into the mysteries
  - Everything is motion
    - Two kinds of motion:
      - 1. Active (sense objects)

- 2. Passive (sense)
  - These kinds are in motion either swift or slow
    - Together they beget a sensible quality and perception
    - Nothing exists in itself: they exist only in union of an active and passive element
  - Everything is always becoming in relation to something
    - Being should be abolished
      - Speech that makes things stand still should be abolished
- Defective Point of argument:
  - Dreams and illusions suggest that there are true as well as false perceptions
    - This cannot be if perception is know-ledge
      - Solution:
        - The perceiver is never the same:
          - Therefore, when dreaming, a dream is true for them
          - When waking, waking is true then for them
            - Socrates-dreaming ≠ Socrates-awake (they are wholly unlike!)
        - The result of solution is that all becoming and knowing is relative to the knower
          - All perceptions can thus be true for *each perceiver*

Following the clue

We often associate clues with detective novels, with the likes of Sherlock Holmes, who uses a clue to deduce (or induce) a solution. But the word 'clue', from the Middle English, refers to a ball of thread.[52] A much older association (as in Theseus's encounter with the Minotaur) is that of a clue and labyrinth. Labyrinths were once regular features of gardens and mosaics. They were even used in spiritual exercises. Make no mistake, real philosophy is a spiritual exercise.

While it is unlikely that a minotaur was any more common in the Middle Ages than today, the idea that a thread might lead one through a winding and bewildering course is readily intelligible. We love something about finding our way through an impasse, about solving riddles and making sense of a complex whole.[53] But to find our way through Plato's *Theatetus*,

---

[52] "Cleue - Middle English Compendium," accessed March 17, 2021, https://quod.lib.umich.edu/m/middle-english-dictionary/dictionary/MED8009/track?counter=1&search_id=5606458.

[53] Thomas Khun characterizes ordinary science as the work of "puzzle solving" (ch.VI); Thomas S. Kuhn, *The Structure of Scientific Revolutions*, 3rd ed. (Chicago, IL: University of Chicago Press, 1996). *Physics* I.1 suggests analysis of the complex whole is characteristic of reason (see Act III). St. Thomas characterizes reason as collative and discursive. See also Summa III, Q.11, a.4. From Thomas's *Commentary on Boethius's de Trinitate*, Ch.2, Q.6:

Now reason differs from intellect as multitude does from unity. Thus Boethius says that reasoning is related to understanding as time to eternity and as a circle to its center. For it is distinctive of reason to disperse itself in the consideration of many things, and then to gather one simple truth from them. Thus Dionysius says, souls have the power of reasoning in that they approach the truth of things from various angles, and in this respect they are inferior to the angels; but inasmuch as they gather a multiplicity into unity they are in a way equal to the angels. It is clear, then, that rational

neither main rational *force* nor haphazard guesswork will suffice. This is because the goal is not just to get somewhere; it is to *know* the way (*Meno* 97a-e). Therefore, it is apropos to recall that a clue is not just something one *uses* but an integral thread which one must *follow*.

To discover such a thread, whether in a difficult text or in our lives, is to discover a cause and justification for hope. This is because in doing so we take hold of a means of navigating and delineating a whole. To discover a unifying thread, a clue, is to discover a logos! Heraclitus states in two fragments:

> Though the logos is common, the many live as if they have their own wisdom.[54]

> The soul is a self-increasing logos.[55]

We must listen to the logos of the *Theaetetus* and let the logos be our clue. Though much that is said will feel somewhat haphazard, there is indeed a thread of reason which runs throughout, weaving together an intelligible whole.

Jacob Klein describes Plato's *Phaedo* as a philosophic labyrinth with fear and death at the Minotaur at the center.[56] The

---

thinking ends in intellectual thinking, Following the process of analysis, in which reason gathers one simple truth from many things. And again, intellectual thinking is the beginning of rational thinking, following the process of synthesis, in which the intellect comprehends a multiplicity in unity. So the thinking that is the terminus of all human reasoning is supremely intellectual.

[54] Fragment 2. This translation is based upon the Greek text and translation found in Heraclitus and Thomas M. Robinson, *Fragments* (Toronto: University of Toronto Press, 1991), 10.

[55] Fragment 115. Ibid., 66.

[56] Plato et al., *Plato's Phaedo*, Focus philosophical library (Newburyport, MA: Focus Publishing /R. Pullins Company, 1998), 1–24. The *Phaedo* recounts Socrates final hours, his execution having

labyrinth of the *Theaetetus*, on the other hand, is not the dread lair of death. It is the tangle of human experience. The clue we must follow, as Heraclitus suggests, is a clue we already each have a share in, one which is common to our nature. We must take hold of ourselves then, of our experience, of the situation in which we exist, and attempt to untangle the confused knot, hopefully without cutting the living cord. We can only do so through logos.

Will the thread(s) of our experience hang together? Will the clue lead us through? Is there anything at the center? If not, what we hold is not one but rather a multitude of disconnected strands, a jumble of unrelated bits and pieces. The world and our cognitive grasp of it, however, does not present itself as alien or fragmented in this manner. The whole of human life, the whole created order is woven together by logos. It has the structure of a word (John 1:1, 3).

Nevertheless, this does not mean the task of learning is easy. Heraclitus also tells us that "nature loves to hide" (B123). And Scripture teaches that "It is the glory of God to conceal a word, but it is the glory of kings to search a word out" (Prov. 25:2).

There is a knack to unravelling a knotted ball of yarn. It takes docility, attention, intuition, steadfastness, prayer, perhaps all the virtues.[57] We will need these virtues as we go forward. In part, this is because we cannot predetermine what it is we shall find. It is also because we do not always lay hold of the argument in the most propitious manner. There are many apparent dead ends, some which only seem so. If we are not careful, we can make the tangle worse.

---

previously been postponed during the religious celebration of the Minotaur's defeat.

[57] For an illustration of such a thread, see chapters 11, 12, and 15 in *The Princess and the Goblin.* George MacDonald, Arthur Hughes, and Ursula K Le Guin, *The Princess and the Goblin*, 2016.

Theaetetus has taken hold of perception as his beginning. This is the first thread or part which he tugs on. In doing so, he begins with what is experientially first to us, though perhaps not with what is most characteristic of human cognition. The very first matters which engage our conscious lives, that stir our thoughts, have a connection to sense experience. It seems that the senses and what we know through them provide a good deal of the *matter* which we attend to.

But are sensations (or even sensible things) the only or ultimate objects of our thinking? Are they the things we know best or that which can be best known? For instance, do I know a sensation of color, flavor, texture, or temperature better than I know the thing which I am eating? Is the thing I eat only a conglomeration of such qualities? Do I know that it is good to eat or only that I feel pleasure? To strictly insist on sensation would mean excluding our knowledge of wholes, of substances and natures (oranges, people, trees, cats), of good and evil, of justice, love, friendship, virtually all that makes human experience truly human.

Still, Theaetetus has not ill chosen where to begin. The unity and analogy of sense with experience, judgment, and all our other forms of cognition is expressed in ordinary words like 'see', 'sense', and 'perceive.' Those words often describe acts which go far beyond the five senses. '*I see what you mean*' only distantly refers to sensation. Such ways of speaking suggest not only an analogy between sense and cognition but an organic link.

In sensing, we grasp that which is greater than sensation. While we may want to modify or nuance the medieval dictum *nihil est in intellectu quod non sit prius in sensu* (nothing is in the intellect which was not first in the senses), we can at least admit that the senses are the profound starting place of human cognition.

Having acknowledged the organic unity of sensing and knowing, we must nor forget that Theaetetus's definition will compel us to explore sensation or perception *per se* (in itself). We are about to examination sensation abstracted from other forms of cognition, insofar as such abstraction is possible. In doing so, we can begin to clarify both what is characteristic of sensation and simultaneously that which goes beyond it.

Socrates will explore the sufficiency of sense experience, whether it alone or even chiefly can account for what we call knowledge. This approach is reasonable if we keep in mind that it simply follows upon Theaetetus's definition. Our question in Act I cannot be then whether perception (sensation) is *related to, a kind of,* or *needed for* knowing; our question in Act I is whether knowledge is *nothing other* than sense perception (151e).

Sensing and seeing are commonly treated as the preeminent source (the cause and measure) of all knowledge. Such an attitude usually goes hand in hand with a commendation of the hard sciences. After all, the hard sciences, the *empirical* sciences, which are based on sense perception, have had countless successes over the centuries. But should we characterize science merely as the development of sense experience?[58] It may depend what *development* or even sense *experience* implies. Further, do the hard sciences exhaust what we can rightly consider the domain of human knowledge?

Human experience, far more complex and wonderous than it may seem at first glance, remains to be analyzed as we

---

[58] As Act I will make clear, the cognitional analysis of sense experience is not the same thing as sensing. Empiricism or scientific empiricism is often described as sense experience, but without due attention to our cognitive and theoretical activity. For accounts concerning the relation between sense and cognition, see *Phaedo* 74b-75b, *Metaphysic* I.1; *Posterior Analytics* II.19; *Physics* I.1; *One the Soul* III.

reflect on the *Theaetetus*. Perhaps in doing so, we shall know ourselves, our sensing, and what it is to know a bit more clearly.

Logic, Conclusions, Dialectic

Plato's dialogues come remarkably close to living speech with all its implicit connections, tentative conclusions, unfollowed leads, occasional non sequiturs, analogical explanations, imagery, emotional coloring, as well as the explicit and implicit use of logic.[59] The logic of a dialogue is the robust logic of living men and women—not solely the formal logic of textbooks. To be sure, as in all life, syllogistic reasoning is necessary, though it is rarely the explicit or foremost tool of inquiry. It serves as a means to test and to order, to ensure that what is said is not nonsense. But it must remain ever subordinate to that greater whole, our "real situation" with which we must reckon.[60] A supposedly logical conclusion that leads to

---

[59] Plato clearly knew the science of logic and the difference between valid and invalid, sound and unsound arguments. However, it is Aristotle who provides our first explicit text on formal logic. See John Deely, *Introducing Semiotic: Its History and Doctrine*, Advances in semiotics (Bloomington: Indiana University Press, 1982), chap. ch.3; 146 n.5; 147 n.1.

[60] Redpath, "The One and the Many." Peter Redpath uses the term 'real situation' to describe the total *situation* in which we live and find ourselves—the actual context in which philosophy and science occur. Philosophy cannot be understood through mental activity alone, apart from the historical, psychological, spiritual, personal context in which it exists. Philosophic inquiry does not begin in abstraction, without rhyme or reason. Further, it succeeds only insofar as it in some manner illuminates our real experience of the world. Redpath explains that this is why the genus of the logician (that which the logician studies) is not precisely the same as that of the

nonsense or the upending of all experience must be treated with skepticism. Though valid, it may not necessarily be true!

Also, it can take considerable imaginative-cognitional work to figure out how one step in the dialogue is related to another. The good news is that we are all familiar with these odd logical dance steps. Conversations with friends often range over wide territory and follow the most subtle of associations, all without our conscious awareness. Our work is to bring, as much as possible, the thread which binds the whole into our conscious thought and to analyze it.

With that said, we need to be attentive not only to stated premises and conclusions at various stages in the dialogue but also to the logical and dramatic context of those steps. While a premise can be stated scientifically (with certainty), much of what is said will be proposed hypothetically. One of the most challenging aspects of reading Plato (or Aristotle) is distinguishing what remains firm, after all is said and done, from what has been rejected (either in part or whole).

Act I explores Theaetetus's first major definition. All that is said in it must be understood in light of his claim about sense perception. The general hypothesis of Act I is that knowledge is *nothing* but perception. From this will flow other hypothetical conclusions, some which are themselves tentative, some which are not. The very meaning of some terms must be understood in light of this hypothesis. Even if we reject the ultimate premise of this Act, it does not mean we will have to reject all that is said within it. This is because there are

---

philosopher. The logician studies essences only as cognitional and in their cognitional relations. The philosopher studies essences and natures insofar as they are causal and constitute real wholes and relations in the world. The philosopher attends not only to logical relations, but to things as they are, in their complex and diverse modes of existence.

more fundamental premises which underlies speech and reason than Theaetetus's definition.

Perception is always true; Man as the measure of all things 151e-152b

The.   Since you are so **encouraging** (παρακελευομένου)...it seems to me that one who knows anything **perceives** that which he **knows** (δοκεῖ οὖν μοι ὁ ἐπιστάμενός τι **αἰσθάνεσθαι** τοῦτο ὃ **ἐπίσταται**)...

- **Encouragement** is one of the prerogatives of teachers and friends.

- **αἴσθησις** can be translated as sensation or perception. I will use them interchangeably throughout the translation and discussion. The Greek has much of the same semantic range we find in English. For instance, 'I see what you mean' captures a metaphorical, synthetic, or wholistic use. However, it is apparent that Theaetetus means sense perception as such or *per se* (hearing, seeing, taste, touch, smell).

- He opens this stage of the dialogue with the phrase 'δοκεῖ οὖν μοι' (it seems to me). This is precisely where genuine dialogue must begin.

...and as it appears now, knowledge is **nothing other** than perception (καὶ ὥς γε νυνὶ φαίνεται, **οὐκ ἄλλο τί** ἐστιν ἐπιστήμη ἢ αἴσθησις).

- To claim that one perceives what one knows would not necessarily be the same as saying that knowledge is *nothing other* than perception. This ambiguity is about to be explored. Theaetetus's *division* may not have been made with sufficient precision.

- Theaetetus has made a division:
  - If something cannot be perceived, it cannot be known.
    - What does this mean for friendship, justice, God, mathematics, or knowledge itself?

So.   <u>Good and **well born** boy…not a trivial saying about knowledge, but what Protagoras said.</u>
- Socrates responds with a twofold comment on *sources*:
  - Theaetetus' source (or genealogy);
  - the source of Theaetetus' definition (Protagoras).

- The order of the inquiry parallels other dialogues. Having begun with examples, it next takes up the opinion of wise or eminent men. Aristotle formalizes this into his general method, a method later taken up in the Scholastic period. One explores what the wise and the many say, uses examples, experience, and logic. Philosophy does not happen in a vacuum but by entering into conversation, into a tradition.[61] Those who have come before do much to make the problems and the way forward clear.

  - As an aside, many of the greatest innovators are terribly difficult to read because they make important and difficult distinctions for the first time. Aristotle and Ludwig von Mises are two examples. It is the relative privilege of following generations to formalize whatever truth they have attained more felicitously.

---

[61] Alasdair C. MacIntyre, *Three Rival Versions of Moral Enquiry*, Reprint. (Notre Dame, Ind: Univ. of Notre Dame Press, 2006).

Commentary

Still, something can be lost in pithy speech (either the precision of distinctions or the ground of reasoning for those distinctions). There is ever a need for *ressourcement.*

<u>...Man is the measure of things, of the things that are, that they are, and of the things that are **not**, that they are not...</u>

- In his maieutic role, Socrates helps Theaetetus formulate his own argument and grasp all its implications.

- Socrates does not just 're-formulate' Theaetetus's definition; he recalls the conclusion of Protagoras whom he recognizes to be the *source* or 'father' of Theaetetus's mental offspring.[62] This formulation is in some manner directly contrary to Parmenides's doctrine which denies that we can *nay-say* (speak about what is not).[63]

- It is perhaps not clear how the statement about perception is *equivalent* to the statement about man being the measure of things. To measure is to judge or give an account of something, to know it in some respect. A true measure fully accounts for a thing, just as the unit perfectly measures every counting number, or as 'rational animal' measures man.[64] Perception however is

---

[62] We might say that Protagoras is materially the father, but not that he is the father of Theaetetus' mental capacity.

[63] An example would be, "That is *not* a cat."

[64] A meter stick is the measure of a meter. An inch can measure a foot in this sense. But an inch could never measure a meter—one cannot divide a meter by an integer quantity of inches. Meters and

something private; it is not a measure that one can share with another. You cannot see my seeing (or feel my feeling). Each man would be the measure of his own perceiving. It is difficult to imagine what it would mean to say a man can be wrong in his very perceiving. In what sense can perception as such be false? Be careful you are not importing something more than sensation into the argument! We will explore this problem throughout Act I (and into Act II).

...<u>You have read that?</u>
- Theaetetus readily admits he has read the *Truth*, Protagoras' treaties, many times. Theodorus, Theaetetus's teacher, was a disciple of Protagoras. Theaetetus begins with what is familiar to him, within the philosophic tradition he has inherited from his own teacher. The opening of the dialogue places this inquiry in the context of discipleship, sources, and intellectual lineage (Megarian, Platonic, the gymnasium, and now Protagorean).

Relative qualities
152b
So. <u>Does it not happen at times, when **the same** (τοῦ αὐτοῦ) wind blows, one of us feels cold, and the other does not, or...Shall we say that the wind is **in itself** (ἑαυτοῦ) cold or not cold or shall we accept Protagoras's saying that it is cold for him who feels cold and not for him who does not?</u>
- Sensing is subjective in at least two ways.

---

inches are incommensurable. If an inch was the unit measure, a meter would be an irrational magnitude.

Commentary

- All sensing requires a sensing *subject* (a person who senses). There are no subjectless-sensations.
  - There is no feeling of cold without someone who feels cold. Perhaps there is *being* cold? Notice how complex this is: "Are you cold, wind?" has a double sense. Cold can mean temperature or how something feels.
- Different people experience things differently. Some feel cold when others are warm. There is not a universally agreed upon thermostat setting (though there is a general rang)!

- **The Same/Itself:** The intensive pronouns (e.g., itself) recall the language Plato typically uses in reference to the eidos or forms (justice *itself*). Here it refers to the wind. Is the wind a thing in itself? The *same* wind is refers to simultaneity of time, but it is tricky to think of wind having strict unity or identity. It is also strange to consider cold as a thing in itself.
  - We can note that Theaetetus's definition is not followed by a discussion of *what* something (the wind) is but *how it is*! Is the wind cold or not? It is no *accident* that Act I begins by attending to *qualities.*

- **It is cold for him who feels cold and not for him who does not**: How would two people argue about whether it is cold? We of course do it all the time. But could I tell someone that he is actually cold when he does not feel cold? If sensation is the sole ground of knowledge, I have no means of argument, I could not distinguish between feeling and being cold. A man in hypothermia who felt a burning sensation would in fact be warm!

- The sensation of hot and cold are immediately cognizable but they are not very intelligible. I am immediately in touch with being cold, but I may be able to know other things better than my sensation of temperature (cf. *Physics* I.1).

So. <u>It **appears** (φαίνεται) that way to each of them? ...Then 'appears' is a perceiving? ...Therefore appearance and perception are the same.</u>
- According to this argument, saying 'the wind is cold' would mean 'the wind **appears** cold **to me**.'
  - We are again at a moment of division which Theaetetus does not sufficiently grasp. Aristotle's *On the Soul* seems to take hints from this dialogue in that it distinguishes the sensible qualities of an object from the sense faculties, as well as the sensations themselves, and the appearances (fantasies, images or percepts) which we have by way of the senses.

- My translation follows Sachs who brings out the complexity of this statement by rendering this as '*a* perceiving'.[65]

152c

So. <u>For as each person perceives a thing, such they are to each person.</u>
- This is the logical conclusion of this doctrine. Sensation radically relativizes and privatizes knowledge.

  - Even if sensation is in fact private, sensing may place me in *a relation* to that which is common

---

[65] Plato and Sachs, *Plato's Theaetetus*, 30.

and objective. It is this alone which would allow for meaningful speech. But sensation *itself* cannot account for this.

> ...Perception is then always of what is, and since it is knowledge, cannot be false.

- Theaetetus' definition excludes the possibility that anyone can be wrong, since each is the measure of their own perceptions! This is a problem, unless we believe no one is ever wrong, even when people contradict one another.

All is in motion; Qualities as the union of active and passive (sensed and sense);
152d

Socrates next develops a consequence of this doctrine. He does not directly attack its coherence yet because Theaetetus has yet to grasp its implications. Socrates instead explores the fact that nothing can be **one thing by itself**. One can not rightly describe **what sort of thing** (ὀποῖος) some*thing* is because the doctrine suggests we do not deal with things, only with appearances which are the momentary result of interaction between a sensible and the senses.

> So. **Nothing whatsoever is one by itself... nor a what sort (ἓν μὲν αὐτὸ καθ' αὐτὸ οὐδέν ἐστιν...οὐδ' ὁποιονοῦν).** It is only by movement and mixture that all thing **become** (γίγνεται). And we wrongly say that they 'are'.

- The unity of each being is done away with. Sensation is the temporal result of motion and change in which two things come together briefly.

- The operation of our sense organs is such as to in fact grasp qualitative opposites (light and dark; soft and hard; sweet and sour). The senses sense these qualities insofar as these qualities are proportional to the organ and also according to the mean condition of that organ itself. For instance, a sound must fall within a certain range to effectively cause hearing. The ear drum must be also be relatively still to hear a new sound. This why the nature of the sensible and the condition of the sense organ matter. Talking sounds quiet after a rock concert. Orange juice tastes bad right after brushing one's teeth. The 'taste' of orange juice to that person is indeed different than to someone else.

<u>So.   All things…are the offspring of flow and motion.</u>

- All is *becoming*; it is the result of motion. Every sense experience springs into being and comes to an end. They are not stable entities. Sensation is often described as a realm or world of *becoming* (cf. *Republic* VI; *Metaphysics* 4 & 6). They are contrasted with and related to a realm of *being*, understood to be constituted for Plato by the forms which are posited as unchanging, eternal, intelligible, and thus the proper objects of knowledge. Aristotle argues this stability belongs first of all to the things or substances to which the forms belong. This dialogue will help us determine why Plato attributes some stability to the physical world. Neither in the *Theaetetus* or elsewhere does Plato suggest that the world of sensation is a mere illusion. It is only unstable, subject to change and confusion. One might wish to distinguish between a world *of sensations* and the *sensible world*.

- o Plato does not reduce the world to mere flux. For instance, the *ousia* of a bee, its form or being, is the form **of** all bees (*Meno* 72b-c). Even the formal quality of color, insofar as we cognize it, extends beyond sensation and must have a share in stability. Yellow is a single stable generic grasp of a qualitative form, known in a multitude of ephemeral sense experiences. Whether or how the 'yellow-itself' might exist by itself apart from particular instances is a different question.

- Philosophy and all science must contend with various contrary opposites and attempt to discover their underlying unity. Philosophy deals preeminently with the one and the many, being and non-being, like and unlike, same and other. We are about to reflect on one of Plato's favorite contraries: change and rest.[66] Change and rest are, after all, constitute not only our earliest, but nearly all our experiences. They are almost universal.

- Philosophy must be able to analyze the world in its complexity without prematurely reducing it to an artificial simplicity which relies on an insufficient principle or set of principles. Theaetetus was praised earlier as a young man who united a variety of apparently contrary qualities in one person. His earlier division of numeric powers united two contrary kinds of square powers (roots). Simplistic character is perhaps just as inadequate as simplistic philosophy. Excellence requires an ordering of various contraries and

---

[66] Cf. Plato's *Sophist* and Aristotle's *Physics*.

differences. All longing, not only philosophic desire, is longing for unity, but not every union is authentic. Motion is here given the 'upper hand'.

- Socrates claims that, excepting Parmenides, a host of philosophers can be marshalled in support of the doctrine of motion, which we could also call the doctrine of *becoming, flux,* or *mixture*. He includes Protagoras, Heraclitus, Empedocles, Epicharmus, and Homer. They stand like an army, *the many* with which one must contend. He then quotes Homer, who states that Ocean is the mother of all. Ocean not only feeds and sustains life but brings about life through her motions. Water and motion therefore seem to be the source of life and being.

Primacy of motion
153a-c
So.   Motion brings forth that which seems to be...rest causes destruction.

- The somewhat Heraclitean formulation, that all is in motion or flux, is ambiguous. Are we dealing with the previous claim that perception is the result of a mixture or is this a claim that all being is *in* motion (or even that there is no being, but only motion)? The second, more extreme claim, is implicated. But Socrates will take up (primarily) the first formula at this stage in the argument. He will deal with the second in our fifth reading. He is following the order of the logos.

...Is not bodily **habit** (ἕξις) destroyed by rest and idleness...and what of the habit (ἕξις) of soul?
Hexis, the habit or active condition (ἕξις) of a thing, will come up repeatedly in this dialogue. It forms a

significant component of Aristotle's *Ethics*, expressing a mode of holding onto something or to some state—a stable con-dition.[67] For more on hexis (habit or habitus), see the Seventh Reading. It appears somewhat ironically here in the context of *motion*. Is even motion a certain kind of stable condition or something which belongs to a stable *thing*? A hexis (ἕξις), related to the verb in Greek meaning 'have' or 'hold', implies something other than absolute motion.

- At this stage of the argument, we are told that motion alone causes things to become and to be. It is motion that is the cause of well-being, being, and becoming. We can make a few initial points.

    o First, we cannot speak of something changing without motion
        - God's ex nihilo creation is not an act of change or motion *in* the things made; it takes us beyond nature or natural occurrences and also beyond what we can rationally comprehend.
    o Second, motion truly can produce health and well-being.
    o Third, atomic science makes clear that matter is in a certain respect always in motion.

    Let us address the latter two points. First, can motion alone be the source of being, becoming, or well-being? It seems that motion and exercise do not *always*

---

[67] Aristotle and Joe Sachs, *Nicomachean Ethics* (Newbury, Mass: Focus Pub./R. Pullins, 2002), 201.

and exclusively cause health. Sleep and rest are equally important.

Second, as will be seen later when the *total flux* doctrine is made explicit, even atoms cannot *only and in every way* be in motion. We will need a doctrine which can consider matter from a higher standpoint (perhaps one which even transcends matter). What would we see or know if everything was always and only in motion in every way? Neither stillness nor motion, decay nor preservation would have meaning if we could only lay hold of motion. In fact, without its contrary (rest or stability), motion cannot be.

153d-154b
Deducing Consequences of the Doctrine of Mixture & Motion

- Socrates concludes that white cannot exist either outside the eyes or in them. Otherwise, it would be in a place, stationary, and not part of a process of becoming. It would be stable, unmixed, and solitary (something which exists in and of itself and not in the very act of perception). Whether or not this is true of white, this does not tell us about all being, unless all being is a quality like color or merely becoming and sensation! [68]

---

[68] Whiteness, Coldness, sweet, and the like have been considered *virtual qualities* in the Aristotelean-Thomistic tradition (but also by Galileo and Locke, though with various nuances). That is because cold is the subjective experience of an objective (secondary) quality. The wind may have a quality or ontological condition which causes someone to experience it as cold, just as a yellow flower has an objective quality which causes one to experience it as yellow, but the yellow precisely *as we experience it* is not out there in the same

- White, and all the experiences of sensation, would be the experience of temporal unity between the sensible (the things sensed) and the sense organ: an experience belonging to an individual in a given moment. This argument is strengthened by the fact that sensibles do not appear the same to all people (much less to various animal species).[69]

- Even more radically, sensibles do not even appear the **same** to one's very self because one is never like oneself in having exact **sameness**.

    - The mystery of same and other, of like and unlike, arises here (though not in the directly ontological manner of the *Sophist* or *Parmenides*). The doctrine of *mixing and motion* at this point ignores that change itself must be **mixed** with something *other* than change if it is to *be* at all.

- Theaetetus is persuaded by what has been said. Yet, judging by what follows, he has not foreseen all that it

---

way as it is in us. The causal quality is objective but one's experience of cold or yellow has something to do with the subjectivity of one's sensing—the way that quality activates and effects one's senses. One knows something real but according to one's mode of apprehension. It is both objective and subjective. The quality is thus virtual because the full meaning of cold or yellow is potentially in the object and fully existing in the unity of sense and sensing subject. The complex objectivity of sensation is hinted at 179c and elsewhere.

[69] This is true but need not lead to radical relativism. See note 68 above. See later discussion on Deely's semiotic approach to sensation in the Fifth Reading.

entails.

154c

So.   Take a **small example** (σμικρὸν λαβὲ παράδειγμα)

- **Change and Dice:** Socrates claims at 154b that change and becoming require coming into contact with something—being affected. Nothing changes without having been 'mixed' with or affected by something else. But then what do we make of the **example** (παράδειγμα) of the dice?

    The pattern or example (παράδειγμα, cf. Republic and Phaedo on the perplexity caused by greater and less): When six dice are compared with four, they are more than the four (twice more), but when the **same** six dice are compared with twelve, they are less (1/2 as many). This should be inadmissible since the six dice themselves did not change! There has not been motion, mixture, or contact. What has changed, or what made the dice larger and then smaller?

    Socrates paradigm has provided a hint, a way to rise higher in the argument. But this hint would take us beyond sense perception. The example also helps us consider what goes into judging the wind to be cold. Both the wind and dice have to do with contraries. With that in mind, it is significant that our example uses something more readily intelligible than coldness—Socrates chooses quantity or number to set a pattern. Theaetetus is directed to math once again. Not all contraries have an identical status—some are contrary in themselves while others are contrary insofar as they have a relation to our thought.[70] The dice

---

[70] Carl Cranney, "Opposites in Plato and Aristotle," 2005. Cf. also Aristotle's *Categories* 10 & 11.

Commentary

change insofar as we relate them to different quantities. Thus, double does not belong to them as such, but relatively. This suggests we must take into account both the relation between perceived and perceiver and even more importantly, the role of the mind!

154d

The. If I am to say what seems to me **now**...but if I consider the earlier question...

- Theaetetus beautifully reflects the complexity of their conversation and his own difficulties. He recognizes that these conclusions somehow conflict with his presuppositions: there appears to be change without alteration or becoming. In this, he shows himself as truly philosophical, rather than merely eristic. He is not just interested in words, in winning a verbal battle, but in knowing the truth! Socrates remarks on this by noting the distinction between that which the tongue says and that which heart & mind (φρήν) think.

- They decide not *battle about* many arguments, but simply to follow the things that have been said and see whether they stand in harmony—whether they *sound together* (συμφωνέω). Socrates says that they will examine *themselves* closely and ask *what sort of things these appearances are.*

155a-b

- Socrates makes three claims (155a-b)
    1. Nothing becomes greater or less as long as it is equal to itself
    2. What is not added to or subtracted from could not increase or decrease, but would always be equal

3. What was not before (what did not exist) is **unable** (ἀδύνατον) to be now without having *become* (undergone a process of coming to be)

One might associate these claims with the principles of contradiction, sufficient reason, or sufficient causality. These assumptions do battle in the soul when we consider the dice.

155c
So.   And there are countless myriads of such contradictions...Theaetetus, you seem to me not to be not **without experience** (οὐκ ἄπειρος) in things of this sort.
- **Not without Experience** is a direct reference back to the unbounded (ἄπειρος) infinities which Theaetetus reduced to their kinds. It seems Theaetetus is familiar with some of these philosophic puzzles. But how are these contradictions to be divided? How can we account for the experience with dice and also hold Socrates to be correct (that without becoming, addition, or subtraction, a thing cannot increase or decrease)? Sense perception will not provide a broad enough genus of knowledge within which to discover the necessary division.

Wonder and philosophy
The.   By the gods, Socrates, I am **growing** in **wonder** (ὑπερφυῶς ὡς θαυμάζω)!
- ὑπερφυῶς is a compound of *over* (ὑπερ) and a world which means *natural growth* (related to *nature*, φυῶς). The word suggests that which is *over-grown*, a kind of tremendous natural development. It is therefore a play upon the previous discussion of *increase* (the dice) as well as the theme of generation,

character, and nature (142c). What is suggested is that wonder contributes to the develop-ment of character. Wonder is perhaps in this sense one of the chief principles of all education.[71] It is generative.

- It is by way of the experience of contraries or apparent contradiction that wonder (and thus philosophy) can begin! (*Republic* 522e-526c; *Phaedo* 96a-97b).[72]

- Change (growth) has happened to Theaetetus without material addition or subtraction!

155d
So.   Theodorus, my friend, appears not to have badly **placed** your **nature** (τοπάζειν... **φύσεως**). For this experience belongs extraordinarily to the philosopher, to **wonder** (τὸ **θαυμάζειν**): For there is **no other source** (οὐ γὰρ ἄλλη **ἀρχὴ** φιλοσοφίας) of philosophy than this.

- 'Nature' is used here to describe Theaetetus's character (142c). The word character (which may refer to a person or a written mark) has in it the idea of a distinctive sign by which something is known (208c). It is also related to the term hexis!

---

[71] Stratford Caldecott, *Beauty for Truth's Sake: On the Re-Enchantment of Education* (Grand Rapids, Mich.: Brazos Press, 2017). See also Charles Dickens's *Hard Times* and *Ephesians* 3:17-21.

[72] Redpath, "The One and the Many." Peter Redpath argues that philosophy for Plato begins in wonder which is caused by an experience of conflicting judgments related to sense experience. Such judgments concern contrary opposites (such as big and small). In Book 7 of the *Republic*, Redpath points out that Socrates proposes that this kind of reflection can convert the soul to the study of being and truth.

- What does Socrates *read* in Theaetetus's wonder? This moment can be contrasted with *Meno* 79e-80e in which Meno insists he is numbed by inquiry with Socrates and attacks him, arguing that learning is impossible.

<u>...There is no other source (ἀρχὴ--principle/beginning) of philosophy than wonder</u>

- An awareness that *there is more to all this than I grasp* is the source or principle of philosophy. Such wonder is not merely an abstract judgment; it is infused with desire.[73] Philosophy, our intellectual longing for wisdom, is initiated in awe and confusion, one which awakens an intellectual appetite for truth. We are of such a *nature* that the strangeness of things can awaken in us a longing to know. We are of beings who can form the remarkable judgment that we do not (or cannot) yet adequately judge things, that we have not yet taken their full *measure* (152a).

The child who looks out of his window and sees snow for the first time; the old man looking into the living eye of a horse; a woman who sees a stick bent by water; Einstein watching a magnet attract a compass needle; the queer moment you ask why anything exist at all; the lover seeing the face of his beloved (or knowing he will never see that face again in this life); the experience of seeing wind and sea obey a man's voice: these are the authentic sources of philosophy. Each of these individuals understand something, even while they are acutely aware that something escapes their

---

[73] Ibid.

comprehension. The world is precisely *un*exhausted for them. Josef Pieper argued that love, poetry, death, art, and religion are the main sources from which wonder and philosophy erupt, which causes us to emerge from the canopy of a limited world.[74]

Our souls are all capable of responding to the world, and all that is, as if it were a question, a form of provocation. In this respect, we are aware that we have not fathomed what we know! We long to look into the *roots of things—into their sources and know them in their causes.* Here I am borrowing from Aristotle. Thus philosophy, or science (episteme) broadly speaking, has no other beginning. The question of wisdom emerges once again at this juncture because an awareness of the world, an awareness of one's limits or imperfections (self-knowledge), and a desire to surpass those limits all intersect in wonder .

Socrates claim about wonder stands in direct opposition to the possibility that philosophy has its true roots or initial impulse in skepticism or even in formal logic. We cannot understand the existence of philosophy apart from a human being in his real situation—situated as one who wishes to understand the world in which he finds himself. Philosophy cannot begin then with the struggle to discover the existence of the world in the first place, or even in proving that it exists—such endeavors can only be secondary. Doubt is, as Wittgenstein states, a secondary psychological phenomenon, presupposing something known. "If you tried to doubt everything you would not get as far as doubting anything. The game of doubting itself

---

[74] Josef Pieper, *In Defense of Philosophy* (San Francisco: Ignatius Press, 1992), chap. II.

presupposes certainty."⁷⁵ There must be a psychological-spiritual impetus for philosophy.⁷⁶ That impetus does not emerge ex nihilo. It is a response to that must be awoken by what is other than us, even strange.⁷⁷

In this light, Socratic doubt (his so called skepticism or ignorance) is chiefly ironic and aporetic in character; it is the result of not being or knowing God in Himself. But the philosopher is moved by a somewhat inordinate hope of laying hold of what lies beyond him, even perhaps beyond his own powers! Philosophy stands then at the threshold of human power. It is no accident that the soul is said to be capable of becoming all things or open to all being. The soul is a search for Truth. Faith too stands with philosophy at that threshold, even as it, in its own manner, lays hold of what is beyond man.⁷⁸

<u>And it is likely that he who said **Iris** is born of **Thaumas** traced her geneology not badly</u>
<u>(καὶ ἔοικεν ὁ τὴν Ἶριν Θαύμαντος ἔκγονον φήσας οὐ κακῶς γενεαλογεῖν).</u>

---

⁷⁵ Ludwig Wittgenstein, G. E. M. Anscombe, and G. H. von Wright, *On Certainty* (Oxford: Blackwell, 1969), §115.

⁷⁶ Peter Redpath suggests wonder, hope, desire, effort must all meet in the character of one who will pursue philosophy. Redpath, "The One and the Many."

⁷⁷ The self can thus also become such an object. One might think of Augustine who said, "I have become a question to myself and that is my sickness" (Augustine, Conf. X.33). Nevertheless, the strangeness of the self only becomes apparent after we have encountered many other things. The strangeness of the self for Augustine was strange chiefly because it could not find its rest in the world but nevertheless sought it there (Conf. I.1).

⁷⁸ *Philippians* 3:7-14

- Mythology has 'philosophic' roots insofar as the source of myth is wonder. Myth is profoundly in touch with our philosophic and scientific spirit. They reveal something about the structure of the world and our experience of it. Story (*muthos*) collects or gathers the world together as a whole, even before we understand all its parts. It is a poetic impulse toward intelligibility, insisting that causes of the things we experience must exist and must even have some relation to a logos.

  Man has what Walker Percy calls a gapless world, a world recognized by us both as known and unknown.[79] We are aware of even those things we do not understand. Our world is therefore truly a world, even while it is not comprehended. It is a world in which we mythically and scientifically dwell in hope. Plato distinguishes between myth and logos, even as he intertwines them and at times treats them as virtually the equivalent (*Phaedo* 108d).[80] Aristotle says this about wonder and myth:

  > For it is because of wonder that men both now and formerly began to philosophize, about less important matters, and then progressing little by little, they raised questions about more important ones, such as the phases of the moon and the courses of the sun and the stars and the generation of the universe. But one who

---

[79] Walker Percy, *The Message in the Bottle: How Queer Man Is, How Queer Language Is, and What One Has to Do with the Other* (New York: Picador USA : Distributed by St. Martin's Press, 2000), 203.

[80] The *Phaedo* examines what lies beyond the threshold of this life, beyond all sense experience. This may explain why myth and logos are so deeply intertwined in it.

raises questions and wonders seems to be ignorant. Hence the philosopher is also to some extent a lover of myth, for myths are composed of wonders. If they philosophized, then, in order to escape from ignorance, they evidently pursued their studies for the sake of knowledge and not for any utility (*Metaphysics* I, 982b; cf. XII, 1047b).

- **Iris**, the messenger goddess who unites human prayer with the divine and communicates divine messages to men is also the goddess of the rainbow.[81] She is a bridge (*poros*) mediating between heaven and earth. Thus aporia and poros touch one another in wonder. For, what kind of bridge is she? she is a wonder to behold! A rainbow is a marvel first known through the senses (perception)! But it is not our senses per se which marvel. Our eyes do not wonder. We do.

  The senses grasp what moves us beyond sensing. This is why Socrates says that whoever made the **genealogy** of Iris did not do a bad job. Thaumos, the father or *source* of the mediator god, is the father of wonder (thaumos). When we encounter a rainbow, we are in some manner imperfectly but provocatively encountering the rainbow's cause or source, insofar as we are moved to wonder. In knowing Iris, we know something of her source and cause—we know it *in* or *through* her. Thus the effects move us through wonder to seek their Cause. What might this suggest about sense perception or about our awareness of the things

---

[81] Mediation is a central theme in Plato. See 'Metaxu' in Simone Weil, *Gravity and Grace* (Lincoln: University of Nebraska Press, 1997).

of this world? Romans 1:20 suggests they should leads us to their first Cause.[82]

...But first do you understand yet why we say this is due to Protagoras?
- Socrates is asking Theaetetus if he understands how the Protagorean doctrine (that knowledge is nothing other than sensation and that man is the measure of all things) has led them to this place of perplexity. Wonder leads to an examination of causes.

...You will be grateful to me if I help you to search out the hidden truth...
- Socrates plays upon the title of Protagoras' work *The Truth*. He is perhaps also playing on the etymology 'truth' which in Greek, as suggested in the *Phaedo*, is 'a-lethia' or the *un-hidden, un-forgotten*. It would be ironic that truth can in any way be hidden if knowledge is nothing but perception.

155e-156b
So.   Look out for any of the uninitiated (ἀμυήτων)
- The uninitiated (ἀμυήτων) refer to those who stand outside the rites or mysteries (mysterion) of the religious cult, such as the cult of Artemis or Aphrodite. The word is derived from the idea of *silence*, the secrets of the cult. Mysteries came to refer to the ways in which by rite, sign, or sacrament something of the invisible and divine is made present—the invisible is made present **through a visible sign** (see the discussion of Iris).

---

[82] Also, Colossians 1:15-17.

- The uninitiated refer to those who insist that only sensible matter exists, that which can be 'grasped with the hands'. This cuts close to Theaetetus's definition. They deny that the following have any share or part in being (οὐσίας μέρει):

    - Actions (praxis)
    - Generation
    - All thing invisible

  As the following interchanges will suggest, they also seem to deny the existence of power or potency. That claim is characteristic of the Megarians.

The.   Clearly, you speak of hard and obstinate men
- They are like the material which they champion, unyielding and repellent. Such men would deny there are forms of any kind.

So.   They are...unmusical (ἄμουσος).
- They are without culture, without muthos or the muses and thus without true science or religion. The word means not just *unmusical*, but *unrefined* or *uncultivated*. It can simply mean that they lack education.

  The mysterious logos...
- The mystery of the refined or cultured turns out to be that of dividing motion into two kinds. There are two forms of motion. We can again hearken back to Theaetetus division of infinite rectilinear figures and their roots.

- There are two kinds of motion, each **infinite (ἄπειρον) in multitude:**

- A **power** that is active (a making or agent power)—ποιεῖν
  - One that is passive (receptive or undergoes)—πάσχειν[83]

- From their intercourse, Socrates tells us, an infinite number of twin offspring are generated: perceived things and acts of perceiving. This is structure is precisely followed in On the Soul, in which the actuality or energeia of the sensible is the energeia of the sensation. The sounding of the guitar *sounds in my ear*. That is, the kind of vibration the guitar causes in the air is precisely undergone by my ear. The motion is the same. It is *sound* when it meets my ear. Thus sound is in this sense composed of the active and passive.

- These perceiving or sense experiences have names (seeing, hearing, smelling, pains, fears). Some are unnamed.

- The objects of sense are kinsman (ὁμόγονος) of the perceptions. In the Meno, Socrates claims that we can recollect all things if we recollect one because all nature is akin (81d, sun-**genos**). He further states here at 156c that these objects indeed spring forth as akin (sungenos) to their twin sense experiences. When such an object or agent acts upon a passive sense, it causes a change. The slow agent, for instance, begets upon things which are faster. This seems to imply that we perceive new things based on a *perceiving of new*

---

[83] Aristotle will make much of the active and passive powers in his metaphysical and natural works: act and potency; form and material, etc.

motions or difference, whether faster and some slower. Perception would be a meeting of change and difference, and all being would be a result of flux.

156d-157c

The name of Being is at last expelled and replaced with Becoming! When the eye and a fitting object meet, they beget whiteness. But whiteness does not come from either one by itself. The sight from the eye and the whiteness are moving (combining), and the eye becomes full of sight. It becomes a seeing eye while simultaneously the object joined in the begetting is filled with color and becomes white. This may have a certain truth to it (see note 68 on virtual quality).

Because of this, Socrates next denies that anything exists in itself. This is the radical conclusion. We only have access to sensations and not to *things which we sense* as a result of Theaetetus's definition. But further, there are no things! Nothing exists in itself. Instead, all arises out of motion. There is not even the active and passive until they are mixing or in union (they are relative only). Thus, nothing in itself exists as one integral being. Therefore, we should remove or abolish being (εἶναι). It is only custom and ignorance which causes us to use the word **being**. Rather, everything is always **becoming**.

Words that imply stability of being, that make things stand still or imply identity, must therefore be false. But as Socrates and Theaetetus abolish words which make things stand still (ἱστῇ), what will happen to knowledge (*epi-steme*)?[84] Nouns, pronouns, and classes have been abolished. They are "easily refuted," we are told. Socrates concludes by asking Theaetetus if such doctrines have a pleasing *taste*.

---

[84] Episteme and the word for stand (ἱστῇ) have the same root.

Commentary

Problem of dreams;
157c-158e

Theaetetus is not sure what he makes of this argument. He is also unsure what Socrates really thinks. He is encouraged to think of this as the result of their (Socrates's and Theaetetus's) *mingling* together. The results (or the state of Theaetetus and Socrates) are compared to the mingling which results in perception. With encouragement, Theaetetus claims the doctrine of becoming *appears wonderfully* and ought to be accepted. However, Socrates suggests there is a way in which the argument falls short or lacks something.

The problem is that we ordinarily distinguish dreams and illusions (such as those of the insane) from true perceptions. We normally say that one who treats illusions and dreams as real has a false opinion. But false opinion is impossible if perception alone is knowledge. Dreams and illusions truly *appear* to men.[85] Are they to be classed among knowledge?

Theaetetus does not see a way out of this. Nor does he know a proof by which to distinguish dreaming from waking. The result is that our dreams will be true for us half the time, and the other half of the time, our waking perceptions will be true for us, exchanging place like choral songs with strophe and antistrophe (158c).

The ability to distinguish between seeming and being, dreams, insanity, and reality has vanished like a phantom under the doctrine of perception!

'Solution' through a deeper relativism
158e-160e

The solution is to goes deeper into the problem. Socrates returns to the theme of same and other, parts and wholes, like

---

[85] Theaetetus virtually equated all appearance and perception at 152b. There may be good reason to distinguish the two.

and unlike, as well as accidents and substances (cf. *Physics* I.4, 5).

He asks, if when one speaks of that which is wholly other, it is in any way the same? He concludes it cannot be. Theaetetus assents that what is wholly other can in no way be same. It is "unable" (ἀδύνατον) to be the same. It does not have that power. This, we can note in passing, will eliminate all explanation of change! Socrates and Theaetetus agree (ὁμολογεῖν) that they must be unlike (ἀνόμοιον). We can also recall the likeness between Socrates and Theaetetus mentioned earlier in the dialogue. That likeness was based precisely on that which *like* without being *wholly the same*.

The first corollary from this is that a thing, when it becomes *like* must become the same (identical). When something becomes unlike, it must be wholly other. But it soon turns out that nothing can ever be like itself then. 'Socrates-sick' is wholly other than 'Socrates-healthy'. Keep in mind that perception as such does not distinguish between substance, accident, qualities, or essences—it only grasps what appears as the whole. When I see Socrates, I see Socrates-Sick or Socrates-Healthy. I never *see* Socrates, the abstract being, apart from these sorts of conditions. I never see Socrates apart from his accidents, any more than I see a freckle apart from a surface. The senses *per se* or of themselves have no way of dividing or abstracting these things.

Thus, what Socrates-healthy experiences must be totally different than what Socrates-sick will experience. The active things which will act on him act on one who is *wholly* other. Otherness, solipsism, lack of persistence (or identity) prevail dialectically at this point in the *Theaetetus*. If we accept this argument, it is *no wonder* that one man thinks the wind cold and another not cold. Rather, the same man can never think the same thoughts for he will never have the same experience. He is not the same man! The very terms 'same' and 'he' are equivocal. Further, the objects of perception which themselves only come to be in the act of mixing have no persistent identity.

Thus while a perception and a perceived are united to each other by the necessity of their substance or being (ousia), each one has no unity in itself and is not even bound to itself. The only things that exist from the mixture or uniting *is* the *becoming*. We cannot even say that such things 'become' for they were not before, nor are they after.

The conclusion (160c) is that one's perceptions are therefore always true and are always part of one's being or substance (ousia). Even dreaming and madness must then be true. A dream is just as real as a waking experience, for it is what *appears* to sleeping-Socrates (no less than waking perception *appears* to waking-Socrates).[86] The concurrent perceiver is the judge, the measure of all that is or is not. Such a person is never false or mistaken, for they must indeed know what they perceive or what appears to them. Therefore, knowledge is nothing but perception and all perception is true.

Socrates then states that their conclusion is *identical* to that of Homer, Heraclitus, and all those who follow the motion

---

[86] Whether dreams, illusions, and waking experience are truly indistinguishable, whether our 'perception' of such appearances is equivalent in each case is questionable. This will be explored in later readings. We can note that most people are not in constant struggle to distinguish dreaming from waking. Our definition of insanity is based on facts like these. At this juncture, Socrates is simply attempting to strengthen Theaetetus's argument, so that they do not examine a straw man. For an analysis of the problem of illusions and dreams, see John R. Searle, *Seeing Things as They Are: A Theory of Perception* (Oxford ; New York: Oxford University Press, 2015). See also John L. Austin and Geoffrey James Warnock, *Sense and Sensibilia*, Repr. (London: Oxford Univ. Press, 2010).

(flux) argument (160d). Having brought this argument out into the full light of their understanding, they are now ready to run this child (the argument) around in a circle and determine if it is well born.

Fourth Reading

160e-177a The Defense & True Wisdom:
Protagoras's Truth—men and animals; Knowing and not knowing; Protagoras's own defense: wisdom is not true but useful; The Truth of Protagoras is true to no one; Political life vs. Philosophy and true wisdom

Focus Questions

1. Socrates claims that Protagoras's *Truth* makes men equal with animals. Is this just an appeal to human pride? What is legitimate about this point?
2. How does Protagoras defend himself?
3. How is philosophy superior to a life of politics, rhetoric, or law? Why might one object to placing philosophy above those occupations?
4. What is leisure? Why does Socrates associate it with human dignity?
5. Is Protagoras's *Truth* true to anyone?
6. What is true wisdom?

General Outline of the Fourth Reading

- Testing the offspring (Theaetetus's first definition): knowledge=perception/man is the measure of all things
    - Protagoras's Truth—men & animals
        - Opposing schools
        - Defending Protagoras's truth
            - Knowing and not knowing
        - Protagoras's own defense: wisdom is not truth; it is useful
        - The truth of Protagoras is true to no one
        - Political life vs. philosophy
            - True wisdom

Our interlocuters are now ready to examine Theaetetus's 'Protagorean' offspring, the thesis that knowledge is nothing other than perception. In its Protagorean form, it states that man is the measure of all things.

Theodoros expresses wonder that after such speeches the argument could still perhaps be wrong 161a). Socrates declares that Theodorus is a *lover of words*. There is a distinction implied here between being the lover of wisdom and the lover of words. Philology is not philosophy, no matter how useful. Skill or victory in debate is certainly not the mark of philosophy or truth. It is not words alone which need to be examined, but rather, the things themselves. The convincing appearance of an argument is not enough. The logos must be tried and tested. It is not by logic or valid speeches alone that we ever arrive at worthwhile truths.[87]

In this narrow but extremely significant sense, truth is subjective. Truth is for Plato something deeply personal. Knowledge, particularly knowledge of the most important things, requires the engagement of heart and mind, perhaps a heart and mind of a certain character. It is easy to forget that one can make all sorts of arguments without distinguishing the true from the *seeming*, or without testing them with heart and mind—as a man and not a mere logician or debater (150b-150d). Right thinking takes more than just ratiocination. It certainly takes more than being satisfied with apparent coherence. Not everything we reason or say is truly or eminently reasonable.

This strikes at the heart of the idea that philosophy is a system, rather than a disposition of heart and mind that longs

---

[87] Cartesian and much contemporary philosophy has often attempted to build whole systems by method or formal logic alone. The first principles of logic are powerful and necessary. But they are empty without the objects of our experience.

for wisdom. Philosophy is for Plato a way of life ordered to the mystery of being and thus to the mystery of truth. A system must begin from premises, comprehended principles, and then works itself out to completion. It may be, however, that the principles which philosophy seeks to know (those things a true lover of wisdom longs to look at) cannot be so comprehended. The highest principles or causes of things may demand a different disposition than one which is solely logistical.

Philosophy (and all true science) is a habit of the heart and mind which grasps the being of things, however imperfectly. Thus Socrates ironically describes Theodorus, an instructor in the liberal arts, as artless (ἀτεχνῶς) and useful (χρηστός). His reply to Theodorus is that he, Socrates, is no 'sack of arguments' (161a). The expression is somewhat reminiscent of book 10 of the *Odyssey* and Aeolus's bag of wind which blew Odysseus and his men hither and thither (cf. Ephesians 4:14). Those men lacked the necessary grounding and self-control to arrive at their journeys end. Perhaps they even lacked a fixed desire for that end. Socrates may be implying here that the logos which one must ultimately follow is not some random account, nor one that is merely convincing or lustrous in appearance. It is not the job of philosophy to cleverly construct or invent, but to listen to the logos, to lovingly follow it home, wherever it leads (Mtt. 6:21).

Socrates than states that he knows nothing, or rather, only just little enough to draw out an argument from someone else. In light of these cautions, they begin to test the Theaetetus's argument.

In previous readings, I have attended to the arguments line-by-line to draw out thematic elements and to provide an example of working through the text. I will continue to do this when appropriate, but, as in this reading, I will often provide

Protagoras's Truth—Men and Animals
161b-e

Socrates expresses wonder that Protagoras claims man is the measure of things. He claims that he might as well say the same about pigs or monkeys (dog-faced baboons). This is because animals also have sense perception. Socrates is honing in on the problem of equating knowledge with perception alone. While this seems like an appeal to shame (to the fact that people don't like being compared to animals), it is also an appeal to common sense. Do we really experience or think knowledge is something common between all species with perception?[88] When we speak of the knowledge of animals, are we not in a very serious respect being equivocal? In reality, knowledge is something which *divides* us from other animals.

If the perception thesis is correct, however, animals and men are simply equal; no one has a greater intellect than anyone else. Further, all knowledge is private and it is impossible to judge whether a perception or thing *known* is true or false (for they are all true). In that case, why would anyone consider

---

[88] Studies and anecdotes which purport to demonstrate animal 'language' are either equivocal or flawed. Animals can indeed use symbols, but only as indexes, not as conceptual signs. A dog may associate the word 'food' with being fed, but it does not recognize that the word *means* food. Hearing the sound 'food', the dog only responds based on appetite. It never asks or discusses, 'what about food' or 'what is food'. The word is as Walker Percy says, following Charles Pierce, an 'index' indicating something *here* and *now* (*hic and nunc*). In "Toward a Triadic Theory of Meaning" Percy quotes Charles Pierce, "The index is physically connected with its object...but the symbol is connected with its object by virtue of...the symbol using mind." Percy, *The Message in the Bottle*, 162.

Commentary

Protagoras wise if what he thought or knew was no more correct than any other man, much less any other animal? Each person would be the measure of knowledge, wise in himself (161e).

Wisdom itself has been reduced to nothing, not merely to a universal human characteristic, but to a necessary condition of sub-rational animal life. The very practice of dialectics, the examination of opinion, is reduced to nonsense.

162a-163c

What could Protagoras mean by proclaiming his *Truth* to be true? Is it a joke, Socrates wonders?

Theodorus does not like the sound of this accusation, but he hesitates to oppose Socrates. He seems almost to wish they could *both* be correct—as if two contradictories could be true![89] But Theodorus will not get away with only being a spectator and escape participating in this dialectical workout.

Socrates states that it seems too wonderful that everyone should become equal to the wisest of men. Under this doctrine, men are even equal to the gods. We can note that a strict doctrine of perception might actually mean the gods are ignorant. For, how could we attribute any knowledge to a being without a body, without the faculty of sense perception?

Theaetetus express wonder that what seemed true to him has suddenly changed into its *opposite*. The argument for perception, which appeared one way, has suddenly rushed to the contrary extreme. The theme of change, motion, and contraries is here touched on.

---

[89] His attitude is worth contrasting with Aristotle's willingness to disagree with his friend (Plato) when inquiring into truth (see *Ethics* I.6). Aristotle insists that truth must be honored even above friendship.

Socrates attributes this surprise to Theaetetus's youth. Youth is easily swayed one way or the other by words. In fact, Socrates warns that men should not begin philosophy until they are in their fifties (*Republic* 540a) and that there is a danger for those who embrace arguments too quickly. One risks being disappointed and becoming someone who ultimately despises reason (*Phaedo* 88c-91c). People who trust arguments too easily may in the end become misalogues and mistrust all philosophy.

Socrates replies in the persona of someone attempting to defend Protagoras's *Truth*. In this persona, he states that he excludes speeches about the gods as well as speeches about being and non-being from the discussion (perhaps because they are not perceptible). In this persona, he also claims that Socrates is pandering to the tendencies of the crowd, making arguments which are merely likely, that is, persuasive but not demonstrative. Such arguments prove nothing. In this persona, he seems to suggest that Socrates has been appealing to the egoism and fear of the many (by suggesting Protagoras's *Truth* would make men and animals equal). Further, this persona argues that just as in geometry, we should not here accept merely probable arguments. This warns us that one should not accept a merely *likely* refutation of Protagoras's doctrine. He is preparing us for a full rebuttal of the doctrine.

As an aside, Aristotle states in the *Nicomachean Ethics* I.5:
> We must remember what was said before, that the same precision is not found in all things, but in each according to the subject matter [underlying matter], and upon this should the way of inquiry [the method] be based. For a carpenter and a geometrician inquire differently into a straight line. The one insofar as it is useful for work; the other into what it is or what sort of thing it is, as one seeking true things...Nor should we seek causes equally in all things.

This is a way of saying that good philosophy is attentive not only to logic, but to context and subject matter. A good argument is precise when its precision corresponds to its field or domain.

Knowing and not knowing;
Socrates restates the question at hand: Is knowledge the same as perception? If it is perception, and hearing is knowledge, what shall we say about someone who overhears another person speaking in a foreign language (a language of which he is ignorant)? Or what if one sees foreign writing? One is perceiving in both those cases, but is one really still knowing?

Theaetetus overcomes this difficulty by dividing. We know, he argues, just so much as we hear or see. We perceive foreign speaking or foreign words (by hearing or sight), but we do not perceive their meaning. This excellent answer not only preserves Protagoras's argument from the attack, but even divides according to the truth of the matter. We indeed know just that much! Nevertheless, one is left wondering how to describe the person who also understands the meaning of language. Does that person 'perceive' something in addition to sights or sounds? Or rather is there something beyond perception which they experience. This is not addressed. Theaetetus is not merely dialectically successful here; his answer is a clue which will be taken up later (Act III).

Socrates does not follow up this suggestive division here. He instead wishes to reveal the perception theory for what it is, to fully unmask the phantom: both its moral and intellectual errors. His next step only tangentially touches upon Theaetetus' *hint* by introducing memory. Memory, after all, is not sensation per se and is closely bound up with the understanding of language or words, with all knowing.

163d

Socrates asks, is a man *able* (δυνατὸν) while knowing something he knows, to not know the very thing he *remembers*? Theaetetus accepts that a man who has learned a thing *must* know it when he remembers it.

But there results the problem that if the man who remembers is not at that time sensing (or only sensing with one of his senses but not another), that even while he remembers, he will be knowing *and not knowing* the same thing at the same time. Because he is not sensing (or not sensing in some manner), he cannot be knowing, even though Theaetetus has said he is knowing something by means of memory. The man therefore knows and simultaneously does not know the same thing. If one traces this back to the definition of knowledge as identical with (and not consequent upon) perception, some of the minutiae of this argument becomes clear. Socrates has snuck in a new 'sense' of knowledge here.[90] He has introduced memory. The problem or paradox occurs because the adopted definition of knowledge conflicts with common sense, experience, and ordinary speech. This is precisely a case where logic alone is not sufficient. The conclusion of this paradox is described as terrible (τέρας) (164b).

164c-d

Socrates accuses himself and Theaetetus of acting as disputative men (ἀντιλογικός), men given to the batting about of arguments in order to win, without a regard for truth. Such men simply play upon words and their similarity, but do not deal with the things themselves. Is Socrates merely being disputative or contrary to reason when he says that the doctrine of perception means we might not know the very thing we are

---

[90] He is sneaking memory into the argument. The covered-eye example escapes this logical *intrusion*.

knowing? Unless we entirely jettison the vast majority of our ordinary experience, unless we are willing to cast memory out from the house of knowledge, Socrates may be on to something.

However, he describes these disputative fellows as terrible or fearful (δεινοῖς). His elevated rhetoric (terrible; fearful) prepares us for a discussion of matters of true consequence: wisdom and divine things.

164e-165a

Socrates suggests this would not have happened if the true father of the argument was alive. He is not satisfied with refuting a straw man or with leaving Protagoras's radical relativism unexplored. This is because his goal, both for himself and Theaetetus, is knowledge of the truth! For this reason, he invokes Protagoras himself to defend his own offspring, in part because guardians (disciples) such as Theodorus will not come to the assistance. Socrates is about to speak in the persona of Protagoras himself.

165b-d

But first he asks, is it possible for a man not to know what he knows at the very moment he is knowing it?

Theaetetus states that it is impossible (ἀδύνατόν). But Socrates counters that this will be the case if you make seeing and knowing identical. He has not yet wholly abandoned ordinary speech (which would indeed be terrible). Theaetetus attempts to conciliate between the two by suggesting that this would be true in *some way* or *somehow* (πως), that is, true in a certain respect, but not true in another (165c). He attempts to introduce a kind of distinction or clarification here. But the argument from perception does not allow for any such nuances or attenuations. Under this doctrine, it is precisely distinction which becomes impossible (ἀδύνατόν). A thing must be either altogether known or altogether unknown. One either sees or one does not. There is no somehow (πως). Under the doctrine of perception, there is no means of adjudicating between the variety of ways something may or may not be cognized. There is no way out from the contradiction of knowing and not knowing the same thing at the same time.

Protagoras's own defense: wisdom is not true but useful
166a-c

Protagoras (Socrates) now objects that Socrates is frightening little boys with words. He reprimands Socrates for not guarding against mere verbal entanglements or arguments which merely *seem* to refute him. Socrates has not taken the perception argument far enough and is still arguing from mere 'common opinion' and ordinary use of speech. He is pandering to the many. Protagoras himself is not afraid of the infinite (ἀπείρους) and many. This parallels the repeated complaints of interlocutors in the Gorgias. They claim Socrates' moral-conservatism only stand unrefuted because the arguments have not yet been 'daring' enough. They accuse Socrates and their peers of being shackled to morality by shame and fear of the many.

166d-168c

Protagoras maintains that what he has written is true. Every man is the measure of that which is and that which is not, and each person differs from every other, precisely in that one thing is perceived and appears to one, while another thing appears to another. Yet he also insists that men are not all equal in wisdom.

When something appears bitter to the sick but sweet to someone healthy, this is not where wisdom comes into play; one cannot and should not even attempt to make such things appear differently. Rather, it is the role of the doctor to produce a change in the condition or the hexis (ἕξις) *of the person* (see 153b). The doctor does this by drugs. Similarly, the wise (the sophist) accomplishes this change in a person's hexis by words (λόγοις.). An evil condition of soul (πονηρᾶς ψυχῆς ἕξει) is thus exchanged for a good.

Still, this does still not mean, he argues, that one is changed from thinking what was false to thinking what is true. This never happens! Everything is true because every man is always a perfect measure of reality, being a perceiver. Yet not everything is useful.[91] Protagoras's daring and staggering conclusion is that it is only by inexperience (ἀπειρίας) that people call such a condition 'true'. He rejects such a division. Rather, the change is from the worse to better (βελτίω) never from the false to the true!

He divides here the true from the good (cf. Meno 81a). It is perhaps this division which is the most dangerous and decisive.

Wisdom has thus nothing to do with truth, according to his argument. Rather wisdom is a knowledge of technique, a technique by which one changes 'bad conditions' to good. It is worth pausing and asking how one judges a condition to be better than another, how we know a condition or situation is bad or good, without knowing the truth about it. This doctrine of utility begs the question and proves itself protean and empty. One cannot proclaim a thing useful or better without determining its end and determining whether that end is *truly* good. Such a monstrous disconnect between truth and goodness places the good in the hands of the powerful, the convincing, the sophistical-rhetor.

'Protagoras' claims that wisdom is like any other technique that can make things better (167b-c). When it has to do with bodies, we call such men doctors; when it has to do with

---

[91] This is not what Paul means in 1 Cor. 10:23.

plants, farmers; when it has to do with the useful (χρηστός) in cities, he calls them rhetors (thus there is an overlap between being a rhetor and a sophist). The sophists make those things which would be useful appear just and lawful. They fashions excuses for whatever policies one might wish to institute. If it should turn out that it is useful to liquidate the elderly, to confiscate private property, to destroy a small city, the sophist is ready to make such acts seem just. It is likely that Socrates has memories of the Peloponnesian war in mind and some of Athens's moral missteps.

Untethered from truth, politics (and all human action) is reduced to might and persuasion—to the whim of desire. Human society and human life stand ready to embrace virtually any evil, when one divides the good from the true. As Socrates insists here and in the Meno, such a *division* is not beautiful (*Meno* 81a).

Socrates is about to shift gears. He will examine the value of the useful (χρηστός). An evaluation of this sort perhaps uniquely belongs to philosophy. In another sense, it also belongs to every single human being. To evaluate is something which we are each responsible for. It matters whether our values, our ordering of the good, is true. Love of wisdom is itself a universal calling.

At the outset, we can note that the useful has rarely been delegated the highest position in the philosophic tradition.[92] This is because the problem of value emerges the moment one asks how we know what is useful. This very problem is about

---

[92] Utilitarianism (Bentham and Mill) and consequentialism represent a major break from the ethical tradition. Such doctrines essentially beg the question of pleasure and the good. They demand that men be economic-prophets concerning the outcomes of their actions; treat human action as essentially exterior; treat individuals as accidents who only gain value in a quantitative assessment.

to be explored in the dialogue, during a discussion of justice, happiness, and God at 175c.[93]

First, Protagoras explains (167c) that whatever is [or seems] beautiful and just to a city is indeed the case, for they perceive it as such. *Notice how far we are from sense perception here.* However, those very things are not always useful. It is the wise man (or rhetor) whose job it is to make what is useful appear to be beautiful and just, rather than evil. Protagoras argues that while some are wiser than others, no one has false opinion (167d). This is, again, because false opinion is impossible. Protagoras than admonishes Socrates (167e-168c) to be careful not to take up strawmen and give philosophy a bad name.

Theodorus now praises Socrates for manfully coming to Protagoras's assistance. Socrates reminds Theodorus that the argument (according to Protagoras) should not be addressed to a mere boy; thereby, finally convincing Theodorus to join in their dialectic exercise for a time.

It is worth underscoring the disjunct Protagoras has established between the useful and true.[94] Men cannot be wrong about what they think, but sometimes what is useful will seem bad to them. Thus the useful will seem untrue (or not truly just). But it is not a matter of truth ultimately for Protagoras. It is a matter of seeming. One might hear Shakespeare's Isabella from *Measure for Measure*, make her accusation in disgust, "Seeming, seeming!" (Act I.III).

The whole argument begs the question of how something can *truly* be useful. That is, how does one determine this, if all is seeming (appearance or perception). The question of utility (usefulness) can ultimately only be answered by knowing

---

[93] This is why the discussion of justice in the *Republic* must ascend to a discussion of the Good.

[94] The disjunct is itself logically difficult to maintain.

which ends are truly good. Otherwise useful merely means mechanical knowhow. One might answer whether a certain device accomplishes a certain end, but not whether an end is worth pursuing. Without a knowledge of the good, one can only equivocate on *useful*.[95]

Being, Truth, Goodness, Unity (transcendentals which belong to all things precisely insofar as they exist) are ordinarily treated as convertible with one another. Their object (or supposit) is the same, differing only according to our mode of consideration. They differ in aspect to us but not in reality. It is no accident that St. Thomas insists there is a logical order for the transcendentals.[96] Being is first, insofar as something must *be* in order to be apprehended at all (we must be aware that something exists). The true is second, insofar as we grasp what a thing is. The good can only then follow upon this, for how can we know the goodness of a thing if we do not know that it exists and also what it truly is. A last note is that we must not only know what a thing is, but what we are, for we only know the goodness of a thing when we know it as good according to reason, according to the ends that properly belong to us. I cannot say if salt is good, unless I know what it is for a man to be healthy, and only then what sort of man I serve it to (one with high or low blood pressure for instance).

Protagoras separates these three, reducing being to seeming, the good to opinion and the useful, and the truth the rhetorical victory. History from the Peloponnesian war to the genocides and 'political experiments' of the 20th century unmask this doctrine for what it is—license for unmitigated criminality and vice.

---

[95] One might argue that it is only a matter of preference, that all is relative to perception. In this case, the sophist is reduced to a changer of feelings or preferences but can never say that one preference is *truly* better than another.

[96] *Summa Theologica* I-I, q.5, a.1-2; q.11, a.1; q.16, a.3-4

The Truth of Protagoras is true to no one;
169b
Socrates, about to take on various *terrible* opponents, compares himself now to a Heracles or Theseus. These men were known for ridding the countryside a variety of thugs who threatened civilized life.

170a-b
Socrates takes up the issue of whether what appears to each person must be true for each. He does this by returning to the existence of experts (techne). This theme was broached earlier in the discussion by Protagoras at 167b-c and by Socrates at 144d-145a.

How can all men equally be a measure of all things if we indeed seek after knowers (experts and artists) to serve us and teach us? After all, why would men seek to be taught geometry by Theodorus if all are equally skilled or knowledgeable? All men believe that wisdom and ignorance (lack of learning ἀμαθίαν) exist. We consider wisdom to be **true thinking (ἀληθῆ διάνοιαν)** and ignorance to be false opinion (ψευδῆ δόξαν). It is worth noting the disjunct here between true *thought* and false *opinion*. The introduction of dianoia is significant.

170c
It seems that nobody would be willing to argue that there are no ignorant people or false opinions.

170d-171c
For instance, many people regularly oppose others whom they accuse of false opinion. In which case, most people agree that everyone cannot be right! Can Protagoras resolve this contradiction by claiming that what is true to him is false to the

many? *The many* are precisely not the experts. And yet, if we make truth a matter of expertise alone, how would the many even recognize expertise? More generally, do the many or only the few have a capacity for truth?

Protagoras could in no way allow the many to be the measure of all things. For the many do not agree with him (insofar as they recognize the existence of expertise, ignorance, and thus objective truth). But then Protagoras's truth must be true to no one because in defending it against the many, he must deny his own claim (that they are indeed the measure of the truth).

Socrates speculates that perhaps Protagoras's opinion is not entirely false, but only *more false* because the many stand against it. It is a *little* true because Protagoras believes it, but not the many. Either way, Protagoras must concede his own opinion is false if he admits that the opinion of others is true. This logical problem of Protagoras's position, its self-refuting circularity, is reminiscent of the more generic problem of asserting any strong form of skepticism or relativism.

The conclusion is that if all men, beginning with Protagoras, grant that the opinions of those who oppose him are true, then he [Protagoras] and they [the many] will all have to grant he is wrong. The truth of Protagoras will be disputed thus by all and be true to none, not even to Protagoras.

Theodorus objects to this treatment of his friend.

171d

Socrates grants that perhaps someone older and wiser could defend the *Truth* better, but he insists that he must depend on what *he* thinks and must speak in accord with that. He insists on being faithful to what he knows to be true and states that he does not know how to defend the claim that man is the measure of things, if indeed one grants that some people are wiser than others.

171e-172b

Yet, he attempts another division to save the argument, dividing on the one side sense perceptions per se (hot, dry, sweet) and on the other, recognized areas of expertise (health and disease). His claim is that the truth of perceptions are true to the perceiver (the many), but the truths belonging to science and art are belong to experts. This is a fascinating and somewhat compelling argument, but not one that can be well defended by one who holds that perception alone is knowledge (cf. 178b).

Still, the division is not entirely without shortcomings. While it accounts for expertise, it treats the beautiful and ugly, the just and unjust, the, pious, etc., as subjective. As each city judges those things, so they are; only, in some cases the laws are more [or less] expedient (συμφέροντα). Thus good and evil, pious and impious, just and unjust are measured by expedience! Socrates is now ready to explore the ultimate consequences of this doctrine.

Political life vs. philosophy and true wisdom
172c

A Greater Argument Overtaking a Lesser. Socrates states that a new argument is emerging. Theodorus encourages him to lead on, since they are at leisure (σχολὴν). Leisure is precisely associated with learning, freedom, education, philosophy, and that which sets human life apart.[97] It has come to be associated with philosophy, contemplation, and is, as Josef Pieper argues, preeminently exemplified in religion, in eucharistic celebration.[98]

---

[97] See Pieper, *Leisure*.
[98] Ibid.

Socrates explains that this leisure is precisely why philosophers look ridiculous when they go to the law courts. He describes those who have knocked about (*just like all those things ever in flux 152d, etc.*) in law courts from their youth. These people are deformed and seem like slaves when they are compared to freemen. This is because they are not free to pursue the logos where it leads. They must stick to their planned arguments in court and obey the flowing water clocks. They are carried along by the *flow* of motion and compulsion (necessity), subject to the rule of *flux* and happenstance in the courtroom. They are not free to seek the truth dialectically and listen to the logos. They must doggedly follow the line of argument which their case demands. This means nothing less than that they cannot think their own thoughts: that their logos is not their own (cf. 171d where Socrates insists that he must say what he thinks).

Such men are obedient to the court and its rules and lack courage and freedom, having grown warped by fear while trying to curry favor with their masters. Their souls are bent and stunted. They have not the minds (διανοίας) of men but delight in being clever and wise.

Philosophers, on the other hand, remain ignorant of all these things and don't even know their way to the courts. They avoid banquets and think all the pride of practical life is trivial nonsense. Philosophers do not recognize any greatness in recounting a few of one's illustrious ancestors or in the possession of some little wealth found in the world. Such possessions are as nothing compared to the whole Earth (which the philosopher thinks of as his own). And such ancestors go back only a few generations and do little to distinguish a man.[99] A politician who brags about his work sounds to them like little

---

[99] Socrates is about to discuss a Source which the philosopher is indeed awed by.

more than a man who has some skill as a caretaker of unruly animals whom he milks!

The philosopher appears a fool to them, much like Thales, who while looking at the stars fell into a well and was laughed at by a servant girl.[100] The philosopher thus appears to be in perplexity about ordinary things. Though, when he draws a man out (ἐκβῆναι, 175b) and performs that anti-strophe to the chorus of the city, it becomes the clever man's time to be perplexed and dizzied.

The clever man who is always asking 'is *this* just', does *not know* what to make of the question, '*what is justice*'. He does not *know* how to answer what man's true happiness is. While the clever man *knows* how to do the works of the city, how to pack his bedding or how to season a sauce. But he yet does **not know** how to live as free man and throw his cloak over his shoulder, nor does he have a harmony of logoi or know how to sing a right-hymn, praising the true life of happy gods and men. The clever man is in fact marked by grievous ignorance; Protagorean wisdom is decisively neither wisdom nor knowledge.

176a-177a
True Wisdom and Virtue.
Socrates states that evil cannot be eradicated in this life on Earth. It is in some respect necessary here and now, but it has no place among the gods. Therefore, one ought to seek to become like God as much as one is able (**ὁμοίωσις θεῷ κατὰ τὸ δυνατόν**) by becoming righteous and holy through wisdom (**δίκαιον καὶ ὅσιον μετὰ φρονήσεως γενέσθαι**).

We have arrived thematically at a radical new kind of likeness, one which is the true end of all virtue and human nature.

---

[100] That women then accused him of looking afar while not knowing what was before him (cf. 1 Cor. 2:2).

We are not to become virtuous so that we might *seem* (δοκῇ) good, but because God is in no way unrighteous. God is supremely righteous and no man is more like God than he who becomes as righteous as he can. This is the true cleverness of man, his true manliness. The knowledge of this is wisdom and true virtue (**γνῶσις σοφία καὶ ἀρετὴ ἀληθινή**), and a lack of this knowledge is ignorance and wickedness. The useful and expedient knowledge of Protagoras is now unveiled as utterly empty and worse than useless.

Those who glory in that cleverness which is truly ignorance do so, her argues, because they do not know the real penalty of unrighteousness (cf. *Gorgias, Phaedo, and Republic*). It is a penalty which non can escape because one cannot escape from one's self. The penalty is not scourging and death, but instead a punishment writ in the very being of the wicked.

> Of patterns, my friend, which are established in the being of things, the one is divine [of God] and most happy, and the other is godless and most wretched (**παραδειγμάτων**, ὦ φίλε, ἐν τῷ **ὄντι ἐστώτων**, τοῦ μὲν θείου **εὐδαιμονεστάτου**, τοῦ δὲ ἀθέου ἀθλιωτάτου, οὐχ ὁρῶντες ὅτι οὕτως ἔχει, ὑπὸ ἠλιθιότητός τε καὶ τῆς ἐσχάτης).

Through unrighteousness, the wicked become like unto one of these patterns and unlike the other; their penalty will be to live ever in conformity to that which they resemble. Their very being will be as they have lived. This cannot be escaped, and God will never receive such a one.

We shall either be like God in eternal justice and glory, or unlike him in misery.

At the center of the dialogue, Socrates introduces this decisive division, distinguishing true wisdom from the false. He implies here that knowledge, whether of politics, or law, or the liberal arts, falls short if it does not culminate in true philosophy. True philosophy leads to theology, to a *knowledge* of our end: what we are made for; what happiness is; and where we are headed.

The question of knowledge, the focus of *Theaetetus*, is thus placed within the context of happiness and again paired with wisdom (145e). In particular, Socrates suggests that self-knowledge and the knowledge of God are united.[101] These two knowledges are united because of what we are and what we are made for. Man is the image of the invisible God, the *imago dei*. Man is that creature whom God has formed for himself, so as to exhibit and rejoice in the divine nature. God made us, as Plato describes, to bear the pattern of righteousness eternally. Nevertheless, it is not necessarily the case that we shall bear that pattern in eternity.

For the Christian than it is no small matter that there is One who has renewed that image, who is the new Man. He has made man over in his divine pattern. Jesus Christ, both God and man, makes the divine life known to us most profoundly. "In this definitive Word of his revelation, God has made himself known in the fullest possible way. He has revealed to mankind who he is."[102] Simultaneously, Christ is the revelation of *man* to *himself*, for he is the true Man—the one who bears the true pattern of glory as the new Adam and rejoices in the

---

[101] John Calvin likewise unites these. Jean Calvin, *Institutes of the Christian Religion*, ed. John Thomas McNeill, The library of Christian classics (Louisville, Ky. London: Westminster John Knox Press, 20), bk. I. Ch.1.

[102] John Paul II, "Redemptoris Missio," December 7, 1990, para. 5, Vatican Archive, http://www.vatican.va/content/john-paul-ii/en/encyclicals/documents/hf_jp-ii_enc_07121990_redemptoris-missio.html.

divine life. It is therefore "in the mystery of the Word made flesh that the mystery of man truly becomes clear."[103]

Christ reveals the radical dignity and destiny of the human race. Every man shall either be conformed to the likeness of God and know life everlasting, or he shall forever bear the shame of sin in everlasting death. Christ, who proclaims this news and accomplishes man's salvation, who is the eternal Son of the Father, is therefore fittingly called the *Wisdom* of God, in every respect.

Plato has claimed that wisdom is a knowledge concerned with the First cause of all Being. Further, this knowledge is bound up with that which is most needful for man to know. True wisdom is not only the *knowledge* of God then, but simultaneously a self-knowledge which makes known our ultimate end, directing us to God as the *true* Good. It is therefore a knowledge which can rightly order all other knowledge and desire.[104] This helps us correlate the various forms of wisdom explored in the digression on wisdom in the First Reading.

The center of the *Theaetetus* culminates then in a remarkable reflection on human destiny, the divine nature, and the need for knowledge—for a divine Wisdom. The dialogue may not yet have sufficiently defined knowledge, but it has shown why we might need it.

---

[103] Pope Paul VI, "Gaudium et Spes," December 7, 1965, para. 22, Vatican Archive, https://www.vatican.va/archive/hist_councils/ii_vatican_council/documents/vat-ii_const_19651207_gaudium-et-spes_en.html.

[104] See *Summa Contra Gentiles* Book I.1, "It belongs to the wise man to order." Cf. *Hebrews* 4:12

Commentary

Second Digression on Wisdom

<u>Plato and Wisdom</u>

The discussion has ceased to be merely academic. Without true wisdom, Socrates insists man cannot be happy. Man will bear in his very being the image of misery and unrighteousness if he fails to know his true end. He will either become like or unlike God. If Socrates is correct, this knowledge is indeed most necessary for us and would render all other knowledge secondary.

Wisdom is here characterized as a controlling virtue, most essential for human happiness. It is worth exploring whether this borders in some respect on a kind of Gnosticism, a hyper intellectual approach to happiness and virtue? Is wisdom truly sufficient for happiness?

In the *Meno*, Socrates makes the claim that if man knew the true good, he would do it; no one, he argues, willingly chooses what is evil but only does so out of ignorance.[105] He implies there too that wisdom is an ultimate virtue.

---

[105] The Reformed doctrine of total depravity does not wholly nullify this conclusion. Total depravity teacj depravity to the utmost degree or that the will ceases to want good generically, only that it ceases to know, desire, will, or to love the *true* good. We no longer rightly specify or designate God as our ultimate good without grace. Just because a will desires good generically does not make the will or the person good.

Augustine's example of the pears is also instructive. In Book II of *Confessions*, he first rules out motives which did not actually move him that day. He then points out possible motives which were yet uncompelling or rationally insufficient, even if they played part of his *rationale*. He then meditates on the folly of failing to seek one's good in God who is the only sufficient source of good. He also wonders whether he sought the pears merely because he desired what

Socrates likely asserts this for two reasons:

1. No man seeks out that which he thinks will be evil *for himself*.
2. The True and unmixed Good is utterly desirable (corresponding to our highest and most ultimate end), such that if one really knew it, one would pursue it.

The first claim (1.) does not mean that a man will seek what is morally good. It merely means that every act is motivated by an opinion that gain or a kind of good will result. A man steals with the hope of gain and that gain is conceived under an aspect of *good* by him, albeit wrongly. This principle is no compliment to human nature or to individual men. It is simply a result of the fact that the will (the intellectual or spiritual appetite) is an appetite for the 'good' generically. The will often fails to specify the good correctly in its various acts. The claim that the will desires what is good generically does not imply that someone's will is good or that individual is a good or moral person.[106] Only when the will desires that which *is actually* good is it (or the person) truly or simply good.

The second claim (2.) is more problematic. It seems to fly in the face of ordinary experience and Christian teaching (*Romans* 7). But before we reject it outright. We can note that we often attribute evil and foolish acts to a kind of ignorance. This

---

was 'unlawful', precisely to exert his power of against the law. In such a case, he would not be seeking evil per se, but his own independence and self-determination in opposition to God. That is, he is seeking a limited good (his self-possession) in a disordered manner, and thus actually undermining his true freedom and happiness. Augustine treats himself, a creature, as his ultimate good and sets himself up as God (*Romans* 1:25). Finally, he suggests that he yet would not have done this without the motive or desire for companionship or unity with his friends.

[106] It is indeed good, however, that he has a will.

ignorance may be in some manner caused even by the will itself; nevertheless, we account for human acts, in part, by what a person knows or fails to know. This of course may mean we need to clarify the various ways in which a thing can be known. It is enough here to see that knowledge (or ignorance) is often associated with good or bad action.

St. John teaches, "by this we *know* that have known him, if we obey his commandments" (1 John 2:3). Christ himself tells us that if we *love* him, we will keep his commandments (John 14:15).[107] Love, knowledge, and action are brought extremely close together in these verses. This makes sense if knowing what is good (the One who is Good) means knowing He who is most worthy of love—one who satisfies every heart's desire. One could *in no way* possess such knowledge if one was not in *some manner* profoundly moved by it, if it did not direct the will.

Plato and Jesus Christ claim that there is a knowledge which eclipses all others (John 17:3). To be ignorant of such knowledge is ultimately to render all other knowledge, all other so-called wisdom or cleverness empty and fruitless. If wisdom truly is determinative of the outcome of our life, should one not sell all to buy her (Proverbs 4:5)?

There are several issues:

1. What is this wisdom? What does it know and what is the mode of its knowing?
2. What does wisdom have to do with making known the true good?
3. Would we in fact do what is right and good if we had this wisdom?

---

[107] It is possible to suggest that these verses prove that we do not *at all* love or know God. However, in doing so, one would undercut the rest of Scripture, our faith, our experience, as well as the purpose of such doctrine.

4. Does placing knowledge or wisdom as the highest virtue make ethics and human behavior too intellectual?
5. Even if this is true, is such wisdom possible?

Let's first outline a few points and questions:
- Plato sees wisdom as responsible for moral or human perfection.
  - He believes this knowledge changes us.
    - But can we come to a sufficient know-ledge of the Good (or God) in this life, such that we are actually changed by what we know?
      - This last question asks us to consider both the manner and purpose of the divine pedagogy. That is, God chooses to reveal himself through the creature, reason, desire, acts, signs, Scripture, and Spirit, but he also chooses to preserve our freedom. Therefore, one might need to judiciously nuance the way that right action is *caused* by know-ledge (or love) of God. Know-ledge can still be a determinate cause without mechanically forcing a man to act.
      - Plato continually emphasizes the significance of the search itself, the need to *seek wisdom* (see 142a, or Meno 81d, 89e). Perhaps this is because seeking already expresses a kind of wisdom, a desire-infused knowledge of the end (however confusedly known). Perhaps seeking also expression a dependence on or trust in God. One who seeks implicitly trusts in the providence and goodness of God. They trust that the

> Lord will withhold no good thing from those who walk uprightly; therefore, they walk in a manner pleasing to God (Psalm 84:11; Romans 1:17; Hebrews 11:6).

Ask, and it will be given to you; seek, and you will find; knock, and it will be opened to you.
--Matthew 7:7

The beginning of wisdom is this: Get wisdom, and whatever you get, get insight.
--Proverbs 4:7

- Because Plato sees wisdom as controlling or causal of good action, the role of practical wisdom, prudence (phronesis), is not clearly distinguished from wisdom proper (sophia). See *Meno* 88-90, 96-90. The distinction may be implied in his work, but it is not developed.[108]
  - Aristotle takes up that distinction as important to understanding human action, differing somewhat from Plato on the matter of prudence and wisdom.

Aristotle and Wisdom

Aristotle follows Plato in affirming that the highest virtues in man are intellectual, that knowledge is in fact the *sine qua non*

---

[108] The virtue of prudence is rejected at the end of the *Meno*. Meno ends up replacing it with opinion. His rejection of prudence (and failure to seek in the manner Socrates suggests) renders their 'search' for virtue a failure. It turns divine grace at the end of the dialogue into a kind of radical deus ex machina (Meno 100b). Opinion will be explored in the last two acts of this commentary.

of a human action. Without knowledge, we act only equivocally or accidentally. Without knowledge, we are as the stone under gravity or the bird who migrates by instinct; we are not a truly or perfectly voluntary agents. This is because knowledge allows us to *know* and thus *choose* what we are doing. Blind choice is rather meaningless. Choice further implies will (over and above sensual appetite). What is preeminent to reason is to know the good and seek it. In doing so, one testifies that one values or loves that thing which they seek. One commits oneself to it in love.

This is why knowledge is so important, why our intellect and rational will are central to our existence. They make it possible for us to commit ourselves freely in love to that which we understand to be worthy of that commitment. They also allow us to judge what is appropriate for us to be committed to and further, what acts appropriately follow upon such a commitment.

This is the heart of spiritual knowledge, love, and action. While animals apprehend particular objects and have sensitive appetites, they do not have knowledge or choice. Knowledge implies universals (concepts) and choice implies a consideration of means and ends as such. A dog may see food and desire to eat it, but he does not know *what* food is, nor does he order his acts according to good and evil. He never asks whether it is *right* to eat. He only assesses his appetite, not whether such an appetite (or lack thereof) is good. Animals are not concerned with truth as truth or the good as good. They cannot as Paul and Augustine say "rejoice in the truth" (1 Cor. 13:6). They desire particular things which seem good to them, but without consciously judging them *as* good. Their appetites have limited ends realized in the objects known through the sense-imagination.

On the other hand, the object of the will is the good as such. The will is not specified to one kind of good or another but has an interest in the good simply. This is why there is no natural or limited object which can exhaust the will and force our choices. Only a universal good would wholly fulfil our spiritual appetite. Similarly, the object of the intellect is truth. Our appetite for knowledge could only be exhausted in a knowledge which somehow included all truth, which was the very Truth.

But these spiritual powers are not like the heart and lungs which merely cooperate. These powers mutually include and move one another—the intellect and will interpenetrate.[109] Thus intellectual desire and knowledge (the good and true) inform one another.[110] The will is blind without the intellect, without intellectual apprehension. One cannot choose what to eat if one does not know what food is or what food is available. One cannot love one's neighbor if one does not know what love is or who one's neighbor is. Thus knowledge (the intellect) informs or illuminates the will. Conversely, man would never seek out knowledge if the will did not move him to do so. The intellect can itself be moved by the will to seek the true.[111] This makes sense if one recalls that the true *is* the good of the intellect, that the will is our intellectual appetite for the good generically, and that the true is ultimately the same as the good (differing only in aspect).

If we turn back to Aristotle, we discover that he considers wisdom as the chief *intellectual* virtue. He claims that the truly virtuous person recognizes wisdom's object as better, greater,

---

[109] *Summa Theologica* I-I q.16, a.4, reply 1.

[110] The term intellect can be used to include intellect and will (just as heart can include heart and mind).

[111] The reciprocal influence of intellect upon will (and vice versa) cause motion in different respects. They therefore do not result in a vicious circle. Sense apprehension actually first informs the intellect, providing material for human action. In knowing something indistinctly, the will moves the intellect to investigate further.

more wonderful and desirable than others. Nevertheless, wisdom, according to Aristotle, does not guarantee that someone will act morally. It is not a *moral* virtue. He argues that this means that all knowledge is not equal when it comes to the realm of action.

Wisdom knows things only in a speculative manner. For instance, it is one thing to know that a certain kind of food is good for a person. It is quite another to know *this food here and now as good*. I may agree salad is healthy, but I may reject the goodness of a salad when it is placed before me. Abstract thoughts are one thing, but the thoughts we think when confronted with real things, within the complex situation in which we actually will and act are quite another. Speculative knowledge is, of course, not wholly unrelated to action, but in our active life, there is much more brought to bear in our judgment than abstract concepts. This is because we choose how we will act, not by theoretical abstraction chiefly, but by a cogitative assessment of the total reality we apprehend right *here and now*. We do that according to habits.

One determines how desirable something is not by an abstract concept of x, but by the habits, attitudes, memories, and situational conditions which surround it. One may recognize that it is a good precept to treat a second cousin with respect, but when seated across from him at Thanksgiving, it is not by precept alone that one judges and acts. It is within the actual experience of sitting across from *that* second cousin (seeing him, remembering experiences with him, experiencing attitudes and habit which have been developed during that history, along with a multitude of other judgments, beliefs, and goals) that one judges how to act.

We do not act upon universals! We act upon real singulars (particular things) which we do not grasp by the speculative intellect. This does not mean an individual is doomed to act by habit or impulse but that our speculative knowledge of the good is not enough to cause action by itself. Precepts of action have to somehow (by interior grace and the other providences of our real situation) become sufficiently desirable or needful to cause us to act contrary to habituated inclination.

Knowledge of God, of the divine nature, or even that one is destined to be like God (or ever unlike and miserable) is not sufficient from this perspective. The Aristotelean moral-psychological model, in this respect, presents a more complex picture of human action.

This is why wisdom for Aristotle is not properly a practical virtue or concerned with human action per se. It is an intellectual virtue, chiefly concerned with knowing as such. It may inform prudence in some manner, but not always decisively.[112]

Insofar as wisdom for Plato is concerned with the highest good, there is agreement between him and Aristotle. But they disagree about the sufficiency or efficacy of wisdom. Aristotle believes that what we can know of God in this life by our natural faculties (without grace) does not rectify our acts. Socratic illumination (morally transformative wisdom) would be something of an anomaly.[113]

This distinction between wisdom and prudence allows us to explain, in part, why someone who knows the good in a certain respect, may yet fail to act upon it. Romans 7 suggests

---

[112] Prudence requires the other moral virtues to make the proximate end clear. Only a virtue higher than the moral virtues could direct it to a higher end. But that virtue would need the appetitive efficacy to direct our actions. Aristotle enumerates in Book VII of the *Ethics* several ways we can know something in a manner insufficient for action.

[113] One might explore the role of ascesis (training or asceticism) in *Phaedo* as purgative: purifying the soul of the philosopher so that he might hope and not fear, so that he might sufficiently desire and attain to union with God in the next life. It is significant that Socrates bases his hope on truths intimated in religion as well as by reason.

further reasons and complications. We need not insist that a person who does not do the good is wholly ignorant of it, but only that they do not know it as they ought (1 Cor. 8:2).

Christian Wisdom

For Plato, *philo-sophy* is *love of wisdom*. It is a way of life whose end is not only the contemplation of the divine nature but a preparation to be with God (*Phaedo* 63b). It is not primarily about asking a bunch of questions; it is an ardent search for the Good with one's whole being, as one's final end. Philosophy culminates for him in knowledge of and ultimately communion with God. Philosophy and the highest knowledge is therefore for Plato always moral and not merely speculative. Its aim is to be with and like God, who is one, true, just, and Good. But Aristotle argues quite persuasively (both through experience and the psychological framework of action) that natural theoretical wisdom is inadequate.

The Christian tradition adds something new to this discussion because it teaches that there is a "wisdom which is from above," one which is "pure... peaceable, gentle, open to reason, full of mercy and good fruits, impartial and sincere" (James 3:17). Aquinas argues that Christian wisdom, that wisdom which is the gift of the Holy Spirit, is not merely speculative; it is also practical and thus influential over human action. The following explanation follows Thomas's account of Christian Wisdom in the Summa Theologica.

While Christian wisdom is still chiefly an intellectual virtue, it also overflows into acts; it informs prudence. This is because it is based upon a knowledge of God which is radically different than that speculative knowledge which philosophy (natural wisdom) can achieve. A Christian knows God as revealed in Jesus Christ and knows him through the very Spirit of God. A Christian attains to a share of that knowledge which God has *of himself*. By faith we *read* this in the face of Jesus

Christ (2 Cor. 4:6). This is a profoundly different kind of knowledge.

Christians do not know God abstractly only by their own speculative judgments, such as Aristotle. Christians know God by being partakers of his divine nature and through the deeds and scriptures by which he has uniquely made himself known (2 Peter 1:4). They know God through the gifts of faith, hope, and love, the supernatural virtues which lay hold of, hope in, and adore the immortal invisible, wise God. They have truly received a special revelation. The grace-given virtues are in this respect more powerful than those of the natural reason—they extend further. "The higher a virtue is, the greater the number of things to which it extends."[114] Therefore, these virtues evoke a more profound love and appetite for the Good. This is why divine wisdom directs human acts.[115]

---

[114] *Summa Theologica* II-II q.45, a.3

[115] This does not mean one is forced to act well. Even while such knowledge moves our will, this does not mean our will is forced. We do not cease to be free. We will not choose otherwise or contrary to God, but we would have discovered the One for whom our freedom was intended. The purpose of freedom is, as John Paul II states, that we might commit ourselves in love. See John Paul II, *Love and Responsibility*. Kierkegaard also argues that freedom as mere choice is empty, "only a formal condition." Soren Kierkegaard, *Provocations: Spiritual Writings of Kierkegaard.* (Plough Publishing House, 2014), chap. 73.

We do not lose our freedom in the commitment of love, but rather freely commit ourselves to that which we love. The virtues are habits of soul. They do not force a man to act a certain way but make him capable of acting well. Because of this, even the Christian or theological virtues of faith, hope, and love, transform man according to a divine *pedagogy and gift*, not by violence or a wave of a wand. This is why Solomon, though the wisest of men, was still capable of sin and of forgetting his God. It is indeed by faith, hope, and love that we

We can now circle back to the pious fear which Socrates seeks to inspire in Theaetetus (176a-177a). The gift of Wisdom for St. Thomas, who is simply following Scripture, goes hand in hand with fear. Fear is a first mover of wisdom. This is not because God himself is one to be evaded as evil, but because as we come to love him more, to realize that he alone is our perfection, our beatitude and joy, we come to fear, above all other things, separation from him, his displeasure. That fear of the Lord which is the root or beginning of wisdom is simply an effect of love (Proverbs 9:10)![116] It is like a child in

---

rely on God's continual aid and turn to him for further graces. Included in true wisdom is the fear of God, the loving recognition that we are not God and can turn from him. In such a recognition we experience that fact that our wisdom is itself as Pieper says, on loan or borrowed. See "The Philosophical Act" in Pieper, *Leisure*.

[116] See *Summa Theologica* II-II, q.19, a.7:

I answer that, A thing may be called the beginning of wisdom in two ways: in one way because it is the beginning of wisdom itself as to its essence; in another way, as to its effect. Thus the beginning of an art as to its essence consists in the principles from which that art proceeds, while the beginning of an art as to its effect is that wherefrom it begins to operate: for instance we might say that the beginning of the art of building is the foundation because that is where the builder begins his work.

Now, since wisdom is the knowledge of Divine things...it is considered by us in one way, and in another way by philosophers. For, seeing that our life is ordained to the enjoyment of God, and is directed thereto according to a participation of the Divine Nature, conferred on us through grace, wisdom, as we look at it, is considered not only as being cognizant of God, as it is with the philosophers, but also as directing human conduct; since this is directed not only by the human law, but also by the Divine law, as Augustine shows (De Trin. xii, 14). Accordingly the beginning of wisdom as to its essence consists in the first principles of wisdom, i.e. the articles of faith, and in this sense faith is said to be the beginning of wisdom. But as

a crowd who sticks close to his father so that he might not be separated, who wants nothing more to be close to him. It is an attitude counterbalanced and impossible without love. The context of Philippians 2:12 suggests just this, and further, that holy fear (the beginning of wisdom) is related to our hope of attainting to the full stature of our Head.

Wisdom is unique because it is a knowledge which attends not only to ultimate Being (the First Cause of all things) but in doing so, attends to the ultimate Good. It is a knowledge of One who is ultimate truth and goodness. Therefore, it is a knowing informed by love and love informed by knowledge. It is no accident that the world is said to have been fashioned through Wisdom (Proverbs 3:19; Jer.10:12). In this respect, wisdom expresses both the mind of the Maker and that all those who love the Logos have some share in his comprehensive Wisdom. They have a share that same mind (Phil. 2:5). This is why it is the office of the wise to order.[117] The wise know the highest good and therefore can direct all subordinate things toward that end.

For Aristotle, wisdom (natural theology) amounted to knowing that God was good, perfect, eternal, wise, blessed,

---

regards the effect, the beginning of wisdom is the point where wisdom begins to work, and in this way fear is the beginning of wisdom, yet servile fear in one way, and filial fear, in another. For servile fear is like a principle disposing a man to wisdom from without, in so far as he refrains from sin through fear of punishment, and is thus fashioned for the effect of wisdom, according to Sirach 1:27, "The fear of the Lord driveth out sin." On the other hand, chaste or filial fear is the beginning of wisdom, as being the first effect of wisdom. For since the regulation of human conduct by the Divine law belongs to wisdom, in order to make a beginning, man must first of all fear God and submit himself to Him: for the result will be that in all things he will be ruled by God.

[117] *Summa Contra* Gentiles I.1

one, and true.[118] This is perhaps the height of human wisdom (natural theology or metaphysics). For St. Thomas, Christian wisdom is not a mere improvement upon this knowledge. It is friendship and kinship with God. The Wisdom from above is a surpassing grace, consequent upon being adopted into the mystery of the godhead through the person of the Son. This means that Christian wisdom will look like foolishness to the world (Col 2:8; 1 Cor. 1:18-2:16). No longer is wisdom chiefly concerned with abstractions, with substance, essence, genus, species, actuality, form and matter (though it does not wholly abandon such things). This new and surpassing wisdom is instead summed up, as St. Thomas argues, by the articles of faith. Christian wisdom speaks not chiefly of metaphysical categories, but when it speaks sounds something like, "I believe in God, the Father almighty…"

Finally, we can note that true wisdom not only orders but unifies. Because the knowledge of God is knowledge of one who is Truth and Good, the heart and mind can be radically united in his worship. Wisdom of God pursues our true unity by seeking union with God, even while it is also a result of that union.

But lest we lose our bearings, we should again recall that wisdom's root is in love. Even that fear which first moves wisdom into action is itself grounded in love. Love is a yet more powerful and more perfect virtue, informing all others, without which there is no true virtue.[119] Love is the fulfilment of the law and God is Love (Romans 13:10; 1 John 4:8; Matthew 22:36-40; Leviticus 19:2).

I have argued that knowledge and love are inseparable, but in God, they are one simply. We proclaim this whenever we proclaim the mysteries of the Faith (Deuteronomy 6:4).

---

[118] See Thomas's Commentary on Book 12 of Aristotle's *Metaphysics* or *Summa Theologica* I-I, q.6, a.4

[119] *Summa Theologica* II-II, q.23, a.6-7

As we explore what it means to know and the various faculties and acts which constitute human knowledge, we can keep in mind that they are all intended to aid us in our love of God. They are to be subordinated to the knowledge of the one True and simple Good. Only then can any knowledge rightly be considered wisdom or in the service of wisdom.

Fifth Reading

177b-187a   Final Refutation:
All is motion and all is rest;
Arriving at being and truth

Focus Questions:

1. Why must an account of knowledge deal with flux and stasis? In other words, why does Socrates take Heraclitus and Parmenides seriously?
2. Why and how does Socrates direct Theaetetus's attention to the soul in this final reading of Act I?
3. Why and how are being and truth introduced here? What do they have to do with the refutation of the doctrine of perception (that knowledge equals perception)?

The middle of the dialogue places us at the center of things—at a consideration of man's final end and the nature of true wisdom. We move on now to pursue the thread, to follow the logos. As Heraclitus exhorts, "Listening not to me but to the logos, it is wise to agree that all things are one."[120]

We might pause for a moment and recognize that Socrates is a disciple of several different traditions. Like Theaetetus, he too is knowledgeable of the doctrines of his predecessors. Even while Heraclitus' doctrine of flux is defeated in our reading (and while we hear hints of the mysteries of Parmenides's doctrine of the Monad), we can keep in mind that Socrates critiques may not mean his wholesale rejection of their teaching, only a rejection of their totalizing claims. Socrates will even

---

[120] Fragment 50. Heraclitus and Robinson, *Fragments*, 37. The Heraclitus of *Theaetetus* is chiefly the expositor of the doctrine of flux, but it is likely Socrates learned much more from him than the idea of change. For instance, the doctrine of the logos. See Paul Friedlander, *Plato: An Introduction* (Princeton University Press, 2016).

Commentary

say here that he holds Parmenides and his teaching in reverence (183e).

Where we begin in our reading, Protagoras's definition of wisdom (the power to change people's opinions) has been rejected; yet, it has not been shown that this also means one must reject the claim that all is in motion or that knowledge is perception. We have repeatedly encountered compelling reasons to do so, but it only here that Theaetetus definitively rejects the perception thesis and brings Act I to a close.

The problem of motion and stasis, of the one and many is prevalent both stylistically and explicitly throughout the dialogue. For example, the etymology of episteme (knowledge) itself is related to *standing* or *stasis*. At 176e, we are told about the two patterns which are *stood up* or e*stabl*ished in the being of things, while at 177b we are told that it is hard to get those clever men to *remain* or *abide*. Socrates at this point fears they will be overwhelmed by a flood of logos (177c). Therefore, they return to the original argument concerning those who say all is in motion.

Those who say all is in motion maintain that whatever seems to each man really is to him. They especially insist that this pertains to justice and law. Socrates holds out that none would yet be so bold as to insist that the good (or at least the advantageous good) really is to each as it seems. He reiterates (178b) that man is the measure of all things, such as of the white, the heavy, and everything of that sort—i.e., the perceptible per se—claiming that each man has the standard or means for judging in himself (ἔχων γὰρ αὐτῶν τὸ **κριτήριον** ἐν αὐτῷ,) these things. We have a ground of judgment regarding the white, the heavy, and such. This admission preserves a way in which (or sphere in which) men can be correct about their own perceptions (cf. 171e) But he asks, does a man have the power to judge the way things will be in the future (178c)? Socrates cleverly eludes the problem of the total subjectivity and privatization of knowledge by reflecting on future possibilities. Accurate reasoning about the future obviously cannot be through sensation.

This dialectical move is based on the fact that one characteristic of those who have knowledge is their ability to predict what *will* happen (cf. 142a-d). Where does this power come from? What kind of knowledge is this based on? If a doctor and a layman predict opposite outcomes, it does not seem possible that they can both be correct. Their opinions are not equal; only one will judge best (178d-e). This is precisely why men pay money to doctors, to musicians, to teachers, and even to Protagoras. Socrates borrows this argument from his dialectical counterpart!

But since law making and the useful (the advantageous) concern the future, in no way do we need to say that every man is truly or equally a measure here (179a-b). Theodorus at last concedes that Protagoras's argument has been defeated. Socrates claims that there are many other ways this could have been shown (179c). He does concedes, however, that the judgment of sense perception as such is either very difficult to show to be false or may in fact turn out to be true for each person. He thus potentially *divides* knowledge or provides a limiting condition to Theaetetus's definition: allowing that it is possible for man to truly measure his own sense perceptions and feelings.[121] Truth belongs perhaps analogically to those powers and experiences.

All is motion and all is rest
Socrates now prepares to examine the argument that motion is the *very being of things* (179d). A host of madmen who espouse various permutations of this doctrine threaten them.

---

[121] See 171e; 178c; 179c regarding judgement of our own perceptions as such.

These men are careful to allow nothing to *stand firm* either in speech or in their souls. They war against that which *stands still* and attempt to cast it out from all sides (180b). There is no established principle they are willing to *hold to*. Theodorus proposes approaching it like a geometrical problem and Socrates responds with the observation that such a speech is *measured* (180c). But before he begins, he shows that the doctrine of flux is but one half of the problem—he again divides. On the other side of the division stands Melissus, Parmenides, and the rest (such as Zeno), who state that All is motionless (180e). Their claim is that everything *stands still.* Everything is one and stationary—it is a **Whole** and has no place to move according to them.

How will our interlocuters contend with these two parties, having fallen between them? After all, in a tug-of-war one is not permitted to stand in the middle. But what about in philosophy? Much of philosophy is precisely the work of making a one out of a many, of showing how contraries can be united by a single logos. That often means harmonizing or uniting contraries or, if not standing in the middle, than showing that extremes can belong in different ways to one subject or reality.

They begin their examination with the doctrine of motion (181a), first asking if there is only one kind of motion or two. In doing so, Socrates divides again. Motion is divided into to species: locomotion and alteration (181d; cf. *Physics* IV). The doctrine of flux demands that everything is moving in *both* kinds of motion *at once*. If not, something would be standing still in some way. They contend for a radical flux in which one cannot step in the same river twice because there is not a *same river* ever! If a river were not altering qua river, it would be something stable and not be in flux (181e). That is, the river must not only change location or temperature but must change even from being a river. Therefore, there are no rivers.

Nothing can be *what it is* but is ever changing in every way. Therefore, there is no being as such.

Socrates then examines the previous division of sense experience into active and passive powers according to this doctrine of total flux. The perceived object has been said not to be a certain quality; it is only endowed with a quality.[122] Socrates reminds us that they had stated that nothing becomes something by itself, but only in the union of two things (182a-b). But since things are undergoing both kinds of alteration all the time, they cannot say what qualities actually belong to them. For it is not just the thing that changes and moves, but the quality itself, such as whiteness (182d). Even more radically, the very perceptions are changing. One cannot even speak of hearing or seeing, or any perception. If perceptions also must be changing in every way, they are no more stable as perceptions than as non-perceptions (182d-e). The world through total flux has become totally unintelligible. It is worth noting that the force of this argument relies on our common experience of the stability, regularity, and the intelligibility of things. The strength of this argument implicitly depends upon the real intelligibility of the world, just as our willingness to engage in discussion does!

But if perception is no more perception than non-perception, when stating that knowledge is perception, we have no more stated what knowledge is than what it is *not* (182e). This 'beautiful' argument, that all things are in motion, would reduce every answer to being equally right and wrong, abolishing all being and leaving only becoming (183a). This even implies that motion itself must change from being motion. It is remarkable that an earlier claim that motion preserves all things (152d-153c) has been reduced to its *contrary*. Absolute

---

[122] Aristotle's terminology such as 'quality' is derived from both ordinary speech and Plato (see *Categories* 8b26).

Commentary

motion is shown to be the abolition of being. This is the result of an overly simplistic analysis. An improper division of things which fails to incorporate contrary but necessary principles (here both motion and rest) has resulted in paradox and absurdity. This is emblematic of bad science and philosophy.

Without its contrary, motion has destroyed itself. One might even wonder whether stasis and motion (as well as being and be-coming) are merely co-equal, or if one of the pair must really *be* primary. For can we not even say that motion *is* in some sense? What has been show is that the flux argument destroys both being and speech, naming and knowledge, ultimately even perception itself.

Insofar as the doctrine that knowledge is perception depends on the argument from motion, it has been wholly refuted. What remains is to explore the doctrine of those who say all things *stand* still (183c-d). But Socrates feels shame about examining Melissus and Parmenides in the manner which he did the doctrine of flux. He reverences and stands in awe or terror of Parmenides.[123] He describes Parmenides as a man of depth, whose doctrine should not be treated lightly.

The refutation of flux has revealed something about the fundamental nature of things: wherever there is anything, we can never wholly abolish stasis, being, or unity. This context allows us to hear with heightened wonder the claim of Parmenides, that all being is one; that non-being cannot be. According to him, if we deny being of anything, we must actually posit that non-being somehow *is*.

Being is a name that somehow belongs to all that is! And everything that *is* is in some manner one. Is this not itself a cause of wonder? This is in part why *being* and the *one* are fundamental questions for both Plato and Aristotle. For

---

[123] This is not fear of defeat, though in *Parmenides* a young Socrates fails to prevail against Parmenides.

instance, the central questions of the *Metaphysics* concern unity and being, the one and many, like and unlike, same and other. There Aristitotle explores the sense in which a thing is one and how that is different from its being. He observes that we predicate unity of a thing in precisely the manner that it *is*. But then that might mean we need to understand the manner in which each thing (or all things?) is one. What is the nature and cause of unity? Is the cause of unity or being a form, a genus, or even something yet *Higher*? One begins to sense why Parmenides's doctrine of the Whole or the All is not just a logical challenge, but ontological—even theological (184a).

We have discovered that hidden within the problem of knowledge and perception lurks the mystery of being!

Arriving at being and truth

Socrates turns the conversation in this direction, albeit gently. He asks Theaetetus to distinguish whether it is *by* or *through* his eyes that he sees. He asks him to distinguish the *kind* of *causality* they have. While doing so, he reminds Theaetetus that the goal is not to be persnickety with words or just to develop technical terminology. Such would be unfitting and contrary to free men. But one must be able to be precise and *more correct* when necessary (184c-d). This is a lesson all philosophers need recourse to.

Socrates asks this about the eye because it would be a terrible thing if a man's soul were like a wooden horse in which sensations were found, but which could not unite them into one form or appearance (184d, εἰς μίαν τινὰ ἰδέαν). He clearly imagines a kind of Trojan horse filled with diverse but unrelated perceptions. It is likely that it is from this that Aristotle derives his *common sense*—that power which unites various sensations in a single percept or phantasm, so that when I see and hear, those sensations put me in touch with one single object (See *De Anima* 425a27).

It is the soul by which we perceive *through* the senses as instruments (or organs to use the English derivative of the Greek). And it is the soul which unites various senses and sense moments in one precept or image. This technical segue has taken the argument an important dialectical step forward by more directly introducing the soul itself and its role in knowing.

Socrates next argues there must be a power by which we distinguish between various kinds of sensations. This is because each sense is itself incapable of making such **distinctions** or divisions; each sense only attends to and is activated by its proper object or sensible—e.g., the eye is activated by light and color, not by the *odiferous*. There must be some other power which distinguishes sight from touch and yet recognizes them both. It is impossible (ἀδύνατον) for one sense to perceive what another does (185a). Thus, if one **thinks** (διανοῇ) about both, it will not be through one of the sense organs. There is a power then which thinks about what is *many and one*, about what is *same and other, like and unlike*, and thinks about it insofar as it is the same and even insofar as it is other!

Now through what does one **think** (διανοῇ) about all these things? What power can grasp what is common, as well as what is and is not (185b-c, πᾶσι **κοινὸν** καὶ τὸ ἐπὶ τούτοις δηλοῖ σοι, ᾧ **τὸ 'ἔστιν'** ἐπονομάζεις καὶ τὸ **'οὐκ ἔστι'**)? What organ (ὄργανα) lays hold of each and every kind, all these things? The use of dianoia is again significant.

Theaetetus responds that Socrates is speaking about *being and not being, likeness and unlikeness, same and other, one and the rest of number*, and asking about an organ which they are perceived through (185c-d, οὐσίαν λέγεις καὶ τὸ μὴ εἶναι...). Socrates is exceedingly impressed by Theaetetus.

"By Zeus," says Theaetetus, ..."It seems there is no unique organ." That is, there is no somatic organ or tool by which this is done, but rather, the soul grasps what all things have in common through herself (185e).[124] It seems that Theaetetus believes the soul has a power over and above its bodily functions, a spiritual act of sorts. Theaetetus is not one of those obdurate and uneducated people who believe in matter alone (155e).

"Kalos!" Socrates rejoices because Theaetetus has saved him a long discussion.

Theaetetus goes on to assign *being* or *substance* (οὐσίαν) to the class of things grasped by the soul because it [being] most of all accompanies or attends (παρέπεται) upon *all things* (186a). Thus the soul is that which knows what is *common*. This breathtaking conclusion might remind us of Parmenides who claims that the Whole or All is one.

Theaetetus continues by assigning the beautiful and ugly to the same class, to those things whose οὐσίαν the soul views in relation to each another. He includes under the purview of the soul, the comparison of all contraries, even those opposites which are related to perception (e.g., hardness and softness). It is the soul which grasps their οὐσίαν, that they *are* and that they *are opposites* of one another. It is the soul that judges (κρίνειν) of them or we might add, divides (186b). We

---

[124] They are not wholly ignorant of the brain but recognize that a material power is not enough to make such universal judgments or hold those judgments with conscious awareness (*Phaedo* 96a-b). If knowing was essentially material, every concept would be a magnitude or extended and could be known only through a span of time. One would move through the concept house, for instance, not grasp it as a whole. Further, to know that color is not sound, I would have to move through both magnitudes at once and instantaneously. There must be a third thing, consciousness of the unity and difference at once, not across a span of time, even while the knower is in time. We know such things, not without images (or the brain), but not by the brain as such. See *On the Soul*, Book III.

Commentary

can note that the potential for division, mental or actual, presuppose opposites or some manner of difference.

All the senses can be perceived by human beings and other animals by nature, but it is only slowly and with difficulty that such things are gathered up by reasoning (ἀναλογίσματα πρός τε οὐσίαν) (186c). What a stunning way to out things, that we *gather up through reason*. It will not be until Act III, that we can gather together the significance of this statement.

SO: <u>Will one happen upon truth who has not happened upon being (οἷόν τε οὖν ἀληθείας τυχεῖν, ᾧ μηδὲ οὐσίας;)</u>?

The: <u>Impossible (ἀδύνατον)</u>.

SO: <u>And will a man have knowledge (ἐπιστήμων) of that of which he has not happened upon the truth?</u>

The: How?

- Socrates seems to have suggested a **measure** of knowledge at this point. It has something to do with being and truth as gathered up by the reasoning soul. System building, logical positivism, idealism, and other pseudo philosophy fails to recognize that before all things must stand being itself!

    The mysterious being of each thing must be grasped first. All doubt, all self-awareness, all knowledge or grasp of the fundamental activity of the soul, even error is consequent upon our contact with what *is*, even in its seeming. We are not even aware of our own minds except through contact with the reality. The mind is not some alienated substance, solipsistic and entrapped in itself. Rather the mind, our spiritual interiority, is precisely our connection with all that is.

186d

So: Then knowledge is not in the affections or experiences but in **reasoning through or with** them [the affections and experiences]. It is possible for **being and truth** to be apprehended in this way, but impossible in the other. (ἐν μὲν ἄρα τοῖς παθήμασιν οὐκ ἔνι ἐπιστήμη, ἐν δὲ τῷ περὶ ἐκείνων **συλλογισμῷ**: **οὐσίας** γὰρ καὶ **ἀληθείας** ἐνταῦθα μέν, ὡς ἔοικε, δυνατὸν ἅψασθαι, ἐκεῖ δὲ ἀδύνατον.)

- Socrates states that it is by reasoning about (with and/or through) what one experiences that one comes to knowledge of being and truth. He refers to the πάθημα rather than to perceptions, perhaps hinting that these things have been established in the soul; they are not merely fleeting bodily event (see *On Interpretation* 16a). Or he may be hearkening back to the passive aspect of those combinations of the perceived and perceiving which occurs in sensation and affect us. It should be noted that he here links perception to knowledge, though not directly as simply equivalent.

  He then makes a division at 186d, asking Theaetetus if he will you then call them (perception and knowledge) by the same **name**? That is, will they fall under the same class? Theaetetus and Socrates now divide perceiving from knowledge. They conclude that perception and knowledge could never be the same (186e).

  He notes that they did not set out to find out what knowledge is *not*, though perhaps they have clarified it by distinguishing it *all together* (τὸ παράπαν) from perception (187a).[125] This last statement is a strong disjunct which we could perhaps nuance. But it makes sense in light of the original definition.

Socrates says, "But knowledge must be in that name, or thing named which the soul has when itself, by itself, comes to be engaged with beings" (187a).[126] He has suggestively used **names** like ἀναλογίσματα, συλλογισμῷ, κρίνειν, and διανοῇ in the preceding interchanges which might help us think about what the soul can do in its engagement with being.

Theaetetus responds, "but this is called *to have opinion* (δοξάζειν), I suppose."

Socrates, in turn, says rather ambiguously, "Rightly, indeed, do you *suppose*."

---

[125] In Thomas's *Summa Contra Gentiles* Book II, Ch. 66, he offers the following reasons why sense perception cannot be the same as knowledge:

1. Sense is found in all animals, but we perform diverse and opposite actions and are not moved by sense nature alone—every swallow builds a nest at certain time of year, but we make all kinds of choices

2. Sense only knows singulars, but we know universals.

3. Sense cognition is limited to corporal things, but we know things like wisdom truth, justice, and the relations of things.

4. Sense does not know itself or its operation (the senses do not know that they 'sense' and sight only recognizes color, without even knowing it as such) cf. Summa I, q.77, a.3, ad.4.

5. Sense is corrupted by excess. A bright sun blinds and makes us less able to see other things. The more intelligible the object of the intellect, the better it understands both it and other things.

[126] Name may be closely associated with *word* and *concept*, but it is distinguished from an account or logos per say in Act III of the dialogue (201e-202b).

The First Act—Simple Apprehension (Understanding)

"The act of understanding, or 'simple apprehension' as it is technically called, produces in our minds a *concept*...we do not merely understand *concepts*, we understand *reality* by means of concepts." -*Socrates Logic*, Peter Kreeft[127]

The sense perception thesis has been rejected by Socrates and Theaetetus; knowledge and sensation are not absolutely identical. Nevertheless, sense perception is not cast out from the dialogue because our senses are so intimately bound up with knowing and learning. We might even describe sensation as a *sort* of knowledge, if we use the term loosely or analogically.[128] It is sense perception which puts us in *touch* with the world. Touch is in fact the most fundamental of all the senses. This is why Aristotle compares the mind to the hand. Our hand, he states, is the tool of all tools.[129] It is the *tool* by which we *take hold* of other instruments and assimilate them to our use.[130] Like the hand which takes on the *shape* of things, so the mind analogously grasps things by *assimilating itself* to their intelligible character in its being con*formed* to them.

---

[127] Kreeft and Dougherty, *Socratic Logic*, 36.

[128] Analogously, Theaetetus was still able to comprehend irrational magnitudes along with the rational powers within the single genus of 'square-roots'. The genus of knowledge may have to unite a multitude of powers which participate unequally in rationality. Peter Redpath argues that a scientific *subject-genus* embraces a multitude which share unequally in the subject. Redpath, "The One and the Many."

[129] *On the Soul*, Book III.8

[130] The hand is almost infinitely conformable to things by virtue of its power of *articulation*.

Commentary

We will explore this intellectual assimilation here, what has come to be called the *first act of the mind* or *simple apprehension*. This is not to suggest that simple apprehension is what Plato 'really' has in mind; nevertheless, the placement of sense perception here in the dialogue and its treatment throughout the rest suggest a strong correspondence to the first act of the mind.[131]

The following account of simple apprehension is from an Aristotelian-Thomistic perspective. Plato and Aristotle generally differ on the role of sense experience: whether it only prompts us to recollect what we already know or whether it is that by which we first come to possess knowledge.[132] Even so, their analysis of the psychological process of sensing and learning is remarkably similar. This is born out in Act I and II of *Theaetetus* where sense impressions, common sense, memory, opinion, judgment, and thinking are explored.

---

[131] Cf. the common sense, being and truth in Act I (184b-187a); the wax and the senses (191c-d); the bird cage which is initially empty (197c-197e).

[132] Plato and Aristotle typically represent two related but distinct schools of learning. Plato is known for recollection and Aristotle for epagoge (a form of empirical induction of universals through experience). *Theaetetus* does not enter explicitly into a discussion of forms or recollection. In some points, the dialogue is quite similar to Aristotelian apprehension. This discussion of apprehension is not intended to suggest that the views of Plato and Aristotle are one and the same. The goal is merely to enrich the reading experience and suggest a direction of possible development. Aristotle gives a generic account of induction in *Metaphysics* I.1; *Physics* I.1; *Posterior Analytics* (esp. II.19); *On the Soul* III.1-8. On recollection and sensation, see Plato's *Phaedo* **96a-b**, 73c-74d; *Seventh Letter* 342a-b; *Meno* 81b-86c. It would also be fruitful to think through the relation of images and dianoia as presented in the divided line in the *Republic*. On dianoia, see Klein, *A Commentary on Plato's Meno*, 108–172.

Bypassing the major differences between Plato and Aristotle, we will focus here on a traditional account of simple apprehension, that act by which we first acquire mental concepts (or the forms of things).

We can begin with an example. Some people can visually identify grapes; they can distinguish them from other fruits by means of specific sensible characteristics. Others can express in words precisely what those distinctive characteristics are. While both classes of people know and recognize grapes as a particular *sort* of thing (a fruit), only one has made the cause of that distinction explicit. But how did either of them begin to recognize grapes *as* grapes? Notice, that the question arises from the real situation we find ourselves in—in which we really do recognize things and know what some of them are.[133] Our lives are based on the common experience of continually making these sorts of distinctions, quite accurately. It is this we attempt to explain her by means of the model of intellectual apprehension.

In order to think about a grape, one must first become aware of it. This does not happen without sensation. Children do not think of grapes until they have somehow encountered them. As Socrates said earlier, human nature is too weak to grasp that of which it has no experience (149c). To experience a grape, awareness of it must somehow happen *inside* a person. An awareness of an object is something interior and therefore subjective; an awareness can only belong to a conscious subject or individual. But the actual grape cannot get inside a person (without one eating it). There is hopefully no material grape in a person's head.

As Lady Philosophy teaches in Boethius's *Consolation of Philosophy*, things are known according to mode of the knower and not according to the mode of existence of the

---

[133] Redpath, "The One and the Many."

thing known.¹³⁴ A human being must therefore come to know a material grape immaterially.¹³⁵ The grape must come to exist in a mind in a different manner than how it exists in the world. This means that the awareness of a grape cannot be the grape *itself*, even while that awareness is *of* the grape.¹³⁶

Like other animals, the beginning of human awareness is sensation. Through sensation, an image of the object comes to be formed within the soul.¹³⁷ And like animals with memory, such an image can now function as a kind of transparent icon (very loosely speaking), an *'idea'*, *look*, or *form* by which one

---

¹³⁴ *Consolation of Philosophy* Book V.4

¹³⁵ See Searle, 2015 (p.24) The so-called mind body problem is perhaps better construed as the mystery of *relation*—the mystery by which any being comes to be aware of another. Consciousness itself demands interiority, thus cognitive relations in any imaginable universe demand that subject and object remain separate from one another, even as some form of assimilation or apprehension occurs. This is C.S. Lewis's point at the beginning of *The Problem of Pain*. C. S. Lewis, *The Problem of Pain* (San Francisco: Harper SanFrancisco, 2001), 20–22.

Thought by its very nature is an act of bridging the distance between subject and object or subject and subject. The mind-body problem might aptly by reframed the *subject-object mystery*, that is the mystery in which a *thou* or *it* exists for an *I*. This resituates the philosophic attitude towards wonder and 'ens' (being).

¹³⁶ I am using the language of intentionality here. The philosophic theories of intentionality can be found in Aristotle (even Plato), Aquinas, or in contemporary thinkers like John Searle. As this Commentary will argue, this sort of intentionality is distinct from Cartesian representationalism which suggests that the objects of our knowledge are ultimately only the ideas themselves and not things.

¹³⁷ This image is also called a 'phantasm', 'likeness', or analogically, an 'idea'. Cf. *On Interpretation* 16a.

may identify other grapes.[138] We can and do treat such images intentionally, as signs of objects in the world.[139] Further, humans beings can even turn their attention to that *icon* or *idea* itself, as we are doing right now. This is something other animals never do.

Unlike other animals, our power of imagination is informed by or infused with reason. This power allows us to treat an image (of a grape for instance) as a remote or stipulative universal. Unlike other animals who simply grasp morphic similarity without an awareness of doing so, we come to consciously identify things as *like*. We can even abstract further to *likeness* itself.[140] But because we can become consciously aware of likeness, we can attend to the grapes *as* such. We not only operate by means of likeness then but can attend to and make explicit those features which constitute that likeness. We can begin to identity a grape precisely as a grape because of those features. In doing so, we have moved far beyond a sensible image in the imagination or memory.

An animal does not know a grape *as a kind of* fruit, nor does it identify consciously to itself that one grape is same in *kind* with or *like* another. An animal establishes a *sensitive-appetitive relation* to the fruit, not an intellectual one. Animals only knows if *this-thing-here* is desirable or undesirable in some particular manner. A dog may relate to a grape by virtue of past experience, but he does this without cognizing, without being able to explicitly treat the grape as a *kind*. He instead

---

[138] This does not mean a literal picture exists in the mind, but a kind of semiotic likeness, either a sense 'idea' or an intellectual concept. There can be an image even of a smell in this respect.

[139] More will be said about signs or semiosis later.

[140] Categories such as genus and species, quality and quantity, or like and unlike, one and many are derivative of our initial cognitive grasp of things.

relates to it as a potential principle of action.[141] Animals never arrive at universals, what we call concepts or ideas in the primary sense.[142] On the other hand, humans can attend to grapes as such, even when we are appetitively indifference to them. We can consider a grape when we are not hungry, when it is not a potential object of desire. The τί ἐστι (*what is...*) question of Plato's dialogues therefore marks the radical difference between perception and reason as such.

To attend to anything in itself, we need a way of treating the grape, other than by means of image and memory, even if image and memory cannot and should not be wholly abandoned. We need a way of abstracting from our memory, from images and experiences, that which is one or universal in them all.[143] Only through a universal do we become capable of making rational, moral, or free judgements about a thing. And only here, do we have what can be called knowledge in the principal sense.

The act by which this occurs is called **apprehension** (the first act of the mind). The intellect (also known as the nous or understanding) is the faculty which *lays hold* of the conceptual qualities of an object present in the sense image.[144] When this occurs, we have not necessarily analyzed it into its essential conceptual constituent(s) but at minimum, the intelligible

---

[141] A dog relates to a sense 'idea' as a potential provocation of action, not as a sign as such. An animal is not and cannot become aware of the sign as such; we are, but only through secondary reflection. Nor does an animal have a concept in the proper sense.

[142] Other terms used are 'species', 'genus', and 'form'.

[143] See *Metaphysis* I.1 or *Posterior Analytics* II.19

[144] One might refer loosely to a sensible act of apprehension, but the term as used here refers to an act of the intelligence. Such an act may happen simultaneously with sense perception, but it is radically different.

whole has in some respect been apprehended. This whole is the beginning of scientific analysis, not the end.

Neither the real grape nor the morphic image in our imagination is this concept. The real grape is a complex being which exists extra-mentally (outside the soul). A real grape is something much more than a pure essence or definition. For instance, a real grape may be one hanging on a particular vine, of a definite shade of burgundy, of a certain size. It is a material grape with properties and accidents. The sense image formed in us will also have definitive features. But a concept analyzes and transcends the image by abstracting various features or qualities from it. This is what makes a person capable of reasoning about those features. The results of abstraction are therefore twofold. First, by means of a concept, one now knows potentially all grapes. A green grape for instance would not necessarily require a wholly new concept. Second, sensible features can become known through abstraction as qualities of various *kinds* belonging to a subject of a certain *kind*. This is how we arrive at meaning and definition (skin, fruit, seed, food, etc.) which extends beyond the sensations (touch, taste, shape, color). The very fact that we are talking about sensation, that touch, taste, and color *mean* something to us is because concepts are something much more than the sense experiences or images.[145] It is an amazing thing that I can think of a color red and know that it is not every single red or every single color, even while there is no such thing as a non-definite shade of red or a color that is not a specific shade!

---

[145] A concept is not just the isolation (abstraction), collection, or naming of sense data. It is that by which we universalize and navigate our experience meaningfully. It is the reason we can intentionally manipulate and imagined what is unreal—for instance, one may imagine a blue grape, a grape the size of New York, or the flavor of grape without the fruit.

Our initial apprehension comprehends various features which belong to a complex whole. The imagination, guided by reason, can then represent one or several of those features at will, apart from others. I can think of color apart from the grape. And through scientific analysis, we can form more or less precise generic concepts.[146] We can discover what belongs necessarily to a grape and what does not. Through our initial sense experience and the consequent (though sometimes simultaneous) mental activity, a concept can be *conceived* or formed within us.[147] We may not yet know the grape scientifically (through its causes), but we can grasp it cognitively in a manner that is unique to our rational nature. Charles Coppens summarizes it this way:

> Simple apprehension is the act of perceiving an object intellectually, without affirming or denying anything concerning it. To apprehend is to take hold of a thing as if with the hand; an apprehension, as an act of the mind, is an intellectual grasping of an object. The mind cannot take an object physically into itself; but it knows an object by taking it in intellectually, in a manner suited to its own nature; forming to itself an intellectual image, called a species of the object. The act of forming this mental image is called a conception, and the fruit of it, the image itself, is the concept, idea or notion of the object. The word simple added to apprehension emphasizes the fact that the apprehension

---

[146] The Greek λαμβάνω, often translated as *take* or *grasp*, can mean either to *apprehend* or *comprehend*. As this paragraph suggests, there is a way in which we must do both, though with various degrees of clarity or precision. Initial apprehension makes possible further analysis through reason and experience.

[147] This partly accounts for the theme of conception (generation) and sources throughout the dialogue.

neither affirms nor denies the existence of the object; it affirms nothing and denies nothing, it simply conceives the idea of the object.[148]

The Light of Apprehension

This *process* involves our exterior senses (smell, taste, touch, sight, hearing), our interior senses (the common sense, memory, and imagination), and specifically our properly intellectual powers, without which this could in no way occur (the active and passive powers of the intellect).[149]

Aristotle describes the intellectual principle of all understanding as a kind of light. This light of what is called the active or agent intellect allows us to abstract the intelligible features of things.[150] Curtis Hancock likens this to the way light passes through frames of film and reveals their inner structure without altering them.[151] Light makes such frames reveal their sensible content or structures. The passive intellect, on the other hand, is that power of the mind by which the mind itself is conformed to the intelligible pattern of a thing. This intelligible likeness is variously referred to as an idea, a concept, a species, or form. A cognitive *idea* is formed and made intelligible

---

[148] Charles Coppens, S.J., *A Brief Text-Book of Logic and Mental Philosophy* (Schwarz, Kirwin, Fauss, 1891).

[149] The Intellect is various called *understanding*, *nous*, and *mind*. On Apprehension, see, D.Q. McInerny, *Philosophical Psychology* (Fraternity Publications, 1999); Kreeft and Dougherty, *Socratic Logic*; Coppens, S.J., *A Brief Text-Book of Logic and Mental Philosophy*; James B. Reichmann, *Philosophy of the Human Person* (Chicago, Ill: Loyola University Press, 1985). The common sense is in Aristotelian psychology that power or faculty by which all our senses are organized into a single percept, so that we are not like Socrates' Trojan horse, full of disconnected sense experiences (184d).

[150] See *Republic* 508a-509d and *On the Soul* III.5

[151] Hancock and Bernot, "The True, the False, the Lie, and the Fake."

by the 'light' of the active or agent intellect which illuminates or abstracts from a sense image.

The intellect requires sense imagination (the sense images or phantasms formed by the common sense) because those sense images serve as material for the mind to operate upon or abstract from. One might compare this to a leaf-rubbing, in which one rubs a pencil on a piece of paper placed over a leaf. In doing so, the geometrical structure of the leaf is *taken away from* or *ab-stracted* from the leaf itself. One can thereby *see* the veins and shape of a leaf on the paper, apart from the leaf-*matter*. In the act of abstraction, one isolates and clarifies in the mind that which is not simple or explicit in a real object. By the light of our intellect, we are capable of turning our attention to all that we experience and attending to its intelligible features.[152] We not only can think each of these features (health) apart from a complex whole (Socrates-healthy); we can, to various degrees, grasp what each feature is. We can even discover their causal relations to one another and to the whole.

One might wonder what kind of 'light' the mind would have to possess in order to draw out and comprehend that which is intelligible in created things. In what light would the things of this world disclose themselves as proportional to mind? And why would the things of this world simultaneously be things which are knowable at all, things somehow related to mind? Why is being intelligible?

We can reflect on Josef Pieper's statement that "things can be known because they are created."[153] The Creator who is Intelligible Being per se has made all things intelligible in some

---

[152] The mind takes on the formal likeness of what it knows; it becomes, in a certain sense, what it knows through formal likeness. Thus, the mind is potentially all things.

[153] Pieper, *The Silence of St. Thomas*, 53.

respect, according to their kinds or insofar as they *are* or are like him. We may add that they can be known by us only because of the *kind* of creature we are.[154] He has made us *intelligent*. St. Thomas describes intelligence or intellect as a power of insight or reading. In *On the Truth*, he plays upon the etymology of 'intellect' when he states that the term intellect arises from its ability to know things most intimately, for to understand (*intelligere*) is as if to read within (*intus legere*) [things].[155] It remains to consider then the nature of such an intelligence or light that is capable of *read* the being of things.

We are made in the image of one who spoke all things into being, who is himself the Logos and in whom all things exist. We are thus *like* God, who is Spirit (John 4:24). The Spirit of God comprehends all that exists and does so preeminently as their Maker and as the Supreme Intelligence.

Because it is in the light of the Divine Mind that a things exists (John 1:3, 9-10), true knowledge of a thing must therefore conform in some manner to God's own knowledge.[156] Made in the image of the God (God who is Logos), we too have a power of understanding, a power of relating to things which themselves have likeness to an intelligible Word (see Psalm 19:1; Rom. 1:20). Therefore, "the essence of things is that they are creatively thought," than the conformity of our mind to a thing must be, by analogy, the conformity of our mind to the Maker.[157] This is possible, only if we possess a unique likeness to our Creator, a likeness to God in the creativity of his thought. St. Thomas says there is a "likeness in us of the

---

[154] Ibid., 110.

[155] St. Thomas Aquinas, "De Veritate," n.d., chap. I. a.12, https://aquinas.cc/la/la/~QDeVer.

[156] Pieper, *The Silence of St. Thomas*, 51.

[157] Ibid.

uncreated truth."[158] Scripture states with greater immediacy, "In your light do we see light" (Psalm 36:9).

Embodied Power

While our spiritual powers (our likeness to God) distinguish us from other animals and radically elevate human life, they also connect us with the whole of the created order. This is because our spiritual power is interwoven with our bodily existence. This means we can only understand human learning and apprehension if we also attend to our bodies.[159] All our

---

[158] *De Veritate*, Q.11, a.1

[159] Aristotle explores the relation of knowing and sensing by analyzing what is common and what is distinctive about human and animal experience. In *Metaphysics* I.1 he states,

By nature animals are born with the faculty of sensation, and from sensation memory is produced in some of them, though not in others. And therefore the former are more intelligent and apt at learning than those which cannot remember; those which are incapable of hearing sounds are intelligent though they cannot be taught, e.g. the bee, and any other race of animals that may be like it; and those which besides memory have this sense of hearing can be taught. The animals other than man live by appearances and memories and have but little of connected experience; but the human race lives also by art and reasonings. Now from memory experience is produced in men; for the several memories of the same thing produce finally the capacity for a single experience. And experience seems pretty much like science and art, but really science and art come to men through experience; for 'experience made art', as Polus says, 'but inexperience luck.' Now art arises when from many notions gained by experience one universal judgement about a class of objects is produced. For to have a judgement that when Callias was ill of this disease this did him good, and similarly in the case of Socrates and in many individual cases, is a matter of experience; but to judge that it has done good to all persons of a certain constitution,

higher acts of judgment and reasoning depend in some manner on the body. This is why Act I of the *Theaetetus* is a necessary beginning place.

It is through the body and its acts (such as sensation and memory) that the mind become aware of its mysterious and wonderful nature. Nevertheless, sensation and the other bodily powers are not sufficient to account for cognition, for life as we actually experience it. Simple apprehension is merely a powerful way of accounting for this experience. Ordinary human life (our recognition of generic kinds and causes) is the reason one might conclude that such a power must exist.

Socrates and Theaetetus have just agreed that if one does not take hold of being and truth, one can in no way have knowledge (186c-d). Apprehension has long been treated as that necessary first act of the mind by which we first lay hold of that which is intelligible (true being). It is fitting to reflect further on apprehension and sensation at this point, before we go on to Act II of the *Theaetetus* because without sense perception, we could never make cognitive contact with the world in the first place.

Object Awareness (Intentionality)
Let's spend a moment reflecting on the relation between sensation and our knowledge of objects (the world and the things

---

marked off in one class, when they were ill of this disease, e.g. to phlegmatic or bilious people when burning with fevers-this is a matter of art.

Experience (empeiria) in this sense, from which we get the term empirical, clarifies that Aristotelian realism (sense realism or empiricism) is radically more robust than how we often conceive of the modern *empirical* sciences. Science is not merely a product of sensation or the analysis of 'discrete sense datum'. Aristotelian science, all true science, is based on real contact and apprehension of substantial wholes in their real situation. See also *Posterior Analytics* II.19.

in it). The framework we will use can be called 'intentionality'. We will revisit this framework from a different perspective in Act II.

Theaetetus's first definition begins precisely where human experience begins, where all of our knowledge has its initial stirrings. This does not mean that we *only* know what we sense, but that the senses initiate our mental activity and provide matter for thought. In this respect, the beginning of the dialogue is an excellent one.

A deep and complex relationship between knowing and sensing can be gleaned from the following sentences:

- Did you *see* me catch that ball?
- Do you *see* what I mean?

Our ordinary language not only characterizes sight as a kind of knowing and knowing as a kind of sight, it also seamlessly unites the two activities. This is because sensation is intimately united and intertwined with our mental powers. Sensing is not just something that happens in the eyes or ears. All our cognitional powers are variously engaged in producing what we recognize as 'sensation'. This is because it is almost meaningless to speak of sensing without awareness. The light may cause me to wake in the morning, but I am 'seeing' that light only equivocally until I am awake. My eyes may have undergone an alteration (a modification) due to the light of the sun but seeing is properly inseparable from the awareness of seeing. This is implicit in Socrates point about seeing *through* the eyes (184c). I may not be aware of *all* that I see or specifically *what* it is I see, but there is a difference between the modifications of a sense organ and the act of sensing.[160] Such

---

[160] See John Deely, *Introducing Semiotic: Its History and Doctrine*, Advances in semiotics (Bloomington: Indiana University Press,

modifications can occur without sensation, such as in the case of physical injury, where the eye still dilates but the person does not see.

Further, it is a mistake to think of sensing as an awareness of the sense organ itself. I do not primarily undergo an awareness of the organ's modification. I do not hear my ears when I hear. Nor when I think my thoughts, do I necessarily think *about* myself. Rather, I hear some *thing* by sensing just as I think *about* something by my thoughts. The modification is that *through* which we become aware of the world, but it is not the modification per se of which I am usually aware. I do not usually notice that my eyes have dilated or that my ear drums are vibrating, but instead, I see or hear something else.[161]

In sensing then, we are aware that we grasp some object (some *thing*) *through* sense experience. As John Searle points out in *Seeing Things as They Are*, when we hit our hand on a table, we become aware of both the table and the pain in our hand, but these are "radically different."[162] He argues that we recognize a difference between the two because the awareness of pain constitutes the experience simply, but the awareness of the table is an intentional relation to an object (the

---

1982), 94. 'Modification' refers to the way the ears, eyes, or skin alter when a sense object acts upon them.

[161] An awareness of the modification as such differs in species and is often more akin to touch and/or pain (as when a noise is very loud). Perhaps touch is the sense in which one have the greatest awareness of the self because one is then most aware of the medium (the organ) by which one is sensing. To feel a rough surface is simultaneously to feel the roughness upon me. This may be part of what makes sight (the least *physical* of the senses) so perfect. With sight I relate to the object most of all as object, as removed from me. Aristotle states that by sight we comes to know *many differences* (*Metaphysics* I.1).

[162] Searle, *Seeing Things as They Are*, 24.

table) which is not simply the experience.[163] It is the intentional relationship which we will focus on here. The experience of the table is not *pain-awareness*. But *by means* of that sense experience, one becomes aware of something other than sensation through an intentional relation. This is the way that sense experience puts me in a relation to real things.[164]

Along these lines, John Deely convincingly argues that both sensing and thinking are intentional.[165] That is, when we sense (or when we think by means of concepts), we *intend* them toward things. This need not be a conscious act of will. It has its roots in an innate disposition. Babies, for instance, do this in the womb when they experience sensations. Contrary to representationalism, which has its roots in Descartes, we do

---

[163] I hope not to be misunderstood here. The word intention simply captures the fact that we intend *to* objects through our awareness of them, both zoosemiotically (by an animal power) and also by judgment of the reality of something and thus anthroposemiotically (see Deely p.197). But to say this is not to explain away the mystery of intention (the subject-object relation). It is no more than to say that there is indeed such a relation. It is to characterize it in terms of sensation and our organismic or cognitive attitude; it is to accurately characterize animal and human experience as intentional and semiotic (significant of objective being). But intention itself borders upon the mystery of all relations.

[164] A lack of immediate judgement or the power to judge means that animals cannot distinguish between dreaming and waking, sane and insane. Animals never judge a thing *to exist as such*. They relate to it insofar as it concerns here and now. While animals are in intentional relations, they do not recognize them as such (cf. Deely p.202). Animals are related to real things by their senses, but without consciously judging them as real. An animal does not fail to attack an image in a mirror because they judge it as *unreal* but only because and when they do not appetitively grasp the object.

[165] Deely distinguishes human and animal experience, but this claim is one he attributes to all animal life.

not primarily think about ideas then or even sense impressions as such, but rather think of things by means of ideas. We relate to sensations (and concepts) as *signs* of *things* and only secondarily turn to those signs into objects of awareness (as we are doing here). Deely argues that both sense images and concepts are semiotic (signs) because through them, we are aware of something other than them.[166] Following Poinsot (John of St. Thomas), Deely states that a sign "bring[s] something other than itself into an organism's awareness."[167]

Imagine someone sneaking up from behind and pouring water on you while you are reading this. You would be surprised and might not know what happened at first. You would not just undergo bodily modifications (such as temperature changes, dilation of the eyes, etc.), but simultaneously would begin to grasp, however confusedly, what has happened to you through those modifications. You would begin to search for *a what* and *a why*. In that radical surprise, you are surprised because and only insofar as you have expectations and now must *intend* your sense-experience toward an imperfectly known cause of change. The bodily modifications, such as change in pulse, breathing, skin temperature, etc., do not constitute surprise as such.

The experience of sensation as pure sensation then, without imaginative and mental characterization, is highly liminal and reductive, something at the very fringes of consciousness

---

[166] Deely cites *On the Soul* 3.8 in this regard, "for it is not the rock in the soul but its form (eidos)." He argues that this is true, not only of the concept rock, but also the morphic form, the phantasm to which he also attributes loosely the term 'idea'.

[167] Deely argues that concepts are only indirectly known (p.115). "The basis for positing the existence of ideas is our awareness of objects, not, as in modern philosophy (cf. Hume 1748: 680) or the introspective psychology that produced behaviorism, the other way around" (p.176).

and awareness. When we grasp something with the senses, we are already grasping it as *a this*, what Aristotle's called 'τόδε'. This is precisely because the mind (not the brain as such but the mind or nous) is not in as "an orange is in a crate."[168] Nous is an intentional and intending 'organ' or power. Therefore, mind is not trapped in the body but is already stretching out toward and in touch with the word *by means of thought*—precisely as mind.[169] The mind then does not need to think itself toward or into the world in an act subsequent to having ideas. Instead, precisely insofar as it is aware, our mind is in cognitional and intentional relation to what is *other*, to a world *through* ideas.

This is why there is no problem of 'getting outside', why the cartesian mind body problem is secondary, perhaps even a false start.[170] The mind is not thinking about its ideas and imagining a world (à la representationalism), but rather thinks of the world by means of ideas and concepts which are transparent to it.[171] In fact, we only become aware of our own

---

[168] Kenneth Gallagher, *The Philosophy of Knowledge* (New York: Sheed and Ward, 1964), 44–47.

[169] Ibid. Deely argues that the brain can never account for the act of intension per se (p.177-198). "Ideas and neural conditions cannot be so identified" because the idea (sense or concept) is precisely that by which we relate to things and thus as a relation cannot be a thing as such (p.140). This might mean however that the intentionality of animals may subsist in the same power which upholds their estimative sense and instinctual life—i.e., God.

[170] Ibid.

[171] Representationalism, espoused by Descartes, Locke, and implicitly by many people today, claims that what we know are our ideas. That is, when we think, we are thinking about ideas, images, and concepts; those are the object of our thought. While it is true that we can indeed turn our attention to such things with difficulty, the

thinking (of concepts and ideas, even sensation as such) secondarily, by reflection on mental activity. The mind does not first think and then discover a world, but by virtue of thinking has a world, a world which it is exists by being embodied!

Trusting the Senses?

There is ordinarily then no *existential* difficulty in trusting our senses. In a very real sense, we have never trusted them. To ascribe trust to sensation is a mischaracterization.[172]

When I think about leaving my son in charge of the house, I do not know what will happen. I first consider whether I can

---

Platonic and Aristotelian tradition argues that we think of things *by means* of ideas (i.e., the divided line). Sense experience and concepts are intentional signs which bring to our awareness something other than them. For instance, I think right now of a potential real reader, not of concepts of readers. Representationalism presupposes the mind-body problem, that we must somehow overcome solipsism. This ultimately has resulted in skepticism. Descartes has been radically influential here.

As Deely argues (placing himself in the Platonic and Aristotelian tradition), we are only aware of concepts and ideas reflexively, after the fact. Plato was interested both in beings and forms. Even forms as the primary beings. One can sense the complication as Socrates attempts to turn Meno's attention away from the world of becoming to concepts! This would not be so hard if it was our ideas which we chiefly attended to: *Is there not some one form by which I know each bee as a bee*? It is *to* this form one must *turn* to define what a bee is, even if one cannot comprehensively turn to that form as such (*Meno* 72b-c). "They [ideas] are cognized, if at all, only on reflection, and as the foundation or ground in the knower of what is apprehend directly...they are not objects at all, but the foundation or basis for relations of cognition to objects" (Deely 176). Plato would not agree with this last statement, or at least not in its Aristotelian sense that ideas do not exist by themselves.

[172] Plato ascribes trust to the divided line, but does so loosely, meaning something like reliance.

trust him. I do not *see* what will happen, but make a judgment based on his character. Based on past experience, I trust him and en*trust* that responsibility to him. Because I trust him, I rely on him for something unknown, something that I do not see or know.

This is not at all the structure of my lived experience with the senses. It is true, I can reflect on my sense experience and doubt their veracity as a kind of 'philosophic' exercise. But in my ordinary experience, I have never once *worked* from sensing *to* the world. I have never once first asked if the sensations I am experiencing connect to a world. I did not *reason* or *believe* from sensation *to* a world. We can say that I rely on sensation, but we cannot ascribe an act of faith to them in which I was moved from the seen to the unseen or from a state of doubt to a state of belief or trust, like a blind man who must learn to use a stick to navigate the world.[173] When I am driving

---

[173] The experience of doubt could only occur long after a history of relying on the senses, in mental illness, during existential doubt, or when a sense organ is damaged. But one would not posit a world or question the world unless one had already intended toward a world initially! This initial intension is never an act of conscious will. When I hear a voice in the dark, I do not ask, are my ears in touch with a world (or, is there a world)? Rather, I ask if I hear with enough clarity to judge what made that noise?

Even with this all said and done, I can still ruminate and feel anxiety about the *realness* of things. How badly I want a proof, a confirmation, something I can rest in. But such anxiety is generally existential in character rather than chiefly theoretical. The question *how can I know that this world-**that-I-know** is real?* is more characteristically answered by love rather than a proof. It is in love that I come home most *certainly* to what I know. This is because love is the perfection and consummation of being.

or walking, or eating, whenever I use my eyes or ears, I have never *entrusted* myself to my sense experience as if there was something *unseen* or *uncertain*. I may question whether my senses are working well, whether I have seen with sufficient clarity, but in ordinary experience I never question whether sense experience is related to things, not in the way that if someone tells me they have a rabbit in their hate I can wonder if the hat is empty or not and then come to a decision. The world is not a second thought in sense experience. It is present immediately to me *through* sensation and not as a

---

What would it mean after all for anyone, even God to 'prove' to me that the world or that He is real? What sign or demonstration, what syllogism would convince me that *I am*; *that I see what I see*; *that the world or God is*? God does not 'overcome' this existential problem with signs or 'proofs' in the logical syllogistic sense. Such proofs would regress into the same problem. The crisis is ultimately a personal crisis, one of faith, hope, and love. I am afraid. It is not my existence but the meaning of my existence I question—the fullness of my existence. It is not proof by way of argument I need, but the love of God. It is the love of God made known in the face of Jesus Christ which puts to rest all these boogeymen. For I *find myself in his love*.

The deepest ground of all being is Being itself; it is God, and God is Love. Therefore, it is in the love of God that I exist and exist most perfectly. When I find myself in his love, doubt is silenced. The intellectual-emotional unrest ceases because it was in fact spiritual unrest. It is not fundamentally a proof of this world I needed and longed for, but the confirmation and realization that I am made in love, by love, for love, and to love. Thus, I can only find true repose, not in my own being but in the Being of another. We exist not only because of Love but in order to live *by* that Love. This is why without an awareness of the love of God, reality becomes unreality. We long for the real, and the real is personal. In heaven, we will stand face to face in the light of that knowledge, that love which is the ground of our being. Outside of that light, there is no truth, and within it all things are made true.

conclusion.174 There exists in me no such *act of faith* which makes the world present. Instead, I rely on sensation intuitively and implicitly. Nor did sensation ever operate at a pre-intentional state in my cognitive development. Perhaps the very experience of a world could never have existed for me if this were the case.

I experience the world, not based on an act of faith (trust) but as immediate. I may not be able to explain this experience. I may not be able to provide a proof of its veracity. It is instead the ground of all other proofs and action.175 There are some things we know without proof. If this were not the case, we would know absolutely nothing. All would be either ignorance or opinion.176 This is not at all our experience.

---

174 If I were ever to try to *test* the senses, I could only do so through the senses. The scientist who argues that experiment has revealed we have no perception of things (due to the physiological mechanisms of sensation) undercuts his own scientific observations. See G. K. Chesterton, George William Rutler, and George J. Marlin, *The Collected Works of G. K. Chesterton. Vol. 2: St. Francis of Assisi* (San Francisco: Ignatius Press, 1986), 515.

175 Sense also requires the logical first principles of reason. These principles are innate and made explicit by reflecting on prior acts of reason which are brought into activity by sensation. They are implied in every judgement, even the judgment that they are true (or false).

176 This is not capable of demonstrative proof but is confirmed as the basis of all experience. The very judgment that my senses are wrong is based on a prior trust of the senses. One who denies this (or his own existence), denies the general principles of reason and cannot be argued with. A Christian who denies that first principles can be known immediately (without proof) might want to consider the following:

How will we know we are in heaven when we get there? If faith passes into sight, it will not be by faith. But if one can know nothing

Semiotic Character of Sensation[177]

Sense experience is therefore intentional or semiotic character. This does not mean that we work to the world by 'reading' strange 'signs' communicated to us by our five senses. Semiosis simply expresses that sensation is inherently *significant*. To sense is to experience a relationship, however obscure, with an object of sensation. When the wind blows, I sense the a thing blowing and not just that I shiver. In fact, to merely shiver is something a bit different because *I* move when I shiver, but the *wind* moves me when I sense it.[178]

Here we will clarify how the intentionality of sensation is related to objective wholes. A falsely characterizes sense experience if one construes merely as a collection of datum, a near infinite multitude of discrete, disorganized, or abstract sensations. When one sees a human face, for instance, one sees shapes and colors, and takes in a vast array of information, but at the same time, and much more definitively, one sees *a face*. This is not the result of cultural practice. It is not even a merely subjective accident belonging to the human creature (though it is subjective in the sense that we are subjects whose constitutions sense discrete wholes).

---

immediately, then one will neither know nor believe one is in heaven. One will simply have opinion at best. But even opinion is based on something known or believed, and belief must always be based on something known, therefore one will not have faith, knowledge, or opinion that one is in heaven when one is in heaven! One will in no way no one is in heaven then. Surely this cannot be correct!

[177] Based on Deely's *Introducing Semiotic*.

[178] One might try to use the theory of relativity to argue that shivering and wind are therefore the same thing viewed from a different perspective, but this is not a precise analogy.

To see shapes or colors apart from wholes (as shapes or colors) takes a special effort. An artist learns to isolate the morphic contours a face as something secondary to their ordinary experience. For this reason, we can argue that we do not 'construct' wholes out of discrete datum or randomly interpret the world. It is not merely because I am a human that I recognize a face, whether the face of a dog or a grasshopper, but because they have faces that I see them as such. We can recall here Jacob Klein's argument that without discrete kinds or features, the world would be infinitely confusing. Without a way a grasping individuality (the indivisibility or undividedness of things), we could not grasp the unity of anything. Without unity, all would be one big undivided mess.

Through the senses, cooperating with our other intellectual powers, the objectivity of the world makes itself known. The objectivity of things is constituted by an intentional encounter with wholes. When one says, 'I see a red ball,' one names the whole which constitutes a human perception. We do not see *a round* or *a red* but *a thing of such a shape and color and size* which we perceive as a ball. This 'perception' involves sensation, but also goes well beyond sensation, including the common sense, imagination, and memory. Part of what makes Act I of *Theaetetus* so difficult is that it attempts to attend to perception isolated from these faculties, as *mere* perception; it attempts to analyze something we are hardly familiar with at all.

Again, the *objectivity* of sensation, that we experience objects or objective wholes through perception is not an after-the-fact construction which we impose on the world. John Deely convincingly argues that it is not even a species-specific construction which we impose on things when we make them *things*, though our understanding of them is indeed unique. Instead, the object-intentionality of sensation is somewhat universal in character—it belongs to all perceiving creatures.[179] It would be hard to see how the more advanced animals would survive if this were not the case. Deely uses the example of camouflage. Camouflage is something which serves to obscure an animal from predators, to hide a certain kind of *object* or whole known through sensation. But camouflage is something which must be (and is) effective across a variety of species in surviving its function. For instance, a mouse has trouble recognizing a snake in the grass. If perception was merely a species-specific construction of sense data, it would be strange that it should succeed in frustrating a variety of predators, despite their differences. We can conclude that our analysis of sensation is not an utter imposition, peculiar to man. Across species, animals read sense data as intentional, and as object-significant, as *signifying* discrete and objective wholes.

> The initial sensory 'data; are not 'atomic in character ('this blue here and now'... 'this noise ...synthesis of sensations formed within cognition is neither arbitrary nor subjectively controlled, but *naturally determined* by semiotic means... since a sign is functioning to bring something other than itself into an organism's awareness, and since colors, sounds, textures, etc., immediately bring along with themselves an awareness of plurality, position, shape, movements, and so on, one has only to regard sensation semiotically in order to realize that we are already given within it an outline of objective structure...Sense data already comprise an objective structure...for all organisms. Species variation, consequently—that is, subjective different sensory range, orientation, and variety—are strictly background phenomena at the level of the sensory core; and that is why biological mechanism of camouflage

---

[179] Searle, *Seeing Things as They Are*, 43, 108–109.

(such as protective coloration) and deception, though principally dependent on the qualitative appearances or 'properties; of bodies, are so widespread and consistently useful across species lines."[180]

This zoological response of objective-intentionality is one grounded in treating sense experience as *significant*. We do not 'learn' this attitude; we only refine it. This is corroborated by an infant's rooting reflect (infants will turn their head when their cheek is stroked) and perhaps more radically by in-utero babies who turn their heads toward noise occurring outside the womb. Cognition then does not add this fact to our experience: it depends upon it as its material precondition, the foundation of all that it may come to clarify.

Sensation is therefore already organized, intentional, and expressive of unified causal sources. This is not something accidental to the kinds of organism we are or the kind of education we have had.[181] The example of

Figure 1: My Wife and Mother-in-Law by W. E. Hill, 1915

---

[180] Deely, *Introducing Semiotic*, 97–98.

[181] A mature person who gains the power of sight for the first time must develop their ability to navigate the information and discern various unities (thus the rapid neural development which

illusions which allow us to move between two different interpretations of a perception (e.g., the old woman and young) are secondary and occasional occurrences (see fig.1). The very fact that we seek to discern 'what' we are looking at is itself noteworthy, far more so than that we can be mistaken, that we must learn to do so effectively, or that in the case of some signs, a thing can have a variety of significations or modes of unity.

What this confirms is the immediate intuition of our experience: that sensing lays hold of that which is not merely sensation. Such an experience is so automatic, so seamless, that we have no awareness of it (prior to the kind of reflection we are doing here). And yet, without intentionality and its objectivity (the grasp of real unified wholes, however vaguely understood) the world would be incompressible. It would not be a world, but a chaos, an overwhelming confusion, utterly unlike our real situation. Disconnected and discrete sensibles, severed from all causal sources and signification, do not constitute the vast majority of what we know as human experience.

The very act of sensing therefore extends beyond sensation per se. And in man, this passes seamlessly from perception to an awareness of *a that* and *a what*. I may not comprehend the experience, but I apprehend it as an experience of a certain *sort*. This is the potential beginning of all higher forms of knowledge including science, art, and wisdom.

> Sense experience is not the totality of knowledge, to be sure, but it an authentic form of it, and one whose role

---

occurs in such moments), but they do not learn to become intentional in their judgment or construct unified sensation or causal relation simply. They may read a face confusedly and learn to do so better, but they do not 'construct' the human face through their sense data.

> must be seen as complimentary to other forms of knowing. It is crucial to appreciate that the total phenomena of human knowing is a harmonious unified process which constitutes a cognitional whole. Our investigation at the sensory level does not prejudice this truth, and above all does not suggest that sensation either precedes intellection at the temporal sense, or that it is a mode of knowing which merely parallels the intellectual process. Human sensation finds its true goal and purpose in understanding. It [sensation] is not an end in itself but contains an inherent order beyond itself.[182]

The mind, its awareness, its knowledge, can be brought to greater explicitness and clarity, but if it had to be brought into activity simply, without recourse to sensation, we would have no hope or means of doing so. This is why philosophy is possible. We begin in sensation and from sensation comes a rudimentary kind of knowledge (*Physics* I.1, *Metaphysics*, I.1, *Posterior Analytics* II.19). It is through the imperfect that we arrive at the perfect. Sensation is therefore the external stimulus and material which constitute the beginning of our cognitive life.

The Whole Person

The centrality of sensation clarifies some of the importance of the human body and bodily experience. We are educated by what we experience. Our experience is not merely *of* sensation, but nevertheless begins there. Therefore, through sensation we learn not only about the world, but even about the sort of being we ourselves are.

---

[182] Reichmann, *Philosophy of the Human Person*, 68.

In Hans Urs von Balthasar's *A Résumé of My Thought*, he states "The infant is brought to consciousness of himself only by love, by the smile of his mother."[183] One might mediate upon such a statement for a lifetime. The mystery of love, of personhood, of communion, and of the Imago Dei is here profoundly laid forth by him. The statement also reveals the enormous loss suffered by those who have not known the smile of their mother (or father), who have not know a friend, who have not been brought into consciousness of themselves and the world by that most fundamental and necessary framework of truth. There is a sense in which such a person has yet to awake to who they truly are. But what does Balthasar's claim suggest about us? It suggests that the meaning of the person is revealed ultimately in love.

But love is known by us because we know one another through the senses. The senses therefore make possible the *here and now* communion of persons. Because we become aware of the self through the things around us, and most profoundly through those things which are not merely things (but persons), knowledge, particularly self-knowledge, is interpersonal. What Balthasar's image suggests, is that true self-knowledge is best arrived at in personal communion.

This puts weight on the significance of intentionality: the realism of sense experience. If I come to doubt the reality of the world around me (if my knowledge of the world somehow

---

[183] *Communio*, Winter 1988. full quote:

"The infant is brought to consciousness of himself only by love, by the smile of his mother. In that encounter the horizon of all unlimited being opens itself for him, revealing four things to him: (i) that he is one in love with the mother, even in being other than his mother, therefore all being is one; (2) that that love is good, therefore all being is good; (3) that that love is true, therefore all being is true; and (4) that that love evokes joy, therefore all being is beautiful."

ceases to place me in relation to something other than me), how can I know myself? The knowledge of love, of being loved, of being in relation to another who loves me must disappear. Conversely, it is perhaps our doubt of such love which makes the world seem unreal to us. We therefore each desperately need a knowledge or revelation of love.

Our lives depend on this knowledge. Again, it is no accident that Jesus Christ is the revelation of divine love, God's love for us. In that revelation, we receive not only a communication of love but a vocation, we find ourselves.[184] Life takes on meaning its true meaning only in the light of his countenance. What a wonder, that this divine love is communicated by means of a human face, by means of a man (2 Cor. 4:6)!

The body and the sense faculties then, through which human communion is made possible, participate essentially in the mystery of love. We must not denigrate what is made known and what we can communicate with our bodies.

Man in his integrity is made to signify the mystery of love, and even the mystery of God (Genesis 1:26; John 14:9, 19:5). Our existence is therefore in a very real sense sacramental or covenantal. We are visible signs which makes present and known invisible realities. Our bodies (and one Man's body in particular) are made to declare a covenant of love. Man, who can act intentionally (with moral-spiritual purpose), can thereby commit himself in love to another. In doing so, he communicates something of that spiritual love through words and gestures, in all that he does. In doing so, he can become, like Christ, a spiritual revelation of love. In this manner, we reveal not just our own hearts, but something of the Source of our very being through the deeds of the body.

What we do and say then truly matters.

---

[184] I take this from the thought of John Paull II.

Act II: True Opinion (Judgment)

Sixth Reading
187b-196c True Opinion (*doxa*) & Wax:
True opinion; The mystery of false opinion—knowing, being; An aside on the *complexity* of knowledge; *Other-opinion; The block of wax; Division (examples); Dialogue within the soul*

Focus Questions:
1. What is a definition of opinion?
2. What are some examples of opinion?
3. How is opinion related to knowledge?
    a. Are they the same?
    b. If not, are like or unlike?
        i. Do they influence or affect each other?
        ii. Which comes first in time?
4. Why does Act II look at false opinion?
    a. Why is this difficult?
5. Why does Socrates introduce the image of the wax?
6. How does the image of wax move the dialogue forward?

This is by far the most technical and perplexing section of the dialogue, due in part to the introduction of opinion (or *doxa* in the Greek). Act II explores that which makes our experience more properly human: learning, forgetting, mistake, *re*cognition, judgment (i.e., the soul and several of its cognitional operations).[185] Opinion is itself a consequence (as well as a sign) of this complexity. Ultimately, if one is to clarify

---

[185] Perception, growth, metabolic functions, reproductive powers, motion, etc., are also caused by the soul. See McInerny, *Philosophical Psychology*; Reichmann, *Philosophy of the Human Person*.

human experience, and knowledge in particular, we need to account for and coordinate these various acts. The soul, introduced at the end of Act I, must for this reason become a more direct object of our inquiry.

Our last interchange (187a) concluded with Theaetetus's rejection of the perception thesis. Socrates then asks him what *we call it when the soul itself by itself is engaged with beings*. Theaetetus *supposes* that such is called *to opine* (δοξάζειν). His response, a bit of a letdown after the mention of reasoning, thinking, and judgment (ἀναλογίσματα; συλλογισμῷ; διανοῇ; κρίνειν), muddies the water, but necessarily if we are to truly distinguish knowledge from other kinds of thinking.

Whether Theaetetus rightly *supposes* that *true opinion* is knowledge, his proposal allows us to reflect upon a new mystery, one previously excluded by the perception thesis. True opinion (or opinion more generally) opens the door to *false opinion*. Opinion, unlike perception, can properly be said to be true or false.[186]

We can state at the outset that to opine means, at the minimum, to have made a judgment of some kind. In this way, opinion is different from mere perception; it implies affirmation or denial. Because of this, opinion (or the act of judgment) belongs more properly to the rational soul as such—it is something the soul or the person does; it is not chiefly somatic. Still, what makes such opinions or judgments possible? They must come from somewhere or be based on something. This is what Socrates wonders, and he proposes several potentials sources:

- Knowledge
- Being

---

[186] In this manner, *Theaetetus* anticipates the succeeding dialogue (the *Sophist*), in which our interlocutors explore image and original, like and unlike, same and other.

- Memory

To account for opinion, we must also account for mistake or false opinion. But where will mistake be located? Will error be the fault of knowledge or of being? This would be strange (*atopos*). Will it then be the fault of memory or something like memory?

As we seek for the source of error, we can recall that truth and falsity belong most of all to an act of affirmation or denial (when we say or think either that something *is* or that it *is not*). This act looms in the background of Act II because we have to reckon with something more than the first of act the mind. We cannot just deal with concepts alone; we must consider the knowing individual—the relationship between the knower and the known. Therefore, we ultimately have to reckon with that act by which we affirm or deny, that act by which we mentally join or divide. Traditionally, this has been called judgment.

True opinion;
187b

<u>The.   To say this about all opinion is impossible, since there is false opinion, but I venture to say that true opinion is knowledge.</u>

- Theaetetus opens this section by making a division. He has *divided* perception *from* knowledge. He then *divides* opinion into two forms (ἰδέαιν), false and true (ψευδής; ἀληθής). Knowledge, he says, is *true* opinion. Knowledge is therefore a *species* of opinion. This division had been excluded by the first definition, for if knowledge is perception (if each man is the measure), there can be no error.

- Theaetetus's assertion is itself an opinion and is asserted as such. Socrates says that in speaking readily in this manner, they will either find what they have been seeking or will be less likely to suppose they know it when they do not. Dialectic is fundamentally an examination of opinions. We cannot arrive at wisdom or acquire adequate knowledge any other way than by examining opinion. This suggests the possibility of learning! It is remarkable that speech can clarify our thinking, that by means of dialogue (interior or exterior), we can learn. God has so structured us that we can and must learn through speech with one another. This also suggests that we might find in opinions which we already possess both false things and true.

- Socrates is troubled, however. He is very much perplexed, not being able to say what sort of thing false opinion is, nor how it comes about (187d). In the vein of Parmenides, naysaying (or something like it) is treated as logically problematic. Negation, non-being, the false, the like and unlike, are a mystery of their own, a mystery intertwined with the mystery of being (see *Sophist*).

The mystery of false opinion—knowing, being;
187e

So.   <u>How then? What are we saying? Are we saying that each time there is a false opinion, someone has a false opinion and someone else a true opinion, as if they were that way by nature?</u>

- Socrates seems to be asserting here that false opinion and true opinion can both exist or be held by individuals. Somehow either of these contraries (true and false opinion) are possible. But what is their cause? What in fact are they? This is about to be explored.

188a
So. ...It is possible with all things and each thing, either to know or not to know? For learning and forgetting, those **middle states** (μεταξύ), I dismiss for the present. For now, they are nothing according to the argument.

- Socrates dismisses these *middle states*, even while Theaetetus himself seems to be in *the middle* by means of opining. Opinion, like learning, means someone is between total ignorance and perfect knowledge. But if Theaetetus is correct in defining knowledge, if opinion (or true opinion) *is* knowledge, one has no means of distinguishing the middle (or imperfect) from the perfect—opinion cannot be said to be *distinct* from knowledge if knowledge *is* opinion.[187] Act I and Act II therefore each suffer from deficiencies of division.

    Under this new hypothesis (the exclusion of learning and forgetting), one must either know or not know. One either has no opinion (ignorance), a true opinion (knowledge), or a false opinion (error). Even with this simplification, the problem of error remains rather mysterious. The problem of error recalls the earlier question, *can one not know what he knows* (163c-d).

The. Nothing is left but knowing and not knowing.

188a-b
So. Then it is necessary for the one opining to have an opinion about what he knows (οἶδεν) or does not

---

[187] Weil, *Gravity and Grace*, 200. Simone Weil explores the mystery of the μεταξύ which concerns middle states and participation in her work. She points out its centrality in the Platonic project.

know...it is impossible (ἀδύνατον) for the one who knows a thing not to know it.
- Socrates uses οἶδεν for knowledge, broader and less technical than ἐπιστήμη.

- Theaetetus allows Socrates to make the following problematic assertions.

   A. One can have an opinion about what one does not know:
   On the one hand, opinion seems to be precisely concerned with what one does not know! Because we do not know, we are forced to opine. On the other hand, it would be strange to have an opinion about something wholly and utterly unknown. But because those *middle states* have been eliminated at this stage in the inquiry, it seems one is left either opining about what one wholly knows or about what one is wholly ignorant of. Are either of these possible?

   B. It is impossible for the one knowing a thing not to know it:
   This seems to preclude error once again and thrust us back on some of the deficiencies of Act I. Of course, this precludes it only insofar as one is a knower. It is possible one can be a knower in one sense, while ignorant (or in error) in another.[188]

- This would be a fitting moment for Theaetetus or Socrates to make another, more careful, dialectical division, perhaps concerning either knowledge itself,

---

[188] Cf. *Posterior Analytics* I.1

opinion, or the human person (the one who knows, opines, or errs). The logos moves forward however. In doing so, it will bring to light various problems: directing us to clarify the nature of opinion, and consequently, knowledge.

So. <u>Then does the one having false opinion think that the things he knows are not these things, but other things he knows, and knowing both he is ignorant of both?</u>
- Socrates asks here if false opinion is the result of thinking that a thing one knows is actually some other thing one knows.

The. <u>But this is impossible (ἀδύνατον), Socrates</u>
- The is impossible only if we insist one either wholly knows or is wholly ignorant. One either knows or does not know if we eliminate the middle ground or take the object of knowledge very precisely. In the ordinary and actual occurrences of life, we often **mistake** one thing we know for another, or know *something* about one thing but not something else about it. Even with this said, there remains the mysterious fact that we err! We actually do make mistakes about what we know. This is precisely the focus of Act II. We do not just know infinite discrete facts; we are capable of knowing in one manner and not another.

188c

The. That would be terrible (τέρας γὰρ ἔσται).
- It seems a terrible thing that a man would:
    a. Think something he knows is something else he knows (for then it seems he does not know either)

> b. Think something he knows is something he doesn't know (for then he does not know the thing he knows, but somehow thinks it is something he does not know at all)
> c. Think something he doesn't know is some other thing he doesn't know (for then something he does not know at all is mistaken for some other wholly unknown thing).

An aside on the *complexity* of knowledge

These last ('b' & 'c') seem to be the most terrible options of all. How could one possibly be mistaken about, much less have any opinion concerning that which one does not know at all? How can error or mistake occur concerning something of which one is in no way cognizant? If we pay attention, we can see that something is beginning to emerge here which is more fundamental than ignorance and error.

> If I do not know what a thing is, how can I know what sort of thing it is? Or does it seem (δοκεῖ) to be to you, Meno, if someone does not know someone altogether (τὸ παράπαν), that one could know whether he is beautiful, or rich or well born, or the opposite (*Meno* 71b).

While Theaetetus and Socrates have simplified our state of cognition to knowing or not knowing, knowledge is by no means so simple. Both the things known to us and our modes of knowing can be complex in a variety of ways. This complexity or ambiguity is hinted at in the opening lies of the *Meno* in Socrates use of τὸ παράπαν. As several interpreters have pointed out, 'τὸ παράπαν' can mean either 'altogether' or 'at all'.[189] The phrase may refer then either to a total ignorance, that is, not knowing a thing 'at all', or it may refer merely to an imperfect state of knowledge which does not grasp its object 'all together', that is, in every respect.

Complexity underlies the whole of Act II (and perhaps Act III). This partly because in the shadow of opinion, lurks judgment. Analysis of judgment and opinion demands a radically more complex psychology than perception alone does. We can start to unpack why.

The objects we reflect on in opinion and judgment have various qualities, states, parts, and relations. We do not look directly into the essences of things but must collate various aspects of our experience. "Every object we know directly is composite."[190] The black cat in my house is both a cat and black (as well *by the window; sleeping; on its back; with a paw up...*). But as stated about *Socrates-healthy* and *Socrates-Sick* (158e-159b), I do not grasp each of these qualities separately. They are known as part of and diversly related to the causal whole, the cat. Our thinking reflects this complexity, particularly in the act of judgment which combines and separates things in the mind.

In addition to qualitative complexity, judgment also concerns itself with existence more directly. For it is by judgment that we affirm whether a thing *is* or *is not*. It is through judgment that we arrive at existence. As Randall Colton puts it,

---

[189] See also *Meno* 80d. See Alfred Mollin, *An Introduction to Ancient Greek*, 4th edition. (Lanham, MD: Hamilton Books, 2018), 313; Plato, George Anastaplo, and Laurence Berns, *Plato's Meno*, The Focus philosophical library (Newburyport, MA: Focus Pub./R. Pullins Co, 2004), 49.

[190] Randall Colton, "Philosophical Anthropology," Course Notes (Holy Apostles College and Seminary, Cromwell, CT, spring 2019). See also *Summa Theologica* I-I q.85, a.1, 3, 5, 8.

Commentary

> We can only know them [the things we experience] in their real existence by means of the synthesis (or division) of a judgment. So in judgment the mind reaches the existence of things. In direct judgment, the mind reaches things in their real existence; in reflex judgment, the mind reaches things as the object of judgment—as second intentions. The capacity for reflex judgments makes it possible to ask the question about truth: I can hold a reflex judgment before my mind while forming a direct judgment and then consider their relation.[191]

Every limited being we actually encounter is not only composite in some manner, but in our minds composed of *what it is* and *that it is*. This is why it is by an act of judgment alone that we arrive at existence, at being—even when that judgment is concurrent with our simple apprehension of it.[192] We apprehend beings directly, but we do not directly apprehend being or existence as such.[193]

---

[191] Ibid. Concepts when considered in their own right are called second intentions because they are secondary ontologically and in our cognitional *intentionality*. The concept of cat is normally that by which I attend to real cats and only secondarily something I consider in its own right. A scientist thinking through the nature of a cat is intending his thought not to a concept but to a real thing. It is a logical question or a second intention when we ask, is 'cat' a genus or a species, universal or particular, negative or positive, concrete or abstract.

[192] We need not consciously initiate such a judgment, though we can turn our awareness to the act of judgment. Judgment need not even occur only 'after' perception or apprehension. It can be simultaneously, though it is something other than (and can indeed follow upon) apprehension.

[193] For an excellent analysis of this from a Thomistic perspective see John Knasas, "Gilson vs. Maritain: The Start of Thomistic Metaphysics," *Communis* 43, no. 3 (1990): 169–183.

- Socrates now proposes (188c-d) that instead of searching for the cause of false opinion in what a man **knows or does not know**, they will seek it in **being and not being** (κατὰ τὸ εἶναι καὶ μή). The mystery of false opinion is thus shifted from the ground of knowledge to the ground of being. Whether this will be fruitful is questionable, but we can recall it was established that one who does not arrive at the *being and truth of a thing* could never arrive at the knowledge of it (186d).

  He states that anyone who has opinions *which are not* has false opinion. And the only way one can opine about something *that is not* is when one opines that which is not true.

  Let's put this in the context of what truth has been said to mean. Based on Aristotle, Thomas Aquinas enumerates three definitions of truth:
  a. The conformity of the mind with what is[194]
  b. To say that what is, *is* or that what is not *is not*
  c. The conformity of a thing with what it is supposed to be

  It is perhaps 'b' which concerns our problem here, the strange fact that we can speak and think truly about things, not only those which are, but even those which

---

[194] Thomas states that it is not enough merely for a likeness of something real to be formed in the mind, but that the mind must be aware of its own conformity with reality. Truth is the conscious and intentional grasp of this conformity. This conscious or self-aware aspect of knowing will come up later in the dialogue. We can state here that it is one thing to be self-aware of this conformity; it is another to be aware of *why* what is known is true.

are not. We speak truly about things which are not insofar as we know or express that they are not.

188e
So. But can a man see something and see nothing? ...surely if he sees one thing, he sees what is one of the beings (τῶν ὄντων)? Or does it seem to you that a thing is a being that is not? (ἢ σὺ οἴει ποτὲ τὸ ἓν ἐν τοῖς μὴ οὖσιν εἶναι;)
- Theaetetus agrees that this cannot be. One does not encounter or see non-being. That which *is* is not a non-being.

189a
So. So then one who is opining is opining about something that is?
- Theaetetus agrees with this. Of course, the ambiguity lies in several areas:
  - Is the opinion about that thing about it *as it actually is*?
  - Does the object of the opinion actually exist?
  - Does it exist just in the way which one opines it?
  - Is the object, in reality, the very object identified in the opinion? For instance, is to opine about *Socrates-sick* when he is healthy to opine about what is not or what is, but not as it is?

So. Then the one having an opinion of what is not is opining about nothing...he who is opining about nothing holds no opinion **at all** (τὸ παράπαν).
- It is clear that a division might be made here by Theaetetus. Without the middle ground of learning and forgetting (or knowing *somewhat* vs. *altogether*) such a distinction might not be possible. Another distinction might be between mental and extramental.

Even while such distinctions might seem obvious, we should not lose site of the fact that when one makes any error, the absolute value of the judgment, the judgment taken as a whole, must either be true or false. The law of the excluded middle (that every proposition is either true or false) necessitates this.

189b

From the conclusion that one would need to be opining about non-being, Socrates concludes that false opinion cannot be holding an opinion about that which *is not*. Therefore, he claims that false opinion is neither caused primarily by what we know nor by being (by that which is).

What has been (and is being) brought to light, somewhat implicitly, is the rather remarkable, if paradoxical fact that all false opinion must somehow be based on being and knowledge! That is, it is unthinkable that anyone could ever, in any way, form an opinion that is based absolutely on non-being or ignorance. Therefore, all error and all opinion are secondary phenomena, dependent upon being, truth, and knowledge. I can mistake or misconnect things. But even if we admit this, we should still keep in mind that this depends on the more mysterious fact that all mistake, all error relies on prior apprehension and knowledge. There can be no error or opinion without knowledge of some kind. Thus opinion and error are shadows cast by the mystery of knowledge and being.

We are neither wholly ignorant, nor perfect knowers when we opine. Along these lines, Aristotle, states in *Metaphysics* II.1:

> Speculative, knowledge of truth is in one sense difficult and in another, easy. An indication of this is found in the fact that, while no one can attain an adequate knowledge

of it, all men together do not fail, because each one is able to say something true about nature. And while each one individually contributes nothing or very little to the truth, still as a result of the combined efforts of all a great amount of truth becomes known. Therefore, if the situation in the case of truth seems to be like the one which we speak of in the proverb "Who will miss a door?" then in this respect it will be easy to know the truth. But the fact that we cannot simultaneously grasp a whole and its parts shows the difficulty involved."

Other-opinion
189b-c

Socrates suggests a new approach, having failed to find the cause of false opinion in being or knowledge as such. He suggests that false (ψευδῆ) opinion might be *other-opinion* (ἀλλοδοξίαν). *Other-opinion* occurs when one exchanges (ἀνταλλαξάμενος) one being for another in one's **thinking** (διανοίᾳ). Thus when one **speaks** within oneself or **vocally** and makes an exchange of one thing for another—aiming at one, and missing (ἁμαρτάνων)—one holds a false opinion.

Theaetetus is delighted with this account and claims ironically that such a person *truly* holds a *false* opinion!

What has not been explained yet is how a knower could yet *mis*-take that which he knows for some other thing, either for something else he knows or something he does not know. *Other-opinion* (ἀλλοδοξίαν) is therefore a problematic step. It is a step forward, however, insofar as it prepares us to consider more directly the interior operations of the soul (memory and judgment).

Socrates picks up on Theaetetus's unintentional irony (189c). The phrase *truly-false* seems self-contradictory. But perhaps something profound is expressed here. Such an expression can actually be meaningfully *combined*! This is because we can know the truth, even about what is untrue. Surprising combinations *truly* occur under certain conditions. Opinion and judgment are complex in precisely this manner. Socrates lets this pass.

189d-190a
Whenever we have *other-opinion*, it is necessary that we have in our thought either one of the things which we exchange for the other or both. Socrates then describes thinking (διανοουμένη) as speech which the soul has with itself about the things it beholds or considers. The soul converses (διαλέγεσθαι) with itself, asks itself questions, affirms and denies. And when it divides or judges (ὁρίσασα) and no longer doubts (διστάζῃ), we set this down as opinion.

This description however does not sound to me like *mere opining*. It seems to boarder on something more certain, perhaps even some fundamental act of the soul. Nevertheless, it might refer to either (opinion or certain knowledge). We can note that there are indeed judgments about which the soul can be and often is wrong. Yet, there are other judgments which seem to virtually exclude the possibility of error (either due to their objects or to the clarity of our thinking). Are there not times when a thing is judged in the full light of the intellect, and others in which we judge that which is less clear to us?

One might contrast the following:

- That odd is the opposite of even (*Not the mere definition, but the knowledge of their contrariety*)
- that 12 is even
- that 144+137.5=281.5

or

- That a triangle has three sides

- That a triangle's three interior angles are equal to two right angles

or

- The recognition that someone is alive
- The recognition that you love them
- That they belong to a certain species or genus

Some of these are not only more immediate known, but almost impossible to be wrong about! Others are less certain. Even as Socrates and Theaetetus explore the ways in which we can err, it is worth asking if error is possible equally and everywhere, whether the soul is always an unwitting dupe of opinion. William James describes cognitional certitude in this manner:

> Of some things we feel that we are certain: we know, and we know that we do know. There is something that gives a click inside of us, a bell that strikes twelve, when the hands of our mental clock have swept the dial and meet over the meridian hour.[195]

---

[195] William James, *The Will to Believe*, n.d., https://www.gutenberg.org/files/26659/26659-h/26659-h.htm. Perhaps James's expression of 'clicking' is too metaphorical. Socrates suggests truth is recognized by means of a *kinship* of the soul with all things (*Meno* 81d). Descartes uses the problematic criteria of *clear and distinct*. Both Plato and Aristotle have also used the analogy of sight. The contrary of some intuitions and judgments are virtually meaningless or unthinkable (*that A is not A; that a whole is less than a part*). The certainty and insight by which we perceive or know each thing may not be of the same degree or of the same character. Some knowledge is more personal; some less; some things more certain; some less. See, Gallagher, *The Philosophy of Knowledge*, 218–289.

There are times we *touch* the whole, when we know that the *fit* of what think is precisely the *fit* of what *is*. Perhaps such moments are not restricted only to mathematics and definitions, but even extend even to music, to love, to the recognition of truth itself, perhaps even to recognition of something writ in the human face. The image of wax will capture something of this experience.

190b
Theaetetus admits that whenever a man *opines* that one thing is another, it seems to that man that one thing *is* the other thing.

Recollect (ἀναμιμνῄσκου), Socrates bids him, whether you have ever said to yourself that the beautiful is shameful or that the unjust is just, or have you tried to convince yourself that the odd is even? Or rather, even in your sleep would you never do such a thing?

You speak the truth, says Theaetetus. He agrees that there is a kind of knowing or thinking that does not readily admit of error. What sort of thinking or knowing would this be? What is its mode and what are its objects? In the *Meno*, Socrates claims there exists a kind of kinship with all things which the soul recognizes. It may be that the intellect (nous) cannot fail in regard to certain kinds of intelligibles, anymore than the eye as such can err in its reception of color.[196] Thinking (dianoia), when guided by such insight, would itself be trustworthy. But surely not all thinking is like this. Not all speech within the soul or inner judgment is of the same quality. Not all inner speech is guided step-by-step by intellectual insight or understanding.

---

[196] Judgment of color is very different than the eye's operation itself. The eye is not subject to fantasy or will power. When healthy and presented with a color, the eye simply operates accordingly.

They do not consider this but will recur to the same theme at 195b-d.

190c-e

They reject the idea that one who forms an opinion of two things and lays hold of (ἐφαπτόμενος) both with the soul could have an opinion that one is really the other. Neither could one who holds an opinion of the other only, have an opinion that it is yet some other thing. Again, this considers opinion and knowing simply or as a whole—that one either knows or does not, without nuance or gradation.

They seem incapable of showing how false opinion can exist in us. Yet, Socrates asserts that many more absurdities shall follow if false opinion is found *not* to exist! An account of knowledge which excludes the possibility of error (i.e., Act I) is wholly inadequate.

191a-b

In an attempt to somehow account for false opinion, Socrates now claims they were perhaps wrong when they said it is impossible for a man to have an opinion that the things he does not know are the things he knows. There may yet be a way that this is in his power.

Theaetetus thoughtfully interjects a *suspicion* or *opinion* (ὑπώπτευσα) of his own, that this may occur when you see someone at a distance and wrongly suppose it to be someone you know. The image is that if *imperfect* or *partial* apprehension. But Socrates objects that this seems to mean that someone knows and does not know the very thing he is knowing; that is, one knows and does not know *the very same thing*. Before such an account can be accepted, a dialectical step is needed.

Theaetetus may have missed an opportunity to make a distinction at this point, to clarify whether his suggestions really means knowing and not knowing the *very* same thing.[197] It matters, after all, that the objects we judge are complex and therefore can be in some manner *like* one another, even as they are also in some manner other or *unlike* (*Socrates-sick* and *Socrates-Healthy*). While such a division or clarification might 'solve' the dilemma, it would also obscure the solution. There is a deeper problem or mystery concerning false opinion that would be concealed by this obvious but premature distinction. Our problem is bound up both in the primacy and complexity of knowledge, as well as in the complexity of the facultative powers involved in knowing.

Concerning the primacy of knowledge, we can note that false opinions can only occur if there is something known. At the same time, knowledge alone is not a sufficient cause of false opinion. If I know that a certain cat is black and I see a small black dog, I am *not* wrong in identifying them both as the same, insofar as they are black. My knowledge of the part, the quality black, is precisely correct! I am only wrong in identifying the dog *as* the cat.[198] Therefore, I am *wrong simply* about

---

[197] It would be a shame to think one had *found* the *sought-for* when in fact one had not (or had not done so adequately), 142a.

[198] It is worth considering that such 'knowledge', fundamental to our experience, is hardly knowledge at all for Plato or Aristotle. When I recognize an individual, I recognize them *in the perceiving*. Perception is not without knowledge, but it is not the same as the knowledge by which I know they are human or some other species. Particulars are never, in the strict sense, episteme. We truly attribute 'knowing' (oida) to such acts, but they are very different than the knowledge by which I know that which is true, necessary, and causal in the more governing sense. There is a science of man; there is no science of Socrates. There is no science of *that* bird, but of birds. This is both a result of the individuality of the thing but also their

the dog and cat. But am I wrong *in my very knowledge* about the cat, or am I wrong *because I have knowledge* of the cat? The first would be the fault of knowledge as such; the second would be a fault in judgment or opinion. Knowledge provides

---

intelligibility. Socrates is intelligible, not by virtue of *that* flesh or being *that* individual, but by virtue of being a creature of a certain *kind* (one who is a specific *form* of living embodied being). It is this formal character and not the particular flesh or individual per se which is known scientifically. We might not have such intelligible forms without particulars, but it would not be qua particular that we know what a thing is. Socrates is intelligible not qua Socrates. This is in part because he is not identical with what he is absolutely, with his essence. He is *a man* and not *man*. For this reason, Plato sometimes referred to apprehension of particulars as opinion (Republic 509d-511e). Aristotle would remind us that there is no definition of Socrates or singulars (of each thing, 'ekaston', as such). Aristotle states this in *Metaphysics* 7.10, 1036a1-10:

But in the case of a concrete whole, for example, this circle, or any singular thing, either sensible or intelligible (by sensible circles I mean those made of bronze and wood, and by intelligible, such as are the objects of mathematics), of these there is no definition; but they are known by intellect or by sense, i.e., when they are actually seen. And when they are removed from a state of actuality, it is not clear whether they exist or not; but they are always known and expressed by a universal formula. Now matter is unknowable in itself. (τοῦ δὲ συνόλου ἤδη, οἷον κύκλου τουδὶ καὶ τῶν καθ' ἕκαστά τινος ἢ αἰσθητοῦ ἢ νοητοῦ—λέγω δὲ νοητοὺς μὲν οἷον τοὺς μαθηματικούς, αἰσθητοὺς δὲ οἷον τοὺς χαλκοῦς [5] καὶ τοὺς ξυλίνους—τούτων δὲ οὐκ ἔστιν ὁρισμός, ἀλλὰ μετὰ νοήσεως ἢ αἰσθήσεως γνωρίζονται, ἀπελθόντες δὲ ἐκ τῆς ἐντελεχείας οὐ δῆλον πότερον εἰσὶν ἢ οὐκ εἰσίν· ἀλλ' ἀεὶ λέγονται καὶ γνωρίζονται τῷ καθόλου λόγῳ. ἡ δ' ὕλη ἄγνωστος καθ' αὑτήν.)

For him, the knowledge of particulars is much more like noetic insight or perception, a kind of perceptive understanding or initial wisdom (apprehension) which can be informed by the higher acts of mind.

a means by which to err but is not itself a sufficient cause. Error is somehow precisely in *me* or in *an act* which belongs to me, which is my own.

Error is never the simple result of knowledge or nous. It has something to do with a more synthetic or analytic activity, a more complex kind of thinking and relating. It is with this in mind that Socrates here introduces the myth (story) or image of the wax to address the complexity at play, not from the perspective of our cognitional objects, but from a facultative perspective: that of memory and judgment.

The block of wax;
191c-d

Socrates asks, could a man who did not know something learn it later? And, can he learn some other thing and then another? Theaetetus admits this. In their desperation to give an account of false opinion, they have at last reintroduced learning and with it, the possibility of giving a more comprehensive treatment of opinion.

Let there be then, for the sake of the argument, Socrates says, a waxen block in the soul, something which receives impressions.[199] It receives images or likeness of sense perceptions and thoughts in the way that one stamps an image upon wax (ὑπέχοντας αὐτὸ **ταῖς αἰσθήσεσι καὶ ἐννοίαις**, ἀποτυποῦσθαι, ὥσπερ δακτυλίων σημεῖα ἐνσημαινομένους). That which it receives as an impression, we can remember.

In some people, this wax is larger; in others, smaller. In some, purer, in others filthy, and in some it is in a state of having a measured quality (μετρίως ἔχοντος). The character of this wax can differ. These various contrary qualities are

---

[199] Cf. On Interpretation; *On the Soul* II, III; *Posterior Analytics* II.19; *Metaphysics* 1.1.

reminiscent of how Theaetetus was described early in the dialogue (144a-b).

The waxen block is the gift of Memory (Μνημοσύνης), the mother of the Muses. Memory is that power by which something becomes present to the soul in an abiding manner, as apart from a things extra mental existence. By memory, something comes to belong to the mind in its own right. Without this gift from the Mother of all arts and sciences, all of our human spheres of knowledge, dependent on experience, could never exist (149c). Without memory, we could not recall the differences between things or their similarities. Without memory, we could not learn or judge. We would never know the difference between accidents and essence. We could not learn from the past or seek into the causes of things. We could never plan, seek means of improvement, or be prudent for ourselves. Therefore, all of our higher mental acts depend in some manner upon this power. Human life, insofar as we know it, cannot exist without memory.

Socrates explains, whenever we wish to commit something to memory, whether things which we think or perceive, we hold the wax under those perceptions or thoughts and impress them upon it, just as one leaves a seal in wax with a signet ring.[200] The impression is a kind of sign and likeness (σημεῖα). And we remember and know (ἐπίστασθαι) whatever is imprinted upon the soul, as long as the image lasts. Whatever is rubbed out or impossible to mold, we forget and do not know.

---

[200] It is worth recalling two moments in *On the Soul*. Early on, Aristotle describes the unity of the body and soul as like that of wax and an impression. Later, he describes the receptive part of the mind (nous) as a blank tablet that can receive the writing or form of things (logos/eidos).

It is through the vehicle of this image that Socrates will attempt to show that a man indeed can have false opinion (191e-196c). By means of the wax, Socrates distinguishes (διοριζομένους) between the original objects and their memorials (μνημεῖον) in the soul. He precedes then to give 17 permutations or possibilities, only three of which admit of false (or other) opinion.

Theaetetus, perhaps like most readers, is perplexed by their variety and significance (192d).[201] Therefore, Socrates will follow this up by repeating the division with examples.

Division (examples);
192d-193e

Before elaborating upon the tortuous line of argument at 192a, Socrates makes two clarifying points:
1. One may perceive or not perceive what one knows
2. One may not perceive or *merely* perceive what one does not know

For instance, Socrates knows Theodorus and remembers within himself what sort of man he is. He also knows Theaetetus in this way. However, sometimes he sees them (or experiences them through one of his senses); sometimes he does not. Sometimes he can remember them without perception and simply know them within himself. The point is that one may perceive or not perceive that which one knows—precisely what was impossible under the Protagorean (perception) account. This Theaetetus admits.

Socrates second points is that one may sometimes not perceive or *only* perceive that which one does not know (192e). Theaetetus also admits this. But is this statement equally

---

[201] Sachs points out that Theaetetus had also made a division of seventeen examples in his mathematical foray. See Plato and Sachs, *Plato's Theaetetus*, 97.

admissible? This places some pressure upon the meaning of 'knowledge' (οἶδε). In the ordinary usage, surely we can admit that there is a difference between the people we know and see and those people we merely see but do not know: e.g., *I don't know that man standing beside the door.* Still, do we want to wholeheartedly state that we do not *know* such people *at all*? Just earlier, the image of the wax allowed us to distinguish between thought impressions and sense impressions—such a distinction, between sense knowledge and a more intimate sort, might be useful here.

Socrates now enumerates the seventeen permutations with greater detail and examples. Each pair joined with '↔' is a set which Socrates claims can either be or not be mistaken for one another:

Key to the list of divisions below:
    K: Known
    P: Perceived
    ↔: Correlating two things which may or may not be mistaken for one another
    ~: Not

Those that Do **not** Admit of *Other-Opinion* (mistaking one for the other)
1. Thing K & has Imprint & ~P ↔ Other thing K & has Imprint of & ~P
   (i.e.: *K Thea. & Theo. & ~ Perceiving them, one cannot mix them up*)
2. Thing one k's ↔ Other thing which one does not k & ~Imprint
   (i.e.: *Knowing only Thea. & ~Perceiving either Thea. or Theo, one cannot mix them up*)
3. Thing ~K ↔ Other thing ~K
   (i.e.: *~Knowing & ~Perceiving either, one cannot mix*

them up)
4. Thing ~K ↔ Other thing K
5. Thing P ↔ Other thing P
6. Thing P ↔ Other thing ~P
7. Thing ~P ↔ Other thing ~P
8. Thing ~P ↔ Other thing P
9. Thing K & P & has imprint which accords w/ P ↔ Other thing K, P, I w a
(more impossible)
10. Thing K & P & correct Imprint ↔ Other thing K
11. Thing K & P & has Imprint ↔ Other thing P
12. Thing ~K & ~P ↔ Other thing ~K & ~P
13. Thing ~K & ~P ↔ Other thing ~K
14. Thing ~K & ~P ↔ Other thing ~P

<u>Those which **do** admit of *Other Opinion*</u> (193c)
15. Thing K ↔ Other thing K & P
(i.e.: Knowing both, Perceiving only one)
16. Thing K ↔ Other thing ~K & P
17. Thing K & P ↔ Other thing K & P
(i.e.: Knowing Thea. & Theo., & having Imprint & Perceiving both at a distance, hasten to assign imprint to each)

Having introduced the device of the wax, Socrates can now distinguish as well as corelate impressions, knowledge, and perceptions. While this distinction could be clarified, it has permitted a dialectical step forward, by means of which Theaetetus's intuition at 191b, that we can too hastily assign an identity to a thing, can be examined.

Socrates explains that error might indeed occur in the last three cases, as when he, knowing two things and having a wax impression of them, sees at a distance, but not sufficiently. If he hastens to assign the imprints, attempting to force them fit and cause recognition (ἀναγνώρισις), error may occur. He would be like an archer who hits the wrong target. In such cases, one either:

1. Thinks the things he knows are some other things he knows and perceives
2. Thinks the things he knows are things he does not know but perceives
3. Thinks the things he knows and perceives are other things he knows and perceives

194b-195
Theaetetus is pleased with this account of the wax and error. He asks Socrates if it is not beautiful. Socrates however suggests they wait until Theaetetus has heard the cause of these mistakes or other-opinions. He insists on this because it is only beautiful to hold a true opinion, but disgraceful to hold a false one.

He then gives an account of the condition of various sorts of souls (learners). The wax block in some is deep, plentiful, smooth, and tempered to a measured condition. In such a case, one is not likely to mistake one impression for another, but instead will preserve the likeness or signs (which he provocatively calls here the *beings*, ὄντα) and will rightly assigns each impression or perception to them. Such a one is called **wise**!

When the condition of one's soul is otherwise, when one is small souled, filled with impurity, or of such a condition that an impression is difficult to make or too easily altered, one does not preserve the sign or likeness—the imprint of the beings. Such a soul (or the wax in it) is earthy and filled with dung (cf. *Republic* 611d-612a). One like this does not receive clear impressions and therefore often has false opinions when he senses and then wrongly assigns things to them. Such men are wrong *about things and unlearned* (τῶν ὄντων καὶ ἀμαθεῖς).

Perhaps we might note that this ingenious account of the soul, a rich introduction of memory and mistake, has yet largely reduced error to a mechanical or material cause. While individual agency is clearly at play, it stands in the background of the material condition of the wax. The inert nature of this image might mislead one into thinking of mistake and knowing as merely mechanical, as wholly apart from the act or agency of a person. It would be interesting to think of the role which moral character and intellectual habit play in this error, perhaps even in the condition of the wax. It is after all a poor craftsman who wholly blames his tools.

Dialogue within the soul
195B-D

Theaetetus, delighted, says that Socrates is exceedingly correct. Socrates turns to Theaetetus and somewhat ironically asks him if we can now say that false opinions are *in us*. Theaetetus affirms this and also affirms that true opinions are also present in them.

Socrates is vexed. He fears that if false opinions are not due to perceptions or thoughts, but found only in their relation or *combination* (συνάψει), they will not be able to account for a certain kind of error which belong to the mind itself. For instance, while a man might think that some multitude is twelve when it is actually eleven, he could never confuse the twelve itself in his mind with the eleven itself (190b). Could any man confuse that? But men often mistake what seven and five add up to, even when they calculate this in the mind alone. Is this not, Socrates asks, an instance in which a man thinks the twelve itself is the eleven itself?

Are we ready to agree with Socrates here? It does not seem one is necessarily knowing and not know the very same thing in the same way. When one misadds for instance, it is not one's concept of a number per se that is mistaken but the act of calculation. The concept of '5' does not morph or go wonky when one errs in one's calculation.

We might ask: is there another similar or *like* division that would help clarify what it is one knows or does not know when one does not add correctly? Does one truly mistake the eleven itself for the twelve itself, or is the error somewhere else? A hasty *combination* might be the fault of the one combining, or to use a prior image, of a bad archer. This may be why Socrates makes the intriguing claim that they should try to show that false opinion is *something other than* the interchange of thought and perception (196c). If it were only the swerving of thought and perception, we would never be wrong in our thoughts (διανοήμασιν), that is, when we are only dealing with thought and not also perceptions. The error in calculation shows that we can err in our very thinking, the kind of thinking that unites or divides things.

Theaetetus sees this is a problem but does not offer a solution. Therefore, Socrates says that they have come back again to where the argument first began; they are forced to admit that someone can both know and not know the very same thing (196b-c).

The Second Act—Judgment

"After the mind has understood...something by forming a concept, it then goes on to relate two of these concepts to each other by making a 'judgment'."
  -*Socrates Logic*, Peter Kreeft[202]

It is no semantic accident that we often qualify an opinion as either 'true' or 'false'.[203] This is partly because opinion requires an act of judgment, the *second act of the mind*. An opinion is a product of an act judgment.

To judge is to affirm or to deny one thing of another. It is a mental act of combination or division. In speech this expressed by predication in a sentence. To judge is therefore to think or say that something *is* or *is not*. It is to combine a subject with a predicate or to assert that something exists simply.[204] Remarkably, the very introduction of the act of judgment, that act which introduces being and existence into our thinking, also introduces that which is *not*!

One does not yet properly have the true or false in perception.[205] Similarly, in apprehension, there may be clarity or lack of clarity, but not the true or false per se.[206] Concepts like 'red',

---

[202] Kreeft and Dougherty, *Socratic Logic*, 140.

[203] Hancock and Bernot, "The True, the False, the Lie, and the Fake."

[204] We assert something is *simply* when we judge that it exists ('that dog over-there *is*'). We assert something is in a *certain respect* when we predicate some quality or condition of its existence (*that dog is black*).

[205] The sense organs do not make 'mistakes' though they can be damaged. They operate mechanically and passively in accordance with their proper sensibles which activate them.

[206] Judgement is sometimes called 'complex apprehension', to distinguish it from the simple apprehension of concepts. It may

'hard', 'loud', 'man', 'truck', 'dog', 'chair' have no truth value. It is only when we make a judgment about what we perceive or about ideas that we think *truly* or *falsely*. It is only in predication or judgment that we combine, that we assert, either mentally or verbally, that one thing *is* (either simply or in some respect). In judgment, we consider a correspondence (or lack thereof) between thought and reality. For all these reasons, Act II marks an important dialectical step forward from simple apprehension.

Socrates has slowly introduced Theaetetus to a more complex framework of perception and memory. We not only have sense experience; we can remember those experiences and remember things about them. Further, we are not merely static receptacles, observers, or minds. Our knowledge is not merely the possession of images and concepts. We are both thinkers and judges. We are thinkers who are in one sense necessarily informed by what we come to known. In another sense, thinking is something *we* must *do*. It may be that I could never really think that *this-dog-I-am-looking-at-right-now* is *some-other-dog-I-am-looking-at-right-now*. Nor could I ever think that *this-thing-I-am-knowing-right-now* is *some-other-thing-I-am-knowing-right-now.* But I can think that *this-dog-I-am-looking-at-right-now* is *some-other-dog-that-I-know*. I can also mistake the relation of a term (or name) to a concept, or the relation of one concept to another. Thus, it is not in the passive act of apprehension (sensual or intellectual) wherein

---

occur consequent to or simultaneously with the first act of the mind. Judgment is also divided into immediate and mediate. We judge immediately that what we perceive really *is*. This is an intentionality that can be brought consciously to mind, and this consciousness of being (existence) as such distinguishes us from animals. Thomas argues it is one of the reasons we desire eternal life (to exist everlastingly). *Summa Theologiae* I-I, q.75, a.6.

error lies, but rather in some dynamic act of the mind. In such an act, the mind actively relates itself, rightly or wrongly, to that which is. Opinion and judgment are therefore necessary components of in inquiry into the character of human knowing.

Digression on Opinion

'Doxa' in Translation

Theaetetus signals the transition to Act II (187a-b) with his proposal that *to know* may be *to opine* (δοξάζειν) or to have a *true opinion* (ἀληθὴς δόξα). Translators have been split on how to render 'δοξάζειν' and 'δόξα. 'Judgment' and 'opinion' have been their chief candidates.

The act of judgment (that is of dividing, joining, predicating, of uniting two concepts or two things in one's mind) is more directly expressed by the Greek 'κρίνω'. 'Κρίνω' expresses the act of a judge in a court, an act of dividing, *distinguishing, separating, picking out, choosing, or passing sentence upon* (see Liddell-Scott on κρίνω & also 201a-c).

On the other hand, 'δοξάζειν' expresses more generally *thinking, imaging, opining,* or *supposing*. The noun 'δόξα' can mean *opinion, conjecture, estimation, expectation, reputation*. In this manner, κρίνω and δόξα are similar and corelated— δόξα expressing a subjective aspect of thinking or judgment somewhat more than κρίνω. In fact, there could be no opinion without judgment. In many cases, either word might be appropriate in the *Theaetetus*. The subjective aspect of thought (that I must think or assent to something) does not stand opposed to the objective act of the mind by which it is decisive in

Commentary

making a distinction.[207] Navigating the relation between the subjective and objective certainly underlies some of the challenges in this section of the dialogue.

The choice to render 'doxa' 'judgment' is one which reflects Greek usage and ordinary speech. In fact, we could never say that someone expressed *good* judgment if the contrary were impossible, that is if judgment were not also treated as a kind of opinion. Yet, judgment has a more formal and precise character, both as an act of the mind and in its explicit decisiveness. It leans toward the objective. Theaetetus is lauded early on in the dialogue for an act of judgement or division (the division of mathematical roots). The need to divide well is at the heart of philosophy, this dialogue in particular, and in general, the whole of human life. While the translation of doxa as 'judgment' loses much significant nuance, it also follows Socrates's analysis which associates the two and explicitly equates them to some degree at 201a-c.

On the other hand, 'opinion' more precisely expresses not just that a mental act has occurred, a measurement, predication, synthesis or analysis, but especially that such an act has been rendered according to the subjective activity of an individual (the agent), even if that subjective activity has occurred without the careful use of judgment. Opinion expresses something more readily associated with error, something open to doubt, or in some manner uncertain. Opinion in both its meaning and its excellence is less definitive than judgment.

---

[207] For instance, the Father states that Jesus is his beloved Son in whom he is *well-pleased* (εὐδόκησα). That is, the Father has a good or pleasing opinion of his Son, an opinion or judgment which is of the highest objectivity, based on the true identity of the Son. In fact, to be the Son is what it is to be Good and glorious, to be perfect. The only begotten Son has true repute or glory (δόξαν) (John 1:14), though this is not yet recognized universally (Philippians 2:9-11).

'Opinion' is therefore a stronger candidate for translators. Nevertheless, if one read doxa in the text as *mere opinion*, if one hears in this term *only* the subjective, or even that which perhaps *cannot be justified* (such as an opinion about what kind of soup is best), one has left behind the necessary semantic range and intention of the dialogue. *Theaetetus* is exploring the way in which an opinion (something held as the result of a judgment of some kind) may or may not obtain to being and to truth—to knowledge.

Opinion: Range of Meaning
Opinion can have a terrific range of meaning which we should perhaps spelled out:
a. Preference (Mondays are the best)
b. Correct preference (It is better to suffer injustice than do it; Bach cello suites are better than the one's I write)
c. A general notion or guess (I think that guy is Arminian)
d. Statements which are probable (It will rain tomorrow)
e. When one grasps or even knows a truth without knowing **why** it is true (It is my opinion that the Four Color Theorem in mathematics is true)
f. Knowledge about changeable things (It is raining, cf. the divided line)
g. The subjective assent to (or judgments of) what one knowns to be in fact true (it is indeed my opinion that 2+2=4, or that human beings are rational animals)

The translation choice favoring 'judgment' gains strength when one realizes that this section of the dialogue has virtually nothing to do with 'a', 'b', or 'd' (cf. 201a-c).

Let me remark that 'f' and 'e' may be related in a special way; they are significant in Plato. The divided line in the

Commentary

Republic is a division between the realm of being and becoming. That division is also marks the distinction between knowledge and opinion. Book 6 of the *Republic* explores how we move from sense experience of changing things to scientific knowledge, both of the world and the forms by which each thing in the world is known and is what it is. It is perhaps no accident that the line is itself a unity, a single line divided proportionally. It is already a whole, but the *relating* of one part of the line to another occurs through an act of thinking and *judgment*.[208] The relation of dianoia, memory, and sensation at the divided line paraells the problem of Act II.[209] How does one relate what one sees to what one knows? How does one make judgments or form opinions about these things? What are the objects of judgment? How does one distinguish them? Without the forms, without such distinctions and relations, perhaps one inevitably must end up in all kinds of difficulties, much like Theaetetus does here.

Borrowing from the divided line, we might keep in mind that opinion is something like the shadow of judgment. Hidden in that shadow is the source of the true and false, the source of error, but also of veracity and rightness. For this very reason, doxa is best rendered as opinion, but readers must keep in mind opinions inseparable relation to the act of judgment (201a-c).

---

[208] Aristotle may draw upon this in *On the Soul* III, 4 where he deals with judgment. He describes our ability to distinguish and relate forms and particulars as judging a line bent over upon itself (a nature in a particular) vs. straightened out (the nature abstracted from a singular), e.g., flesh vs. the being (form/essence) of flesh.

[209] See Klein, *A Commentary on Plato's Meno*, 108–157.

Some Technical Clarifications of Opinion

In Thomas Aquinas's *Commentary on De Caelo*, he reminds us that it is not enough to investigate a thing insofar as one satisfies the objections of an adversary. Rather, we must investigate a thing insofar as it is possible for us to inquire into the matter (Bk. 2, Lect. 22, n.10). If one is to know something scientifically, if one is not just to defeat an opponent rhetorically, one must not be "content with merely answering the objections."[210] We must not mistake the persuading of others for knowledge. We have to be careful not only to avoid sophistry, but to avoid being satisfied with superficial solutions. Therefore, one must be ready "to object against himself and others, not with sophistries but with real and reasonable objections."[211] When a man loses sight of this, he has lost sight not only of the structure of science, but the real earmarks of knowledge; he has forgotten that knowledge and opinion are indeed different.

Opinion has a wide semantic range which makes it difficult to analyze. Yet such an analysis is illuminating.[212] It is useful to clarify the meaning of knowledge and its twin. Opinion is not a contrary opposite of knowledge, in the way that black is of white or good is evil.[213] Strictly, ignorance is the opposite of knowledge, whereas opinion refers to a middle state. This does not mean it is always better to opine than to be ignorant, for opinion and error can go hand in hand. In fact, it is often more difficult to escape error than ignorance. Socrates is well aware of this danger! It is the thematic and logic problem

---

[210] St. Thomas Aquinas, "Commentary on Aristotle's De Caelo," n.d., https://isidore.co/aquinas/DeCoelo.htm.

[211] Ibid.

[212] Hancock and Bernot, "The True, the False, the Lie, and the Fake." I am indebted to a course developed by Curtis Hancock and taught by Eduardo Bernot for much of this analysis.

[213] Ibid.

which shapes the trajectory of the *Meno* and many of his aporetic exchanges.

Opinion, as opposed to knowledge (using the term more precisely), refers to that which can admit of doubt.[214] As said above, this is expressed in the very word 'doxa' (related to 'repute' or 'reputation'). A given person is not always aware that what he holds can admit of reasonable doubt, but we can objectively distinguish opinion from knowledge by clarifying that opinion does not know precisely *why* something must be the case.[215] Whether opinion holds that something exists, has occurred, that something is a certain kind of being, or that something is the cause of something else, by its nature, opinion falls short of obtaining the *why* with necessity (through a sure knowledge of principles or premises which are prior, necessary, and truly causal). Thus opinion does not stand on a known foundation—it is not *epi-steme*. Of course, it might become episteme later; this is the hope present in all dialectic. It can also be called episteme, somewhat less strictly, if by opinion we refer merely to the subjective grasp of an objective fact (it is my opinion that China exists, though I have never been there).

---

[214] Ibid.

[215] Reasonable doubt should be distinguished from radical, willful, or naïve skepticism. One earmark is that reasonable doubt is not merely a logical possibility. That my aunt will become a coal miner may be virtually impossible but admits of possibility. That I am the only person who exists or that Earth rests upon a space dog is logically conceivable, but not a viable possibility right now. That something can be articulated mentally or verbally does not make it logical in the robust sense. It is no accident that the Cartesian thought experiment can only be sustained by an act of will or insanity. This is because it is a 'logical' but not an ontological possibility. A willful skeptic cannot always be answered because they have put themselves beyond the full range of reason.

Opinion is not evil. To have a good opinion can, in fact, be very good. Much of our life, perhaps most of it, depends upon thousands of opinions of all kinds. An opinion may stand upon authority, upon an intuited foundation, a guess, or a desire. One may have very good reasons to hold one. Still, in such cases, one has not yet bound to a foundation what one judges by means logos and causes (*Meno* 97e-98a). In this respect, all opinion, true or false, admits of doubt! Opinion therefore makes disagreement possible, both about things that can be known (if we are not dealing with knowers) and about those things which are in themselves conjectural to human beings (either in a given circumstance or always).[216] The very subjects which belong to these two categories (that which is potentially knowable and that which must by its nature be opined by us) can themselves be matters of opinion. Please note however that this very distinction itself presupposes knowledge.

Opinion is like knowledge under tutelage, it is not the state of the master or teacher, but of the disciple. Theaetetus's docility suggests he recognizes this; it is even a kind of wisdom on his part.[217] The philosopher is, after all, one who desires wisdom: he or she is not a god. Perhaps Socrates also recognizes this, that while he guides Theaetetus and functions as a

---

[216] Hancock and Bernot, "The True, the False, the Lie, and the Fake." Curtis Hancock points out that it is generally matters of opinion that stir up the greatest ire and emotion.

[217] "The question of how initial learning comes about is not even raised in the *Theaetetus*...the *Theaetetus* ignores that problem altogether. Instead, the *Theaetetus*...deals with the ways we err: its immediate concerns are 'false opinions,'...the ἀνάμνησις story [on the other hand] presupposes...that there is knowledge 'in' us, which proper questioning...might bring to light. This knowledge 'in' us is not supposed to be 'fathered' [by the teacher]." Klein, *A Commentary on Plato's Meno*, 165–166.

teacher, he is not his master. There are no 'masters of philosophy' here on Earth then because we are all, in a certain, respect disciples who are "pilgrims on this earth," who are of the "*status viatoris.*"[218]

Opinion vs. Faith

To clarify the overlap and distinction between ordinary opinion and Christian theological virtue of faith, we can distinguish between three acts. Direct or unreflective reliance (intentionality) is our fundamental attitude to reality. I do not *believe* or *opine* the reality of the world (or my sense experience) in the strict sense. Rather, it is the principle of all my action and practical thought. It is also the premise of nearly all my theoretical thinking. All my acting and thinking occurs within this framework. I do not question it ordinarily or initially. I *can* question it, but I do not arrive at certainty about the world through those questions. I may clarify my right to rely on sensation, but I will never get to a proof for it because it is the first principle of intentional cognition, one which begins in utero. The very questioning of sense experience presupposes the experience itself and even the experience of its object or world-connectedness. So it was never by faith that I began to rely on the world. No one ever first doubted and only *then* began to have an opinion or belief about a world. This is an illusion of modern and post-modern skepticism—the idea that we somehow have to work from our minds to the world to prove it exists.[219] Such an attitude is secondary and often related to spiritual disquietude and disorientation. It is ultimately the compass of love and peace which rectify this, not a logical argument alone.

---

[218] Josef Pieper, *Faith, Hope, Love* (San Francisco: Ignatius Press, 1997), 91.

[219] In ordinary discourse and experience, we clearly distinguish dreams and illusions from reality.

For this reason, I do not sit in reality as upon an old creaky chair which I feel will give way at every moment. I may be shocked into realizing that some aspect of the world is not fully what I thought it to be, or I may come to believe that some greater reality is coming, but I never strictly hold reality in faith!

Opinion (what we might call natural belief, trust, or faith in a generic sense) is what makes much of our life possible. I trust maps, doctors, recipes, that my employer will pay me, that my house will not collapse. Some of these are better founded than others. In none of these cases, however, do I immediately see that such *must be* the case or *go on being* the case. I can imagine and it is indeed possible that something will change or fail to come to pass. Still, one can see how these are all predicated or premised on a prior grasp of reality. That grasp can be more or less perfect.

Faith, the supernatural virtue, is a gift of God. It is a habit of the soul by which the Christian lays hold of things invisible, even of God himself. In that contact with God, we know peace in his unshakeable goodness. Just like I have never been to China, I have never seen God. Supernatural faith is the grasp of God's reality, an apprehension (through a glass darkly) of who he is and that what he says is true. It is not without evidence, but that evidence which precedes faith does not and cannot command assent. Such evidence does not amount to the sight, but to a sort of clue, worthy of assent. It is faith which recognize the goodness and trustworthiness of that intuition and lays firm hold of God.

The evidence which serves as a kind of proximate matter for faith is not proportional to the thing which it reveals. It therefore cannot cause necessary conclusions in the way that the mind necessarily sees that two plus two will always and everywhere equal four. Faith and its conclusions are in a way more certain than any natural knowledge because of its

Source and Object. For this reason, Paul freely uses the term 'knowledge'. But it is not knowledge in the strict sense: we do not see the very thing we believe or comprehend its very Foundation.

However, because faith lays hold of God who knows all things, because faith apprehends its object through a spiritual union and kinship with God, it has a certainty which ordinary opinion and even natural science cannot. It is, as Thomas teaches, a kind of quasi-science (knowledge).[220] It is a science possessed most perfectly by God himself, and secondarily by the faithful who are united to him. It is something like when a musician relies on the principles known by the mathematician, but without knowing them himself.[221]

---

[220] St. Thomas Aquinas and Armand Mauer, "Commentary on Boethius's De Trinitate" (Toronto: Pontifical Institute of Mediaeval Studies, 1953, n.d.), https://aquinas.cc/la/en/~DeTrin.Q.2, a.2.

[221] Ibid.

Seventh Reading

196c-201c   True Opinion and the Aviary:
Shameless dialectic; Having vs. holding; The aviary; Recapturing birds; False birds and infinite regress; True opinion cannot be knowledge

Focus Questions:

1. Do all fruitful discussions have to begin with definitions? How is dialogue possible if they begin without them? What might be another starting point?
2. How does the distinction between *having* and *holding* help?
3. How does the image of the aviary work?
4. What are its weaknesses?
5. Is there a way to prevent an infinite regress of aviaries?
6. Are there things we are never wrong about?
    a. Can we ever be certain that we know something? Are there certain states, conditions, or experiences in which we truly know that we know?
7. Why do they conclude that true opinion cannot be knowledge?

Socrates has thus far preserved a tension between fallibility and certainty. It is easy to be aloof to this tension or to reject it outright. It is easy to be skeptical about knowing, considering how prone we are to error. But Socrates suggests that there are certain conversations within the soul when we indeed know we have touched upon that which *is*, when we both know what is true and *know that we know it*. The soul seems to have an inner eye by which it sees.[222] At 190b they reflect

---

[222] Recently, some have used 'inner eye' to describe the imagination. That is not how it is being used here.

upon the soul's inner dialogue with itself about the beautiful and the good, the odd and even (they do this again and at 195b-d just before the conclusion of the previous section). Both Theaetetus and Socrates find it hard to imagine being wrong about some things.

Consider the remarkable degree of certainty with which we carry on most of our lives. Even in reading Plato, do we not bring to this task the assumption that we have some capacity for knowing—for judging when we really do know (and even when do not)? It does not seem we believe that our judgment is entirely subject to whim or error. We do not treat everything as opinion. If we did, we would never try to know anything. Is this merely naïveté, stubborn blindness, or perhaps bowing to the practical necessities of life? Or rather, do we have firsthand experience of knowing what it is to know, however limited?

The tension between infallibility and error stands front and center in Act II. It forces us to reckon with the wonderous reality, that somehow every man and woman can be and is a knower. Yet, these very same persons, these *knowers* are also in some respect *non-knowers*, maybe in some manner even regarding those very things which they know.

Socrates attempts to account for this mystery. But before he does, he proposes to do something *shameless* (ἀναισχυντεῖν, 196d). We can recall that just prior, it seemed for a moment that they had succeeded in giving an account of false opinion as the mismatching of perceptions and thoughts. Were we entirely fooled if we found that account somewhat compelling? Its weakness was, in part, a failure to explain *all* error. It did not account for mistakes which occur in thought alone. The argument may have needed a further division. Error (or false opinion) can itself be *divided* into various *kinds*. The kinds (and thus the *causes*) of false opinion might have been examined more carefully. This means that Socrates and Theaetetus were not entirely wrong or ignorant.

As we attempt to account for false opinion in our very thinking, we approach a yet greater crisis. It is one thing to *mismatch* a perception with a mental impression (or a perceived thing with that which I know about it). It is quite another to be wrong about that very thing which I know. If I am wrong in my very knowing, knowledge might turn out to be unequivocally the cause of ignorance; knowing may be no different than not-knowing (error or ignorance)!

Shameless dialectic;
Socrates proposes to *shamelessly* say what it is to know, even while they remain ignorant of knowledge (196d). This proposal gives the dialogue a similar hypothetical character to that of *Meno* 86e-87b. In both dialogues, the interlocutors assume a conclusion (the *sought for* 142a) hypothetically in order to examine the results of the assumption, to test the hypothesis and its consequences. This method is traditionally called analysis.[223] It is no accident that both this section of the dialogue and the final third of the *Meno* concern opinion. Merely hypothetical analysis cannot arrive at knowledge unless it is based on something more profound than opinion or assumption. Dialectic is itself hypothetical in character; yet, it has a power to turn one towards that which is not merely hypothesis (*Republic* 518b-d).[224]

As Socrates is about to imply (and as he explores more explicitly in the *Meno*), all dialectical inquiry, all philosophy relies not only on analysis, but upon a prior foundation. It

---

[223] See https://plato.stanford.edu/entries/analysis/; George Pólya, *How to Solve It* (Princeton University Press, 2004), 141–148.

[224] See also Aristotle's treatment of dialectic in *Posterior Analytics*.

belongs especially to philosophy to make this foundation as explicit as possible.

He states here that they have all along been polluted by **unclean talk** (μὴ καθαρῶς διαλέγεσθαι). They have used the word 'knowledge' from the get-go and have acted as if they understood what it meant. The various words they have used for being 'ignorant' and 'knowing' are examples of this impurity.

Theaetetus asks, *in what manner could one talk or inquire if one held back from such words?* To which Socrates replies that one could say nothing (197a). Inquiry would be impossible.

Yet, Socrates is not disheartened. He claims only a disputatious person, a professional debater (ἀντιλογικός, 197a; cf. Meno 71b, 75c-d, 80d-81d) would maintain such an objection. Being simple or lowly individuals, he suggests they may venture onward and even attempt to say what knowing is. If what follows is in anyway meaningful, if what has preceded is meaningful at all—that is, if our use of 'knowledge' does not first depend on us having a precise definition of it— we must be able to proceed in this dialectical manner. In fact, we must somehow already *know* knowledge in some manner.[225] All

---

[225] Stewart Umphrey makes this point. Umphrey, *Is Knowledge True Opinion with a Logos?*

As an aside, students often think we need to define terms first during conversations. This may be true, but we have to hold such early definitions loosely, so that we do not cut off such terms from ordinary discourse. When inquiring dialectically into the nature of a things, to prematurely cling to a strict definition would be question begging. Such would amount to blind system building. Essential definitions (rather than ostensive or stipulative ones used in dialectic) should follow upon inquiry and cannot precede it. Real science depends on this order. A scientific textbook presents the results of such inquiry. A dialogue is its beginning.

meaningful philosophy and science hinges on whether a man is able to affirm some possession, some real share in the truth, however meager and imperfect. Without this, one is just an opiner, a sophist, or even a *misalogue* and *antilogikos*.

Theaetetus assures Socrates that he will receive a lenient judgment or **pardon** (συγγνώμη) for not holding back from speech. Theaetetus's willingness to engage in dialectic is characterized as a kind of wisdom regarding the law, perhaps the law of human nature.[226]

Having vs. holding;

The previous account of false opinion relied on a rather static device, an image of wax in the soul. As Socrates attempts to clarify how we can be mistaken in our very thinking (not just in the relating of thought and perception), a new, more dynamic image will be developed. This image will attempt to bring to light the role of human agency.

With Theaetetus's permission, Socrates offers the following unremarkable definition: *people say knowledge is **a having of some knowledge*** (ἐπιστήμης που ἕξιν, 197b).[227]

He then amends this popular, even circular definition by stating that it is rather a **possessing** (κτῆσιν) of knowledge. He then provides an analogy: a man can *possess* a cloak but may or may not *have* it on him. The man may or may not have it *in hand*. Theaetetus declares this to be a *right* distinction.

---

[226] 'Συγγνώμη' is a virtue needed by judges. See *Nicomachean Ethics* V.4 1132a

[227] For other significant uses of *hexis*, see 153b, 167a-b, 208a.

Commentary

The aviary;

Perhaps, says Socrates, something like this is also **possible** (δυνατὸν) for one who possesses knowledge. Such a man might be like one who hunts wild birds and keeps them in an aviary (197c).[228] We might say of such a man that while he *possesses* the birds which he has caught, he *has* none of them. Rather, he has come to have a **power** over them. (ἀλλὰ **δύναμιν** μὲν αὑτῷ περὶ αὐτὰς παραγεγονέναι). He is able to take hold of them by hand when he wills (197d).[229] The distinction is something like that of knowing something versus actively thinking about the knowledge one has. This distinction (this *having* (ἕξιν) would be impossible without memory.

The notion of hexis (197b) is developed, perhaps most notably in Aristotle's *Nicomachean Ethics*.[230] However, the distinction between habit and use is also found in his *On the Soul* II.1. There, Aristotle distinguishes and correlates various powers and acts of the soul (what are called first and second actuality). He analogically compares a person who *is* sleeping (but with the *ability* to wake) to one who *has* knowledge (but with the *ability* to contemplate). Both of these possess a power or actuality which is in potency—which *can* but is not currently at work (in act). They have this only because of some prior state of the soul (living or knowing). Those first acts are analogous to life itself (the first actuality of a soul) without which a living creature could not perform any other operations (secondary acts) because it would not even be alive. A soul causes an organic body to live (to exist simply). Only by possessing life is a living or ensouled being *capable* of or in potency to

---

[228] See the *Sophist* on hunting.

[229] This is perhaps the source of Aristotle's analogy of the mind to the hand in *On the Soul*, III. 8.

[230] Habit from *habitus* is derived from *habeo*, meaning *to have*, just as hexis comes from exein.

other acts (operations). Because of this, the soul can possess a power or habit (a *hexis*) without taking that very power in hand at every moment.

Aristotle's distinction is clearly derived from Plato. Thus Aristotle (and St. Thomas following him) follow Plato when they describe both virtue and knowledge (science) as *habitus*. To know is therefore the active condition of a knower, the formation of character and not just a body of knowledge. Science is chiefly not the facts one knows (the *birds*); it is the condition of a soul which can intelligently take such things in hand and think about them.

Flocks

Instead of a waxen substance, Socrates has established an aviary in the soul, filled with all sorts (παντοδαπῶν) of birds. Some of these birds are in flocks (ἀγέλας οὔσας χωρὶς τῶν ἄλλων), others are in small groups (τὰς δὲ κατ᾽ ὀλίγας), while other ones are alone, happening to fly through them all (**ἐνίας δὲ μόνας διὰ πασῶν** ὅπῃ ἂν τύχωσι πετομένας), 197d.

What is the significance of the flocks, the small groups, or most provocatively, the *ones alone* flying *through them all*? These birds represent knowledge, impressions, concepts, or forms which have been captured or taken possession of by the soul. Some knowledge is divided into *flocks or* **kinds** and thus collected together into families, that which might be logically characterized as genus's. Some are in smaller groups or even by themselves. For instance, one's knowledge of animals might be in one group, while one's knowledge of math or painting would be in another.

But what sort of knowledge is flying about *through them all*? The knowledge of a *one* which is through the many would seem to be a kind of preeminent or fundamental knowledge.

The language of genus and species is worth playing with. Would those knowledges which are *through them all* be of the ultimate genera or universals? Perhaps knowledge that flies through the *whole* would even surpass or *transcend* genus in the ordinary sense (see *Republic* 509a-b; *Metaphysics* III). If so, what would that *one* be that belongs to all the knowledges of things that *are*? It was agreed, earlier that one could never know the truth of anything without touching upon its being (186c). Parmenides who argued mysteriously that all is one is making his presence felt. It is no accident that he should appear when we are about to consider the knower and what is demanded of him—a single power of taking in hand the many and unifying the multitude.

As commentators point out, the aviary is initially empty in childhood (197e). On the surface, this conflicts with the doctrine of recollection, which is conspicuously absent in *Theaetetus*. For some, this is a sign that Plato has abandoned recollection at this stage in his thinking. For others, this is only because the mimetic and logical context of the dialogue—the youthfulness of Theaetetus and the dialogue's exploratory nature.[231] Whatever the reason, recollection, an innate possession of the 'birds' (or knowledge), would not of itself, without further analysis, solve the problem which we are about to confront: the possession of *many knowledges*, innate or otherwise, does not explain how it is that we *know what we know when we take it in hand*.

---

[231] Their exploration here, which first began in the context of the gymnasium, focuses not on initial learning, nous, or wisdom, nor even on the forms or objects of knowledge directly, but on science as such (here loosely including art). *Theaetetus* can by no means be considered a complete discourse on knowledge, learning, the forms, or the human soul. It is preliminary. See Klein, *A Commentary on Plato's Meno*, 165–166.

Recapturing birds;
197eb

Socrates explains that whenever one places knowledge in the aviary, one has learned and found that very thing which is knowledge of some being (μεμαθηκέναι ἢ ηὑρηκέναι τὸ πρᾶγμα οὗ ἦν αὕτη ἡ ἐπιστήμη, καὶ τὸ ἐπίστασθαι τοῦτ' εἶναι, 197e).

They next need to examine how to speak of re-capturing or taking hold *again* of those things in the soul. That is, after one has captured some knowledge, what shall we call it when one takes it up again, to use that knowledge or reflect upon it at some present moment? Should this be called learning or finding (μεμαθηκέναι ἢ ηὑρηκέναι)? This seems problematic because one has already *learned* and *found* the thing. If we had to hunt all over again, memory and knowing would be almost worthless.

To clarify the issue, Socrates returns to number, using the example the arithmetic art (ἀριθμητικὴν τέχνην). He states that the arithmetic art hunts for all the knowledge concerning even and odd. It is by that art that a man has the science of number. It is by the arithmetic art that one has knowledge of arithmetic and also can hand it on to another (ὑποχειρίους ἐπιστήμας τῶν ἀριθμῶν ἔχει καὶ ἄλλῳ παραδίδωσιν ὁ παραδιδούς.). To hand over is to teach and to take hold of is to learn. The man perfect (τελέως) in arithmetic knows all numbers. We can note that whether the arithmetician knows each number actually or potentially, he *has a power* which others do not.

198c

Then would such a person ever count either number itself or those things outside [his soul]? It seems obvious to Theaetetus that the arithmetician would be just the man to do so. He is precisely the man most likely to be counting. But would this

Commentary

man then be treating what he knows as if he did not know it? The reader perhaps senses the ambiguity or disputative nature (ἀμφισβητήσεις) of the question. The old problem (knowing and not knowing the very same thing) is raised again here.

198d

Socrates next makes the division which this image has been aiming at: hunting is therefore **twofold** (διττή; cf. *Sophist* 219e). One kind of hunting is for the sake of possessing; the other kind is for taking in hand what one already possesses.

Significantly, they do not consider whether this first hunting itself require a kind of prior knowledge. That question might force us to seek recourse in recollection or that wisdom first described at the opening of *Theaetetus*—that power by which we learn and grow wise about what we learn (145d).[232]

The second kind of hunting takes hold of that which one already possesses but does not currently have *in one's thinking* (οὐκ εἶχε τῇ διανοίᾳ). It is in this way that a man who knows, who possesses knowledge will be able to count or think. This is what it is for the arithmetician (or knower) to *use* or revisit what he knows. The arithmetician *takes up again* that knowledge he has—taking in hand what he already possesses.

Re-cognizing

Is it not remarkable that we indeed must often search for or take up what we already know? If this were not the case, our cognition would be much less complicated. But our thinking would lack that reflective and discursive quality with which we are so familiar. We regularly take up, again and again,

---

[232] See also *Posterior Analytics* II.19

those things we know in order to think them again or to know things by them. How cumbersome and overwhelming it would be to always have to be thinking every single thing we know. It would be an unnecessary encumbrance because we have no need to be thinking all that we know at every single moment. When cooking eggs, I do not need my trout fishing knowledge.

This partly distinguishes human from divine knowledge. We know a vast multitude of things by many and various principles. For instance, the principles of music composition are distinct from the principles of chemistry or running. We only trace these many principles back with difficulty to God, either by an act of judgement and philosophic reasoning or by faith. God, however, knows all things through his very essence, through the one ultimate cause and principle of all being. Knowing all things by a knowledge of himself, God, from all eternity, comprehends in a single non-discursive glance every single thing immediately and at once. Human contemplation is only a very distant likeness to the simplicity of the divine mind.

Yet there may be a knowledge which we do not take up and put down over and over again. For without something we held fast to, we would be incapable of taking hold of anything at all, even that first truth. There must be some first act or hexis of the mind. Therefore, we have good reason to suppose that there might be something known, something more fundamental than all our many knowledges or *birds*.

False birds and infinite regress;
199a-d

But when a knower, such as one who can read or count, reads or counts, are they reading or counting what they do not know? This is again, the familiar ambiguity of knowing and not knowing.

Commentary

Theaetetus insists this is unreasonable, for one to read or count (to know) that which they do not known. In what manner do we agree with him? Is there a distinction he might have made? Theaetetus is himself a mathematician and is quite familiar with the fact that knowing number, he also must continually take up and examine what he knows in various ways, such as when he determines the count of some quantity. Human thinking is complex. We have to consider not only the various things in our mind, but the various ways we apprehend and judge them, as well as the ways we relate them to other things which we see or know.

Ultimately, there is something going on in our thought, in our knowing, that is not just *a thing*. We will fail to account for know-ledge if we do not account for the knowing subject. Knowledge is ultimately an intentional spiritual act. The mind is not just a repository of facts (an aviary); it is a spiritual power by which we consciously, purposefully *relate* to the world.

We can keep in mind that their inquiry into false opinion is itself somewhat of a digression. In the *hunt* for knowledge, Theaetetus suggested that true opinion might be what they were after. But to clarify *true* opinion, our hunters began to track down *error*. The wax and the aviary were contrived, partly, to do just this. The device of the aviary permits us to state that while it is impossible (ἀδύνατόν) for a knower not

Figure 2 Ringdove (left); Pigeon (right)

to know (possess) what he knows, he can still have false opinion. He may take up the wrong knowledge when hunting again for a knowledge he already possesses. He can mistake (ἁμαρτὼν) it for some other knowledge—like a man who catches a ringdove, instead of a pigeon.233

Theaetetus describes this account as *reasonable* (λόγον.). It is indeed! It is no accident that one might mistake two birds which are so similar, which are *generically* the same. Still, there is a problem. On one hand, how can it be that the one who knows *both* these two birds should mistake them? On other hand, who else could even make such a mistake but the man who knows both?

Part of the problem is that we are looking into what it means to have a false opinion *about* something one knows, particularly when the knowledge and the knowing are characterized merely as *things* in the soul.

This mis-catching suggests that false opinion is not caused by the *very same* knowledge (mistaking a pigeon by one's very knowledge of a pigeon). It has not fallen into the prior problem. But the result is something even more terrible. The knower now fails to know what they know *because* of something else they know (some *other* knowledge). Knowledge is again the cause error or ignorance. If so, nothing will prevent the soul, once it has acquired all knowledge, from being completely ignorant or errant about everything.

199e-200c

Theaetetus makes a clever attempt to recover the account by suggesting that the cause of false opinion may not be the catching of the wrong (unwonted) knowledge but instead the

---

[233]James St. John - Ectopistes migratorius (passenger pigeon) 5, from https://commons.wikimedia.org/wiki/File:Ectopistes_migratorius_(passenger_pigeon).jpg#/media/File:Ectopistes_migratorius_(passenger_pigeon).jpg

catching of *non-* or *not-knowing's*. He now posits there are not only knowledge-birds in the soul, but also birds of ignorance or *non-knowing* flying about with them. Such a man *knows* (or possesses) both knowledge and non-knowledge.

Socrates is truly impressed with this account, but he sees a problem. The knower, the one who possesses knowledge, now also possess non-knowledge. But when he takes hold of the non-knowledge, he does not *know* that it is non-knowledge. They are therefore thrust back upon the previous problem: how can a man who knows two things mistake them (not know them both)? Or how can he, knowing one, mistake what he does not know for what he knows? Could such a man ever distinguish what he knows from his non-knowledge?

Socrates says, as an aside, that Theaetetus might say that there is yet *another aviary* in the soul which holds knowledge *about* the knowledge *and* non-knowledge. But this knowledge would also have to be *taken* in hand when it is needed. Yet another aviary would then be needed for that knowledge, and yet subsequent aviary for that one, ad infinitum. An infinite regress threatens the account. But something crucial has been implied.

There must be a way for the man who possesses knowledge to know that which he knows. This power cannot be univocally similar in kind to the discrete *knowledges* (the birds); otherwise, one would need yet another knowledge to know that knowledge by—one would never arrive at knowing in such a case.

Theaetetus's solution and the aviary fails to account for this. It perhaps cannot succeed because it is still too mechanical in nature. The mystery, not only of error but of knowing, must somehow account for the very knower himself. There must be a means by which our knowledge transcends the individually known things. But this requires a consideration of the spiritual reality of the human person.

One who knows only begins to learn and can only takes up again what has been learned, if one already possesses a light which ever shines within, which never needs to be *taken in hand*. Such an unfailing light would be that by which one would judge all one knows or comes to know in this life.[234] Without an initial and ever active power, a hexis possessed from the beginning and always, we could never judge anything because every judgement presupposes a principle of judgment (something already known). If there is not a *light* which illuminates judgment, we act in the dark from the beginning. Therefore, there must already be a kind of innate intelligence or wisdom, loosely speaking, which we possess (145c, Gen. 1:26; Psalm 36:9; John 1:9). Whether we characterize that primal hexis as recollection, nous, an inner eye, or a light of the soul, it is this which accounts for our power of judgment. For if we had no innate power, by what means would we ever know or judge that which we first come to know? One cannot see or judge something to be true (acquire new knowledge) if one needs yet to acquire some knowledge by which to judge. Sense perception can provide new matter for the mind but not its primal intellectual capacity for being and truth The agent must be capable, not only of knowing, but of knowing that he knows. There must be a knowledge or understanding (nous), an intellection or intuition already possessed by which one sees and also sees that he sees.

Aristotle compares the mind to a hand in *On the Soul*, but this 'hand' is a spiritual power of the living center of the individual, a power of nous by which it consciously takes hold of things. It is a *tool of tools* because unlike other organs or instruments, the mind is not just a means knowledge but the knowing-self. Such a capacity or light avoids the regress which

---

[234] Cf. Psalm 36:9; Plato, *Republic* VI; *Meno* 81a-d; Aristotle, *Posterior Analytics* II.19; *On the Soul* III.

threatens the aviary-account in the reading. When I use a hammer, I take up what is *other* than me to do my work. When I think, I do not take up what is other than myself. My mind is essentially my own, and the mind is potentially all that it knows—it is potentially all things.[235]

This is a way of expressing the unique *interiority* of the spiritual soul (the person). We are not just a depository of things such as sense experiences or concepts. Rather, by a life which infinitely exceeds mere mechanical or material existence, we extend ourselves relationally into the world. We can do this because we comprehend to some limited degree what is in ourselves. The spirit alone has such *depth* or interiority.[236] This is not unrelated to the way in which will and intellect mutually include one another. Spiritual life extends itself across a virtually infinite domain because of this self-possession or interiority—it consciously knows what it knows, know that it knows, and know what its knowledge is about. The person is thereby truly a being in relationship—intentional, conscious, and free.

With this before us, we can appreciate the simplicity, but also the richness of St. Thomas Aquinas's definition of truth: the conformity (adequation) of the intellect with the thing.[237] Truth, for him, is marked by the *intentional* conformity or relation of the mind with a thing known. Therefore, truth is a relationship. A mind is true or knows truth only when it is conformed to the way a thing is and, further, only when it is aware of this relationship. That is, when our mind is in conformity with what is and also knows this, only then do we have knowledge. It is not enough for us to unconsciously or

---

[235] Aristotle, *On the Soul*, III.4

[236] I take the term 'interiority' from Kierkegaard and John Paul II.

[237] Thomas Aquinas, *Summa Theologica* I-I q.6, a.2

mechanically mirror the world, to merely form concepts.[238] Knowledge is *conscious* conformity.[239] Knowledge is therefore a truly spiritual act in which we come into a cognitional relationship with the world. This is partly why it is so desirable! It is a kind spiritual expansion or extension, an inclining unto (πρὸς) the reality of things (John 1:1). The mind, conformed to things as they are, becomes capable of touching them, measuring them, judging them as they are and, ultimately, placing them under an order of love (152a).[240] Both truth and love are intentional.

This is partly why truth is most properly related to the act of judgment, that act of the mind by which place ourself in relation to the world. Thomas puts it this way in Summa Theologiae q.16, a.2:

> Although sight has the likeness of a visible thing, yet it does not know the comparison which exists between the thing seen and that which itself apprehends concerning it. But the intellect can know its own conformity with the intelligible thing; yet it does not apprehend it by knowing of a thing "what a thing is." When, however, it judges that a thing corresponds to the form which it apprehends about that thing, then first it knows and expresses truth. This it does by composing and dividing: for in every proposition it either applies to, or removes from the thing signified by the subject, some form signified by the predicate...Truth

---

[238] John Paul II, *Love and Responsibility*, chap. 1.

[239] Thomas Aquinas, *De Veritate* I, 3; *Summa Theologica* I-I, q.16, a.2

[240] It is no accident that Jesus Christ is very Truth (John 14:6). He is the eternally begotten Son of God, the express image of the Father. From the beginning, the Son, the Logos was essentially God and *toward* or *unto* **(πρὸς)** God, lovingly, knowingly inclined unto him. Even very Truth is a relation. Conformity with the Christ would make possible a new kind of judgment (1 Cor. 2:15, 6:3; 2 Tim. 2:15).

therefore may be in the senses, or in the intellect knowing "what a thing is," as in anything that is true; yet not as the thing known in the knower, which is implied by the word "truth"; for the perfection of the intellect is truth *as known* (emphasis mine).

"What a piece of work is a man! How noble in reason, how infinite in faculty".[241] And yet, this very same creature who possesses such a remarkable capacity, who is potentially a knower of all things, is yet capable of error.

Man is a fallible spirit! Even as we share in some limited way in the divine light (Gen. 1:26), we remain prone to mistake and false opinion. This hunter who takes hold of knowledge must therefore be capable both of the true and the false.[242] We are spirits, participants in the divine nature, rational creatures, and also fallible opiners (Acts 17:28).

And yet, we err only because and when we know something!

True opinion cannot be knowledge
200d-201c

Theaetetus's suggestion fails; the *non-knowledges* cannot overcome the threat of the infinite regress or prevent knowledge from becoming non-knowledge. Socrates therefore argues that the search for false opinion should not have come prior to finding knowledge.

But has this been a total failure? Has the search for false opinion truly *come before all knowledge*? We have perhaps not precisely analyzed every form of error, but surely, we have

---

[241] Shakespeare, *Hamlet* Act II.2

[242] Cf. John 1:9-10. Sin has not eviscerated man's rational nature but injured it and turned it from its source. It is one thing to see things in the light of reason, another to recognize the very character of that light and turn to its Source (Psalm 36:9).

been clarifying (negatively and positively) what is required for knowledge and a knowing agent, and even what is required for false opinion. We have reflected upon opinion, memory, judgment, and certainty.

Theaetetus is steadfast and unwilling to give up the search. Yet he does not know what else knowledge might be, other than true opinion, for surely that is without **mistake** (ἀναμάρτητόν). But being without error does not go far enough. Being without error does not yet account for what it is to know a thing. A machine can be without error. Knowledge remains merely accidental to true opinion. Knowledge for such a person is more like a thing and less like a proper habit (hexis), though perhaps not entirely.[243]

If we follow Meno, who treats prudence as opinion (97a-98c), if we define knowledge as opinion, we precisely empty it of that quality which is characteristic of its excellence and constitutes it as such. Opinion can be true and can be based on things known, but it is not itself knowledge. To merely be free from error is not the preeminent way in which the human soul is capable of possessing the truth, even if true opinion is often necessary and good.

This section concludes by showing that there is an art which indicates (σημαίνει) that knowledge and opinion are in fact two different things. Rhetors and lawyers persuade men without teaching them. Jurors must *judge* by means of opinion because they judge that which can be known only by others, those who have perceived the events in question. In such acts

---

[243] Opinion is used in various ways. According to one of its meanings, one might distinguish between an opinion as such and the knowledge which it is based upon. According to another, one might distinguish knowing *that a thing is* from knowing *why it is* (see Act III).

of judgment (κρίνοντες), jurors have hearsay and opinion but not knowledge. This is because they judge that which is:

- Contingent
- Unobserved
- And argued quickly

In this example, we might find a suggestion for thinking through the problem of false opinion or even a further way of dividing it. There are certain cases, situations, or objects which not only lend themselves to opinion, but perhaps can only be opined.

Socrates concludes that in such cases, when one has a true opinion based on hearsay, one judges without knowledge. Therefore, true opinion and knowledge are different.

Act III: True Opinion + an account (logos)

Eighth Reading

201c-206b　　True opinion with an account (logos): *Hearsay and a dream—logos, elements, & composites; Names & logos; Syllables & Letters; Whole, All, Parts; Reversal—letters as the most knowable*

Focus Questions:
1. What do you think Socrates means by logos (λόγος)? What various things do you hear in 'account', 'reason', 'definition', or 'description'?
2. In what way is an account (logos) something *additional* to an opinion?
3. If an account makes an opinion knowledge, is it all still an opinion in some sense?
4. What would make a good account? What *parts* would it have?
   a. Are there different kinds of accounts?
5. How do syllables and elements help us think about definitions?
6. How do syllables and elements help us think about the *things* we try to define?
7. Do we know elements, syllables, or wholes better?
   a. Which do we know first? Are they all know in the same way?
8. Is an *all* the same as a *whole*?

Act III is the last and shortest of the three major division of the dialogue. It is also the most metaphysically *pregnant*, introducing elements (letters) and their composites (syllables). Having spent time reflecting on the soul and its interior powers in Act II, Socrates and Theaetetus now begin to think about

Commentary

the relationship between the constitution of things and what we can say about those things through logos (λόγος).

In Act I, Protagoras's theory of perception led Socrates to briefly argue that things in themselves are unknowable and do not even exist by themselves—they were said to exist and to be known only in their combining, in the coming together of active and passive 'elements'. Act II also addressed combination, chiefly the combining of perceptions and impressions (or more generally, any combination which occurs through judgment). Act III, which focuses on logos, will attend to combination also, to those combinations which constitute the objects of the world and, in tandem, to those combinations which attend our acts of speech and reasoning (logos).

Logos is difficult to translate because of its rich semantic range. It is used in Act III to express *rational thought* and *speech*. Previously, *Theaetetus* reflected on the speech or inner dia*logue* of the soul (Act I & II). Logos or reason is that power by which we consider, order, and combine thoughts and thus words.[244] While logos can refer merely to a word or name, even to a concept or form, here it explicitly concerns the act of speech in which one gives an account of some thing. In this context, logos has the connotation of 'defining', reasoning, and syllogism, rather than that of simple apprehension, as it does elsewhere. The problem of definition is explored in our last two readings Such speech or logos is the communication of rational thought.[245] Therefore, I have often used 'account' for my

---

[244] Cf. φημί vs. λόγος (logos): the former attends more to the manifestation or vocalization of thought; the later to the fact that such vocalization is rational or even to an interior word or reason.

[245] The Latin *verbum, nomen,* and *ratio* can be compared to the Greek ὄνομα, ῥῆμα, λόγος. John uses logos in the opening of his Gospel, not nomen, conveying an express intelligible unity. Logos

translations, as it comes close to capturing the general range of meaning (*intelligent speech*, *reason*, and *definition*) focused on in Act III.

Keep in mind that Act III investigates what it is we can meaningfully think and say about things. It therefore investigates both the nature of an account *and* the nature of things themselves (those things about which we speak).

Hearsay and a dream—logos, elements, and composites; 201c-d

The.   That is I **heard one say** (εἰπόντος του ἀκούσας) at any rate, Socrates. I forgot but now it is in my mind. He said that knowledge is **true opinion** with an **account** (λόγου), but opinion without an account (ἄλογον) is **beyond** (ἐκτὸς) knowledge—and of things which have not an account, they are not **knowables** (μὴ ἐπιστητὰ), he named them thus, but those which have [a logos] are knowables.

---

captures both the sense of word and intelligible communication. For us, speech can be interior or exterior, an interior word of the heart or the exterior word of the lips. But the Word is the eternally begotten image of the Father, begotten not in time or place, not by an afterthought or by an utterance of the lips. He is without letter, syllable, or part. The Word is not vocal or temporal, surpassing and excelling all human and limited expression, for he is and expresses the fullness of all reality, being very Being or very God. The Vulgate translates logos as *verbum*. *Ratio* would be too intellectual and abstract, *nomen* merely a denomination. The idea of a logos as an intelligible word is by no means foreign to philosophy, ordinary speech, or the Bible. Heraclitus discusses the logos. Men of old asked for a 'good word' when they wanted favorable news or judgment. The Book of Deuteronomy is known in the Hebrew by the name, *Words*. The ten commandments are literary *the ten words*, having much of the same import as logos or ῥῆμα. The expression 'your word is good' refers not merely to a single word but to intelligible whole.

Commentary

- Having denied that true opinion is knowledge, Theaetetus now offers one last definition in this dialogue, perhaps his most compelling. It is certainly the most *complex*. 'Logos' or 'account' means here something like 'definition'. However, not every account or logos is a definition. Further, not every definition is equal. There are all sorts of ways to define or give an account of a thing. 'Logos' is by no means *simple*. Act III will bring to light some of the problems and complexity of speaking and giving rational accounts.

- **I heard one say:** Theaetetus only vaguely remember having heard this before; his definition is based on hearsay. The conclusion of Act II has warned us to be wary of judgment concerning hearsay (201a-c). Nevertheless, Socrates and he are not like the jury who must decide on hearsay alone. Nor are they like lawyers who are limited by the clock and court procedures. They can examine for themselves at leisure these *sayings*. The remaining sections are thus devoted to a dia*logue* about logos. Theaetetus has after all given something like a definition of definition. They are therefore inquiring into *a logos of logos*. It should be no surprise then that such an inquiry is far reaching, even if it must necessarily fall short of ultimate explanations.

    This is not the only moment in Plato's corpus that a major stride forward occurs through hearsay (cf. *Meno, Gorgias, Phaedrus, Symposium, Phaedo*). Hearsay can have the character of tradition, even sacred tradition. It has the character of gift, even a divine gift whose source and nature somewhat escapes our comprehension. Both gift and tradition stand in contrast to that which an individual discovers or establishes for himself. Logos is itself precisely something we receive as handed down to us. We find ourselves already located within a tradition whose roots we do not comprehend—we exist within a speaking community which itself exists *by means of logos*. Further, logos is itself something godlike, even if it is also specifically human. It is therefore in this double sense a thing given to or handed down to us. Inquiry into logos can be said then to uniquely concern man, even if such an inquiry directs us beyond ourselves, to the sources of things and to that which, contrary to Protagoras, man *cannot* measure.[246]

- **Opinion:** Theaetetus' new definition or division still includes opinion (doxa). Socrates does not directly address this, but we might ask whether opinion remains opinion if/when it becomes knowledge. What happens when an opining individual acquires a logos?
    - Does he have a *new* opinion or only think better of the old one?
    - Does he have something else than opinion?
    - Logos might be:
        - part of an opinion
        - something in addition to it

---

[246] The possibility of knowledge, of philosophy, and of virtue are rooted in gift. The end of the *Meno* is not Plato throwing up his hands in defeat or claiming that the philosophic and ethical project is impossible or random. Rather, he is pointing to the source and end of our capacity, to our limits and also to the gifts we have received. He is precisely affirming these as specific human ends, even while the cause, goal, and perhaps ultimate achievement of such ends lay higher than human nature. He is also constrained by Meno's attitudes and intellectual faults.

- or even constitute a specific difference—cause a person to have knowledge *rather than* opinion.

In other words, it is unclear whether a logos is simply more information or a thing which establish in the individual a new *relation* to what they think. Opinion and knowledge may be two distinct ways of *having* or *holding* (197b). Consider how different these are:

"It is my *opinion* that it will rain tomorrow."

"It is my *opinion* (as one who has studied geometry) that the square on a right triangle's hypotenuse equals the squares on its sides ($c^2 = a^2 + b^2$)."

Opinion is not being used univocally in these two sentences.

In the *Meno*, Socrates describes true opinions as beautiful but not worth much until they are tied down or bound by *logos and causes* (98a). Without such binding, they are wont to run off. It may be in such cases that the opinion itself has changed, the way it is held, or perhaps both. We can keep in mind that Socrates says this in the *Meno* only after Meno has given up on knowledge and prudence! (See **Digression on Opinion** in the Sixth Reading).

- Theaetetus claims that opinions without logos are *without* or *beyond* (ἐκτὸς) knowledge. A thing may be 'beyond' knowledge:
    - Because it happens to currently lack a logos
    - Because it is so simple or indefinite that one could never give a logos of it—it falls short of being intelligible.

- Because it stands beyond our power of logos—it excels our intellectual power (*Republic* 509b-c; *Meno* 82b-85b).

  Some things which currently lack a logos might yet come to have one; other things might be beneath our power to describe or investigate them; still others might surpass our power to give an account. Theaetetus' division, which underlies Act III, is therefore ambiguous.

- **Knowledge** (ἐπιστήμη, *episteme*) is used somewhat precisely both here and in Socrates coming reiteration of the definition (201c-202c). Plato's vocabulary is rarely systematic, though it is purposeful. Theaetetus's precision is significant; it sharply contrasts the investigation which will follow. This contrast may help us account for some of the reversals and failures which will occur.

  Episteme, when used more precisely, means something like scientific knowledge—a knowledge *de jure*. For instance, episteme or scientific-knowledge in Aristotle, is associated with definitions, a comprehension of causes, principles, elements, and, therefore, certainty. It is for him demonstrative knowledge, based on premises or principles which are necessary, immediate, indemonstrable, better known, and prior. *Theaetetus* clearly is exploring the significance and possibility of acquiring such a logos.

  Because 'science' from the Latin '*scientia*' means 'knowledge', 'scientific knowledge' is verbally redundant, even while it marks a real division between specific kinds of knowing.

Commentary

So.   "You are speaking beautifully. But the knowable things and those that are not, say how he **divided** (διῄρει) them, if you and I also have heard these same things."

- Socrates is interested in this division between the knowable and unknowable. Theaetetus, switching to a less technical term, responds that he does not **know** (οἶδα) if he can find out what was said. He asks for Socrates help. It hearkens back to Theaetetus' earlier work of division, the dividing of rational and irrational (**logon and alogon**) powers!

201e-202c

Socrates tells Theaetetus to *listen to a dream in return for a dream*. Odysseus might warn us to take care to distinguish (to divide) those dreams which come through gates of horn from those which pass through the gates of ivory—the true dreams, from the false (*Odyssey* 19.560-569).[247]

Socrates frames his *account* in the context of a dream because Theaetetus himself only vaguely remembers what he has heard. The framework also suggests that there is something dreamlike about the way in which we happen upon truth. It is not always easy to explain how it is that we solve a riddle or gain insight into the heart of a matter. It is certainly not by always wrestling a problem to the ground or through a 'method' we fully comprehend. Solutions and insights come to us at notoriously unexpected times and from strangely unexpected places (such as during sleep, when in a shower, from an overheard phrase, or even through the play of light and shadow).[248] Many insights come on the wings of prayer or in the unasked-for providences of life. The mystery of human

---

[247] Plato himself takes this up in *Charmides* 173a.
[248] August Kekulé's insight into the structure of the Benzene Ring was arrived at, in part, through dream.

reason (its successes, its leaps and intuitions, even and especially its sources) is irreducible, and thus for all its clarity, also dreamlike or wonderful. Are these sources sub-intelligible or supra-intelligible?

Socrates says that he has dreamed or heard that:

> So. "The **primary things** are, as it were, **elements**, out of which we and all things are **compounded**; These can have no **articulation**. For each of them are only **named**, but nothing else can one say about them..." (τὰ μὲν **πρῶτα** οἱονπερεὶ **στοιχεῖα**, ἐξ ὧν ἡμεῖς τε **συγκείμεθα** καὶ τἆλλα, **λόγον οὐκ ἔχοι**. αὐτὸ γὰρ καθ' αὐτὸ ἕκαστον **ὀνομάσαι μόνον** εἴη, προσειπεῖν δὲ οὐδὲν ἄλλο δυνατόν)

- **The Primary things**: What are these first things (πρῶτα)? They might be the principles or sources of things, prior in time or in causality—something like Aristotle's *ἀρχαί* (Physics I.1). Or they might be prior only in our knowledge (logically). It is the work of philosophy to seeks first principles. In fact, it is philosophy which discovers or clarifies what it is *to be first*. At this point in the account, these *first things* are described as less intelligible but causal (in at least two ways). That is, while they cannot be described by a logos, they form the material composition of things and also cause us to be capable of giving an account of the composite beings.

- **The Elements**: Socrates calls these first thing *elements* (στοιχεῖα). The elements or *stoicheia* are the fundamental components, perhaps the irreducible material constituents of things—their elements. Hence, we have a branch of chemistry called *stoichiometry* and also refer to a Periodic Table of *Elements*. We will have to consider the sense in which any such elements are first.

The *stoicheia* or elements of the universe were explored by various pre-Socratic and Greek philosophers, just as they are still explored today, particularly in chemistry and quantum physics.[249] The four elements (water, earth, air, and fire) were recognized by many, though different thinkers believed one or another of four to be more fundamental than the others. Some physicists posited various contraries as prior to the four elements, such as the limited and unlimited, or the dry, the wet, the hot, the cold. Democritus and Leucippus, on the other hand, argued for an atomic theory (that atoms and void were the fundamental constituents of all being). In each case, various elements were considered by their proponents to be at the very 'limits of analysis'.[250] They were thought to be the final point of material and/or metaphysical division and therefore *elemental*. Aristotle describes this in *On the Heavens*:

> An element, we take it, is a body into which other bodies may be analyzed, present in them potentially or in actuality (which of these is still disputable), and not itself divisible into bodies different in form. That, or something like it, is what all men in every case mean by element (*De caelo*, III.3, 302a15ff).

---

[249] Physics, the study of nature, through atomic theory quantum theory, has once again returned from a concern merely with mechanics, to an inquiry into the material constituents of the universe.

[250] See https://plato.stanford.edu/entries/chemistry/

An element would be that which a thing could be broken-down or *divisible into*, while the element itself would be *indivisible*. An element would mark the final or ultimate division of things.

But division is quite ambiguous. It is one thing to divide a man logically (in speech); it is another to do so actually! Further, how the division is made is not an indifferent matter, either in reality or scientifically. For instance, it is not the same to divide an animal by their various organs, by body and soul, by their constituent molecules, or by something even more elementals, such as electrons, protons, etc. We will have opportunity to explore this problem.

Aristotle states in the *Physics* that a person thinks he knows a thing scientifically when he knows its principles, causes, and elements (I.1). He clearly does not consider elements, causes, principles, and parts to be precisely the same. *Theaetetus* is challenging because it makes no systematical distinctions among these. There is therefore some *substantial* and, perhaps, intentional ambiguity in Act III.

- **Elements & Letters:** Στοιχεῖα, the plural of στοιχεῖον, can also mean the 'letters' or 'sounds' of the alphabet.[251] Socrates will employ this denotation to explore an analogy and connection between the primary elements of being and those of speech. The analogical character of speech, even its parallelism to being, is a presupposition of Heraclitus, Plato, Aristotle, and perhaps all of us (to some degree).

    Here Socrates will explore the connection somewhat strictly and materially, according to its material

---

[251] This may be true of the Latin 'elementum' also.

Commentary

parts (letters and syllables). He suggests these parts have an analogical correspondence to the things we know. This is partly because being *communicates* or *speaks* to us as something like an intelligible word. It is, after all, words which we use when we want to communicate or make ourselves intelligible—when we want to speak about beings. This is perhaps the most immediate connection we experience between being and speech (logos).[252]

- **Euclid, *The Elements*, and the Cosmos:** Euclid of Alexandria (post-Plato) wrote the great mathematical textbook known as the *Elements* (Στοιχεῖα). In his text, we find further parallelism to the argument in Act III. In Euclid's text, there are those things which are first and relatively simple, as well as accounts (logos or propositions) which follow upon those principles. Euclid then also distinguishes between definitions (*horoi*, which are also known as axioms or principles), common notions, postulates, and propositions. Definitions and common notions are fundamental principles which are either proper to a science (such as Geometry) or common to many. Lines and points are proper to geometry; that a whole is greater than a part pertains to almost all sciences. Definitions and common notions are not subject to demonstration.[253] They are

---

[252] Plato and Aristotle sometimes refer to the form (εἶδος), the nature of a thing, as kinds of logos. It is quite a different move to work from the top down, from God who is the Word and who has made all things in or through his Image, thus as kinds of *logoi*. Included in God's work is of course our own power of logos.

[253] A concept can be defined through analysis and judgment but is grasped by apprehension.

not proven but are instead the necessary 'sources' of all that will be proven in a science. They come *first*. This does not mean they are utterly simple, but that they are not arrived at by prior proof. A geometer does not prove triangles or their definition, nor does a person who studies whales prove their existence.[254] The demonstrative conclusions of a proof depend on definitions, the *elemental* first principles of a science. Propositions are more *complex*. In fact, propositions or demonstrations have the structure of a syllogism.[255] They are the product of *the third act of the mind*—reason (logos).

Euclid's *Elements* culminates in the construction of the five regular solids, also known as the *Platonic solids*. They are inscribed into a sphere in the final propositions and compared to one another. These solids are treated in Plato's *Timaeus* as the underlying geometric structures of water, earth, air, and fire (the four material elements of the whole cosmos). Therefore, Euclid's *Elements* concludes with what can be considered a construction of the *elements* (and if so, a representation of the cosmos—a mathematical representation of the *Whole*).

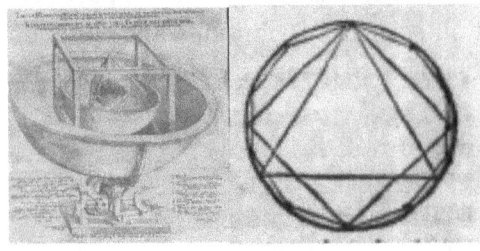

Figure 3: *Kepler's diagram of the Cosmos (the planetary orbits) as nested platonic solids inscribed in a sphere from his Cosmographic Mysteries (left); Three of the solids are depicted as inscribed in a sphere from a two-dimensionally perspective (right).*

---

[254] There are cases where proof belongs to a prior science, but infinite regress is not possible or necessary.

[255] More complex propositions, such as sorites, can have more than two premises.

Commentary

The tradition, accurate or not, has associated Theaetetus with these propositions. These geometric elements, like their counterparts of water, air, earth, and fire, are ambiguously elemental. Euclid is drawing not only from presocratic philosophy, but most of all form a Pythagorean and Platonic tradition. In the *Timaeus*, Plato constructs the universe and its elements out of these solids (32c-40d, 49a-61c).

As an historical notes, Johannes Kepler (1571-1630), a Platonist of sorts, takes up these elements in his work in Astronomy. He attempts to account for the various speeds of planetary orbits. His *Harmonies of the World* and *Cosmographic Mystery* are, partly, an attempt to unify mathematics, astronomy, and music. He shows a correspondence between the ratio or speeds of planetary orbits to one another and places them in correspondence to the side lengths of various platonic solids. Following the *Timaeus*, he relates those speeds or 'intervals' to musical intervals such as the fifth, the octave, etc.[256]

 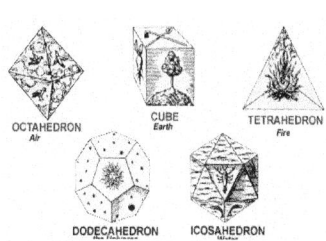

Figure 4: *Kepler's sketch of the platonic solids from his Harmonies of the World (right); A public domain image of his*

---

[256] To read further on Plato's cosmology, see: Plato and Peter Kalkavage, *Timaeus*, Second edition. (Indianapolis: Focus, 2016); Plato and Francis Macdonald Cornford, *Plato's Cosmology: The Timaeus of Plato*, 2014. For an interesting take on Kepler, see D. P. Walker, "Kepler's Celestial Music," *Journal of the Warburg and Courtauld Institutes* 30 (1967): 228–250.

- **Composed:** Socrates, Theaetetus, and all things are composed (συγκείμεθα) out of elements. Early in the dialogue, clay was defined as a complex of earth and moisture (147c). Such an account is perhaps suggestive of a kind of atomism, but it also extends analogically to other kinds of composition. A man is not made of carbon, hydrogen, etc., in the same way that he is made of arms, legs, torso, head, nor in the same way that he is composed of body and soul, matter and form, accidents and substance, or essence and existence. These distinctions (these various kinds of parts or elements) need to be taken into consideration if we are to understand what constitutes a good account (or what constitutes knowledge).

    Combination here indicates the *composition* of a thing, that a thing has parts and is not utterly simple. 'Composite being' comes to be a semi-technical term expressing what Aristotle deduces in his *Physics*—that all natural or changeable being is in some respect composed (or a *combination*) of form and matter (*Physics* I). This known as his hylomorphic (matter-form) theory. *Composite* is later analogically used to describe all created or limited being by St. Thomas.[257]

Names and logos;

Named: The elements are named. We cannot predicate anything of them other than names because they are simple. Since knowledge is here defined as a logos expressive of elements, the elements must be *unknown*. Nevertheless, it seems strange to say that something I name, I in no way know. I am at least acquainted with such things; surely, one does not name that

---

[257] It is used analogically sometimes to refer to sub-lunar substances, treating angels as *relatively* simple.

which is utterly unknown. Part of our difficulty here in the dialogue is that while we are distinguishing knowledge from non-knowledge (mere opinion), we may also be distinguishing, somewhat implicitly, one *kind* of knowledge (episteme), from other *kinds*, such as apprehension, judgment, even opinion.

Socrates, in this first account (201e-202a), denies that we can even apply terms like 'each', 'alone', or even 'is' or 'is not' to elements; otherwise, we make them complex and given them being (οὐσίαν) or non-being.[258] It is as if every element must share or mix with being if it is to exist. The doctrine of participation is perhaps suggested here.

Because of their simplicity, elements would have to be explained or given a logos apart from any combination whatsoever, and this is impossible. Therefore, they can have only a name. On the other hand, those things composed out of elements are complex. Therefore, their names are **complex** (πέπλεκται, twined, plaited, entangled); their names are mixed (plaited or twined) together to become a logos (οὕτω καὶ τὰ ὀνόματα αὐτῶν **συμπλακέντα** λόγον γεγονέναι).

---

[258] At least here, the elements sound very different than the forms which are often described as οὐσίαν and as being a thing itself by itself. Nevertheless, Plato sometimes ascribes οὐσίαν in a limited sense to the composite things we encounter, as belonging to them by participation (*Meno* 72b; *Theaetetus* 186a; *Phaedo* 65d-e). Why would being or non-being be composite? There are several possible interpretations:

a. The act of predication (judgment) would be an act of joining: an element or a form + is (or *is not*).

b. Being (ousia) as form or as things we encounter is itself composite in some manner, not wholly simple.

c. Being (ousia) is definitionally considered here to be a substantial whole rather than a simple element.

The name of a thing is said to express what it is. That is not to say that etymology (or philology) amounts to knowing the essence of a thing. Nor does it mean that a name is a mystical talisman of essence. Rather, names are signs of an essence, of that which a thing is. Names call to mind the being of a thing. One can take this doctrine naïvely and absolutely (cf. *Cratylus*). Or one may take it moderately, in which etymology (or phonology) may or may not indicate some aspect of the nature of a thing. At the very least, a name is the way in which we point something out in speech, and to point out is in some respect to define.

A final distinction we might make is that between the outer word (the spoken name) and the inner word (the concept) of which it is a sign.[259] The concept may also be a sign, although in a different manner, that is, as a *formal* sign (see 197e, or Deely, 44-45, 162 n.2). Whether we consider this from the standpoint of spoken words or concepts, if we treat something which is wholly indivisible, it must indeed be inexpressible other than by a name (a word).[260] It remains somewhat ambiguous here whether such a name should still be considered as in any sense meaningful or knowable.

So. "...The **twining** of names is the **substance** of a logos."(ὀνομάτων γὰρ **συμπλοκὴν** εἶναι **λόγου οὐσίαν**.)
- This is rather a stunning statement. A parallel passage is found in the *Sophist* 259e. There, parallelism

---

[259] Thomas distinguishes between a "word of the heart" and a "word of the voice." See *Summa Theologica* I-I, q.27, a.1

[260] If a name is a word, there is a meaningful sense in which it does not lack a logos.

between an *interweaving* of forms and that of speech is made explicit:

> The complete destruction of all speeches is to sunder each thing from all things; for through the **intertwining of the forms** with each other, **speech** has come to be. (τελεωτάτη πάντων λόγων ἐστὶν ἀφάνισις τὸ διαλύειν ἕκαστον ἀπὸ πάντων: διὰ γὰρ τὴν ἀλλήλων τῶν **εἰδῶν συμπλοκὴν** ὁ **λόγος γέγονεν** ἡμῖν.)

The connection between logos and forms implied here is perhaps the ontological, psychological, and epistemic justification for Socrates *second sailing*, his inquiry into nature by means of speech (*Phaedo* 99d-e).

Ousia (substance or being) is used by Socrates, suggesting that being, as it is considered here is somehow composite or complex. One might, compare these passages to *Phaedo* 65d-e where the οὐσία are equated with the forms (with the truth and being of each thing).[261] In the *Republic*, however, it is suggested there is a reality, the Good, that is, very Being, which is beyond ousia, surpassing all formal limitation or composition *Republic* (509b-c). See the use of ousia at (186c-d).

---

[261] It may be that the *Phaedo* speaks more precisely about the true ousia according to Plato, while ousia here refers to those things which are ousia by participation (composition). Plato does not explore this systematically. Ousia could refer to a matter-form composition or to a form properly and/or preeminently. All these considerations take us well beyond what *Theaetetus* makes explicit. See the use of ἀναλογίσματα, συλλογισμῷ, at 186c-d.

So. "Thus, the elements are **without logos** and **unknown, but perceived; whereas, the combinations** (syllables, or conceptions) are **knowables**." (οὕτω δὴ τὰ μὲν στοιχεῖα **ἄλογα** καὶ **ἄγνωστα** εἶναι, αἰσθητὰ δέ: τὰς δὲ **συλλαβὰς γνωστάς**...)[262]

- **Without logos** (ἄλογα) has a double sense. It may mean merely *lacking a logos* or that a thing is intrinsically *irrational*. To accept the first sense does not mean to accept the second. To be irrational in a strict or radical way would mean that such things have no measure and are in no way grasped by the intellect at all. A problem will result if we make the elements too radically unintelligible. We would not even name them in such a case.

    In mathematics, ἄλογα has a definite meaning. All counting or natural numbers are rational because they can be measured by the unit (see *Elements* VII; *Metaphysics* V.6). This is not the case with magnitudes. While magnitudes are not numbers per se, we can apply numbers to them. For instance, we can apply the number ration 1:2 to a set of lines in which the second is twice as long as the first, or 11:14 to lines when one is $11/14^{ths}$ of the other. However, the moment we apply a unit measure to a given magnitude, some magnitudes cease to be rational or commensurable to that selected unit. That is, some magnitude will not have to that chosen magnitude the ratio which a number has to a number (see *Elements* X; *Meno* 82b-85b). There is no single quantitative unit measure which will measure every single possible magnitude. Again, this is unlike the natural numbers. The unit is a *logos* or measure which measures every single counting number.

---

[262] See the use of ἀναλογίσματα, συλλογισμῷ, at 186c-d.

But we can find no such universal numeric measure for magnitudes. While every magnitude can be said to have a size relation to every other, their relation cannot always be quantified by rational numbers; they do not always have the *ratio* which a number has to a number.[263] Irrational numbers (or magnitudes) are precisely those that cannot be measured by the unit.[264] Thus some magnitudes are *incommensurable* with others. What this means is that is no single **logos** by which we can measure or given an **account** of every magnitude together.

This 'crisis' in mathematics occurs when the discrete (number) is put in relation with the continuous (magnitude/geometry). Mathematicians thus take the **genus** of magnitude and **divide** it into rational and irrational because there is not some one quantitative measure or **analysis** (logos) that can belong to them all. However, they are all comprehended under the genus of magnitude! We still know something about them. Socrates, it seems then, selected his 'demonstration' of recollection in the *Meno* carefully. The *sought-for*, the root of the double square, is by nature irrational. Nevertheless, while it is irrational, it does not prevent him from finding, *pointing out* and *naming* the line. That line or power (the root of the double square) is named the dia-metros (the *through* **measure** or diagonal) because the diagonal of the unit square is

---

[263] 'Ratio' is a Latin term that whose meaning overlaps *somewhat* with logos.

[264] Irrational 'numbers' are not the same as counting numbers. They are measures of magnitude. We can precisely locate an irrational number or magnitude on a number line, but we can never univocally quantify it in the same manner as a counting number.

always the power or root of the double. Therefore, Socrates is able to employ the magnitude in a proof, even while he is wholly incapable of *calculating* or analyzing it quantitatively.[265] While the magnitude is irrational (as compared to the unit), it does not stand outside the realm of all reason or logos.

We can summarize then that the irrational line in *Meno* serves as an example, a *sign* that learning is truly possible. That one can learn or come to know something, even about that which cannot be given a certain kind of logos. This dialogue also began with a proof concerning rational and irrational lines. If we take the idea of *irrational* too radically, we may end up cutting the ground out from under us. To lack a definitional or complex logos may not mean that something eludes reason *altogether*. This is a sign that knowledge itself might be divided into kinds. It is no accident that the *Theaetetus* is divided into three acts.

- ἄγνωστα: Socrates selects a much broader word than episteme here. One might compare the words for knowing used in *Meno* 71a-b.

- αἰσθητὰ (perceptible): These 'unknown' elements are assigned to the domain of the perceptible as such. This is somewhat surprising. We might want to amend this in some manner, but this certainly makes sense insofar as perception is not by itself properly knowledge or episteme. We might even consider a bolder claim, consonant with Plato, Aristotle and Thomas: matter as such, insofar as it is merely matter

---

[265] *Calculate* (like 'reckon') is an appropriate and common translations of *logos*.

(apart from all form), is unintelligible. Matter is always composite or hylomorphic. The elements, as wholly uncombined, are here described as perceptible only.[266] What remains problematic is that it seems that whenever we perceive, we perceive some *kind of thing*, that is, something composite. One might take perception here as the strict perceptible, or perhaps even analogically. Of course, all this analysis goes way beyond perception and beyond the initial definition of Act III.

So. "When someone **apprehends (λάβῃ) without reasoning the true opinion** about a thing, his soul tells the **truth** about it, but is **not knowing** it (γιγνώσκειν δ' οὔ)."

- **Apprehend:** This word can mean to take or acquire. This statement, perhaps intentionally, complicates our interpretation. We are suddenly told that there are things we can apprehend the truth of apart from reason! We were told earlier that truth and being were inseparable. Is it accidental that the term apprehend is used? Socrates does not state whether:

    a. This apprehension without reason is of an object that *could* have a logos but subjectively does not (as Act II might suggest by distinguishing perceptions and impressions).
    b. This is an apprehension of an element that is inherently without reason. In such a case, should we consider this as *irrational* in the radical (unknowable at all) or limited sense

---

[266] Aristotle, *Metaphysics* 7.10, 1036a1-10

(without account)? It seems only the later is appropriate here.

How would someone grasp the truth of a thing if it is only an element (and thus perceptible only)? It would be interesting to put this problem in the context of the divided line, particularly what Jacob Klein refers to as *dianoetic eikasia*.[267] The divided line relegates perception to opinion, perhaps because it is not perception per se which renders a thing intelligible. It may also be because of the limited ontological stability of material being whose intelligible and ontological causes are formal. Though I see a cat, it is not by perception alone that I know it as a cat. 'Cat' is an intelligible look by which I know that perceptible thing. Further, that cat *there* will not be a cat forever. It is a cat because it has a certain form. It is *a* cat but not *cat*.

However this step of the dialogue is understood, Socrates states that the individual indeed grasps some truth about these elements or perceptible things! It would be inappropriate to put too much systematic pressure on the text here.

So. <u>"The one who is unable to give or receive a logos is without knowledge (ἀνεπιστήμονα) of that thing. But having grasped a logos, he may both come to have a rational power (λόγον δυνατόν) over all these things and become perfect in knowledge" (γεγονέναι καὶ τελείως πρὸς ἐπιστήμην ἔχειν).</u>

- For all its clarity, this again complicates things. On the one hand, a scientific knower is precisely one who can

---

[267] Klein, *A Commentary on Plato's Meno*, 108–157.

Commentary

articulate, define, and teach a subject—one who can communicate what they know in words. On the other hand, this suggests that someone could *come to possess* a logos! One can *become perfect in knowledge through a power of logos*. This suggests there are degrees or kinds of knowledge, the most perfect of which is through logos. Has Socrates shifted attention to those things that can *come* be scientifically knowable or is he still simply distinguishing perceptible things and elements from knowable things? It very much seems to be the former.

- Theaetetus affirms that Socrates has reproduced what he had heard *altogether* (παντάπασιν), perhaps anticipating with his phrase the coming discussion of the *all* and *whole*.

Syllables and Letters;
202d

Theaetetus is satisfied with this account. He believes it is exact (κομιδῇ, 202c) and beautiful (καλῶς, 202d): true opinion with a logos is knowledge. Socrates, however, is not convinced yet. He is not confident they have truly just found what many wise men have grown old seeking. He concedes that:

So. "Indeed, it is likely it holds this way, for what knowledge could there be **separated** from a logos (**χωρὶς** τοῦ λόγου) and right opinion?"
- Is there knowledge apart from logos and must that logos be connected to *right opinion*?[268] Both these claims will be tested for the remainder of the dialogue.

---

[268] This partly depends whether opinion means:

So. "The things of writing, both letters and syllables" (τὰ τῶν γραμμάτων στοιχεῖά τε καὶ συλλαβάς.)

- Socrates questions the element-combination account of logos (and knowledge) by using the elements of speech analogically, by taking the alphabet (στοιχεῖά) and the syllables (συλλαβάς) as pledges or hostages by which to evaluate the account (logos). Just as with the pattern or paradigm of clay at the beginning, he is using examples.

- **Γραμμάτων:** This word refers primarily to writing, though it is not in opposition to speech. Writing is the means by which we scientifically know syllables. They now begin to examine the way in which reading is learned, the nature of letters and syllables.

203a

So. "Grant first, the syllables have a logos, but the letters (elements) are without a logos (irrational)?" (φέρε πρῶτον: ἆρ' αἱ μὲν **συλλαβαὶ λόγον ἔχουσι**, τὰ δὲ **στοιχεῖα ἄλογα;**)

- **συλλαβαὶ:** Socrates has introduced the term συλλαβή-*syllable* at 202b, 202c, and 202e, anticipating this discission here. He used it as a synonym for συγκείμεθα (composed, compounded, lie together) and συμπλακέντα (twined, plaited, intertwined). All three of these terms can mean sexual intercourse. There is throughout this dialogue the idea of

---

- The subjective assent or commitment to a thing consciously grasped in its objectivity
- The subjective assent or commitment to a thing grasped subjectively or with uncertainty

generation or productivity in relation to various things being combined. The first meaning of syllable in Greek is provocatively: 'conception' or 'pregnancy'. Other meanings include 'that which holds together', 'grasping', 'an apex'.[269] See the use of ἀναλογίσματα, συλλογισμῷ, at 186c-d.

This section of the dialogue will examine both the sources of things and those things which they generate. For instance, can the individual elements produce knowledge by themselves? If not, why can they produce knowledge of syllables?

A note on grammar: Students who are accustomed to dividing words into syllables may be confused by this discussion. We normally say that the word 'atom' has two syllables ('a' and 'tom'). The Greeks might recognize this usage also, but Socrates is relying on the etymological meaning of 'syllable' which implies *standing or gathering together* (συλλαμβάνω). Thus a syllable is primarily and definitionally letters or elements that have been gathered together. The fact that alpha or the letter 'a' could stand by itself is rather an accident. A syllable here is not, first and foremost, a distinct phoneme (a sound unit or division in our pronunciation); it is precisely something combined (at least in the initial part of the argument).

The argument is not that human beings cannot express single letters or use single letters to signify but that we cannot *give a logos* of single letters, just as we

---

[269] συλλαβή can also mean a perfect fourth, the musical ratio of 4:3 with which Plato is clearly familiar with (see *Timaeus*). What to make, if anything, of this provocative fact is unclear to me.

cannot give a logos of utterly simple things—both called or characterized as elements.

- Syllables and logos are similar. An account (reason/logos) would express the way something is composed or bound together. Reason, as the third act of the mind, *syl*-logizes. It draws a conclusion from prior premises. Syllogism is etymology related to collecting and gathering—it refers to the act of inference. As Curtis. Hancock puts it, to syllogize is "to draw out unity from plurality or to make one out of many".[270] It is the nature of a syllogism to take that which is *relatively* simple and deduce that which is contained implicitly in that whole, either actually or potentially. For instance, man is implicitly contained in animal. In a different way, animal is implicit in man. To syllogize is in a way to *syllabize* (to gather), but it is to mentally gather together various implicit elements of a *thing* rather than a word.

  All A is B
  All B is C
  ∴ All A is C

  'A' is a complex whole whose parts or elements include 'B' and 'C'. 'B' and 'C' are like the letters which become a syllable when joined (A & B) which implicitly constitute 'A' or some part of A. It is the act of reason (syllogism) which makes this explicit. This is somewhat different than saying that the logos of clay is earth+moisture. Earth and moisture would be two distinct elements, unless one claimed that there was moisture *in* the earth in an analogous way that 'B' is *in*

---

[270] Hancock and Bernot, "The True, the False, the Lie, and the Fake."

'C'. Even so, the statement that clay is water+earth would still be an analysis by reason of clay into elements.

So.   "What is '*SO*'?"
- Theaetetus *defines* the 'SO' of 'Socrates' as 's' and 'o' (sigma and omicron). This is the logos of the syllable, the twining together of the names or letters, in this case sigma and omicron (202b).[271] Such a definition is much like earth + moisture.

203b
So.   "...say also in this way the logos for sigma."

The.   "And how can one give a letter (element) of a letter (element)?"
- There is no primary or prior element with which to divide 's'. At least, one cannot define 's' in terms of parts. Nevertheless, there is a way to say what *kind* of thing 's' is.

    The implication or problem suggested here is perhaps less obvious to those familiar with the modern Periodic Table of Elements. The modern elements are (no longer) consider fundamental (the ultimate constituents of physical analysis). Carbon can be analyzed into protons, electrons, etc. The modern elements were once considered fundamental. The fundamentality of elements of being (whether form and matter;

---

[271] For the use of the term name (ὄνομα) in *Theaetetus*: 144b, 144c, 144d, 147b, 150a, 156b, 157b, 160b, 164c, 166c, 168c, 177d, 177e, 180e, 182a, 184c, 186d, 187a, 194a, 195c, 198a, 198e, 199a, 201d, 201e, 202b, 203c, 206d, 207a, 207b, 208a.

water and fire; or some other grouping) are implicated in the elementality of the letters.

If knowing something means being able to give a logos of it through its elements, it matters whether there are or are not fundamental elements. In that case, it matters if there is no known or actual stopping point of analysis—if all things are equally divisible or if the final elements are unknown. In other words, if we only know a thing by its elements, we cannot know it if we do not know the elements! Or, we know it only provisionally by what are only provisionally fundamental. We need to think carefully about what constitutes true knowledge of a thing. In other words, the element-syllable thesis could mean that we don't know anything at all if we don't know the ultimate elements! At the very least, it means we should think carefully about what constitutes the true division of a thing into parts.

For instance, if a dog is ultimately atoms but atoms can be further subdivided, we will not know the dog until we reach those subdivisions because knowledge of the atoms is itself provisional or will require knowledge of subatomic particles. In fact, it seems that either:
  a. knowledge of the dog would be only provisional (depending on further analysis)
  b. empty (if we had no knowledge without knowing ultimate elements)
  c. or empty and utterly impossible if there is in fact an infinite regress of elements.

In any of these cases, a person who did not know the material elements which compose the dog would be not have episteme of the dog. Would such elements (those of the periodic table) properly inform one's knowledge about dogs. In what sense would we really say that in knowing carbon or oxygen we know what a dog is? Atomic theory might be a key to all knowledge, if Theaetetus and Socrates division is correct. Again, this may depend on what sort of 'elements' we are thinking of.

The problem of the infinite, of endless division or the continuous, is masterfully treated in chapter six of Jacob Klein's *Greek Mathematics*. We explored his analysis of the infinite (ἄπειροι) in the second reading, in light of Theaetetus's division, where he reduced unlimited powers to unity by means of gathering them together into one (συλλαβεῖν εἰς ἕν) through a discrete division:

> Now it occurred to us, since the number of powers appeared to be infinite, to try to **collect** them all under **one thing**, 147d. (ἐπειδὴ ἄπειροι τὸ πλῆθος αἱ δυνάμεις ἐφαίνοντο, πειραθῆναι **συλλαβεῖν** εἰς **ἕν**, ὅτῳ πάσας)

Theaetetus reduced the infinity of these line by means of a formal division into **kinds**. What would have happened if he had tried to divide them by their material constitution or by the actual number of square roots which exist? The problem of elements and proper analysis is at the heart of good science. One might again compare this to a statement by Socrates at 148d in which he employs *eidos* and places it in parallel with logos:

> "Try, imitating the answer about the powers, so as to embrace the many beings in **one form**, thus also speaking **one logos** of the **many knowledges**." (πειρῶ μιμούμενος τὴν περὶ τῶν **δυνάμεων** ἀπόκρισιν, ὥσπερ ταύτας

πολλὰς **οὔσας ἐνὶ εἴδει περιέλαβες**, οὕτω καὶ **τὰς πολλὰς ἐπιστήμας ἐνὶ λόγῳ προσειπεῖν**.)

The. "For indeed, Socrates, the sigma is voiceless, a noise only..."

- Theaetetus describes the voiced letters (vowels) and unvoiced letters (consonants). He *divides* the class of letters (or elements) into kinds! Thus, while he may not be able to subdivide a letter itself, he has said something *about* them. They are a species in a genus. We may not always be able to define a thing (or prove it), but that does not mean we are wholly ignorant or that we can say nothing about them. It does suggest that we cannot speak the *same way* about all things. We may not be able to define or speak about one thing in precisely the same way we speak of another. Knowledge is not univocal then, but this would be because being itself is not univocal, because all being is not the same. This is why Aristotle divides nous (knowledge of principles) from episteme (demonstrative-syllogistic knowledge of causes).

  What would it mean to define letters? To define is at minimum to predicate one thing of another, insofar as that thing is a certain *kind of being*. Therefore, definition always implies something more than judgment. It implies reason or syllogism (the third act of the mind). We properly can only define a thing if it is a species of a genus.[272] Whenever we answer the question, 'what is it', we must always answer by way of composition or by a name which expresses composition. *What is that in your hands? A basket (a woven*

---

[272] Aristotle, *Metaphysics* 7.4

container). The *ti esti* question is therefore a demand for analysis, or at least can only be comprehensively answered about things we can analyze. I have been suggesting there may be various forms of analysis, some more excellent than others.

What is clay?	Earth and humidity
What is 's'?	A letter; a consonant
What is Justice?	A virtue; giving what is owed; harmony of the soul
What is knowledge?	
What is the Good?	

The analysis of clay is very different than that of 's' or that of knowledge.

- Theaetetus goes on to give a phonetic division of the letters. Such knowledge today generally belongs to those who study speech (linguistics), but it is also used by those who study the history of semiotics, language, grammar, and those who teach language. The distribution and use of various articulations (stops, plosives, fricatives, etc.) characterize various languages. This is why Hebrew, Russian, German, English, and French all sound different and why someone who does not speak German can make up *German sounding* words. The basic principles of articulation depend upon the part of the mouth a sound is made and the means of making that sound (whether it involves lips, teeth, tongue, etc. For instance, 'f' is a fricative which requires the teeth to be placed on the lips. It is therefore called a labial-dental. 'b' is a labial stop. There is a remarkable range of sounding or articulation-locations, including the glottis, pharynx, the nasal cavity, the front or back of the mouth, and the palate.

Joe Sachs states:

> Theaetetus, as accurate a grammarian as he is a mathematician, is referring to the seven distinctly voiced vowels...of seventeen consonants, nine are mutes or stops that cannot even be pronounced in isolation from a vowel.[273]

This is the third recurrence of seventeen (as the power of squares, as conditions of false opinion, and now, as elements of speech). In each case, an attempt to give a logos has been made with more or less success. In each case, Socrates and Theaetetus are concerned with the ability to articulate the rational and irrational (powers, errors, and elements).

203c-d
So. "...have we **shown** (ἀποδεδείγμεθα) rightly that the elements are **not knowable** (μὴ γνωστὸν) but only the syllables?"
- **ἀποδεδείγμεθα:** Socrates draws upon the language of proof or demonstration with which Theaetetus the mathematician is familiar. We are considering, by means of letters, the axiomatic or elemental principles which would constitute the parts of a proof (a logos).
- **γνωστὸν:** He elects not to use episteme here,

Whole, All, Parts;
So. "Mind this, whether we shall say the syllable is both letters...or some **single form** (ἰδέαν) that has come to

---
[273] Plato and Sachs, *Plato's Theaetetus*, 115.

be **established** (i.e., constructed, συντεθέντων) from them?"
- All the ambiguity of elements and logos comes to a head here. This also happens to be where the problem of the forms makes itself known.[274] Though Socrates does not develop this explicitly, at stake are the following issues:

    a. Is our knowledge ultimately knowledge of the elements of matter, formal elements, or both?
    b. If we need some kind of formal knowledge, what is a form's relation to the material and to the material parts. Either those parts or the form could be considered *elemental*, but with somewhat different results, as the following exchange is about to demonstrate.
    c. What is the relation between elements and the whole? Which is first and which is more intelligible?

    Also raised here is what comes to be called the problem of the communion or participation of the forms:
    d. What things participate in forms and how?
    e. Do some forms participate in other forms?
    f. If so, can some forms be analyzed?
    g. Would there then be a hierarchy of forms?
    h. Would there be some one form through all are what they are (197d)?

    All of these question takes us well beyond the question of definition as presented here through the alphabet.

---

[274] For other occurrences of eidos, see **148d, 156a**, 157c, 162b (cf. *Gorgias* 524d; *Republic* 588a), 169c, 178a, 181c-d, 184d, 187c, 203c, 203e, 204a, 205c, 205d.

It is a good time to remember that this dialogue is Theaetetus's first formal foray into philosophy.

- The question closest to hand is whether a syllable is merely the combination of letters or some unique form which is nevertheless analyzable. When I say or read the syllable 'SO', I am hardly conscious of the fact that it is two. It is one idea in my head, though I am capable of analyzing it into its parts. Nevertheless, one can consider a syllable as its elements *or* as a unit. But is a syllable its elements and a unit in the same way at the same time? What is it *actually*? We can extrapolate this question to being by thinking of our dog. Is a dog:
    - Body +Tail+ Feet+ Head
    - Carbon+ Oxygen...
    - Body & Soul
    - Canis...Animalia

Is the dog the sum total of its elements or some one thing over and above the *elements*? Depending how we approach this, the dog is either a mixture, a single simple thing, a unified whole or a composite.

Aristotle takes up the example of the syllables the *Metaphysics* (Book 7.10, 17; 12.5). His analysis focuses on determining what constitute the proper parts of a thing, what is rightly included in a thing's definition! This forms part of an exploration of essence, substance, being, and unity. His work on the *Categories* is also helpful here.

The.   "To me it seems we mean all of them."
- Theaetetus claims the syllable is nothing but the composition of its elements, it is a composite thing.

Socrates asks: how can someone know (γιγνώσκω) the syllable without also knowing both letters? That is, if a syllable is nothing but the combination of its elements, but one can have no knowledge of letters, how can a person who is ignorant of each letter (when considered individually) have knowledge when he knows them both? One who knows neither 's' nor 'o' somehow knows 'S' + 'O'![275]

The.
- "But that is terrible and irrational (ἄλογον), Socrates."
- Theaetetus shifts the meaning of ἄλογον. It does not mean *lacking an account*, but lacking a reasonable account, a good explanation.

Perhaps here more than anywhere else in the dialogue, the analogy of being is important to take into account. Are we really willing to say we do not have any knowledge whatsoever of these elements? But if we do have knowledge of letters, it seems we cannot insist that knowledge is precisely the same in kind as our knowledge of syllables. After all, what is the purpose of knowing letters? Why is it we read? The end of our knowledge of letters (or syllables) is that we might read things yet more intelligible (words)! And we read words for the sake of logos (the interweaving of words or names). It is no accident that in dealing only with letters and syllables, Theaetetus never arrives at a true whole. The analysis fails to negotiate between proper parts and wholes, between form and material, and this problem plagues the remainder of our reading.

---

[275] A man who knew neither the word 'hot' nor the word 'day' would be ignorant of 'hot day'. Is this the same situation as that described in the dialogue?

203e-204c
Theaetetus proposes that perhaps the syllable should instead be treated as one *form* (εἶδος), having its very own *single look or idea* (ἰδέαν μίαν), different from that of the letters of which it is composed. When mature readers read, they do not in fact see or read letter-by-letter but grasp things as words; they only secondarily spell out a word, when they fail to see or know it as a whole.

Socrates says they must *look* into this (σκεπτέον) because the theory of the elements they are exploring is a great and august *logos*. It is incumbent upon them to do their best here and to follow the logos as far as they are able. Therefore, they will now say that from a combination of each of the elements, a single form comes to be (the syllable). And this he claims is the case in writing and in all other things.

- So. <u>"Therefore, it is necessary that it have no **parts (μέρη)**...This is because if there are parts, the **whole (ὅλον) must necessarily be all the parts. Or, do you say that the whole, having come from these parts, is a form (εἶδος) which is other than the parts."</u>
  - **Parts:** The problem of substance theory, of atomism, of parts, elements, principles, essence, and accidents has now been fully set before us through this rudimentary analogy.

    We have been dealing with elements and syllables, but Socrates now introduces *parts* (μέρη) and *wholes* (ὅλον).[276] I have been suggesting that much of the ambiguity of Act III hinges on whether a whole is nothing but the composition of its parts and whether a part

---

[276] Cf. "οὐσίας μέρει" at 155e in which μέρει suggests participation in being.

and an element are precisely the same thing. Our answers may depend on the kind of parts and wholes we are considering: e.g., *a syllable, a word, a man, a dog, an atom, a cake, a sandwich.*

Socrates is about to use **number** to help us think about this. Math is familiar and clear cut. That is one reason why he chose geometry in *Meno*. But there may be something about number which will actually obscure the question of part and whole. The *parts* of a number may not be precisely like all other parts.

Part (μέρη) comes to take on a quasi-technical use in Aristotle. Euclid also uses 'part' (μέρη) in a technical sense in Book V and VII of the *Elements*. If Theaetetus is familiar with Euclid's usage, he does not give any indication here. Μέρη has various meanings which include 'share' 'portion' 'section', 'part of a whole, and 'class'. The word part in English means something like 'share' or 'division'. From it, we derive our words *par*ticipate and *par*ticular. They imply a **relation** to a **whole**. Examples would include:

- A limb is part of an animal's body
- Dogs are a part of the genus animal
- *That* dog is a part of the species dog

Notice that the limb which makes up a body as one of its parts is not truly a limb without participating in the life and physical continuity of the animal's body. A body (the whole) may, however, be able to continue to exist without that limb. The whole in this case is not merely the composition of its parts.

Dogs *partake of* or are *in* the genus animal. But they are not *in* or *parts* of a genus in the way a limb is a part of a body. We could ask whether their participation is logical or also ontological. If dogs did not exist, the genus 'animal' as such is not in *any way* injured or changed.

A singular dog (a *particular*) is a part of the species dog as a sharer in the whole. That dog is himself a whole. But should we say that an electron (or a nitrogen atom) is a *part* of the human body in the same way as the examples above? The distinction between parts, wholes, elements and an all is meaningful and not an accident of language.

- Theaetetus accepts that the whole is some unique look (*eidos*), distinct from its parts. But Socrates will now ask if the *whole* and *all* are the same. Theaetetus goes out on a limb and suggests that they are different. He will not be successful in maintaining this distinction. Because of that, he will eventually reject his claim that the whole is a distinct form (if being a whole means having parts). The one and the many are not sufficiently analyzed and ordered here. We must pay attention to the argument.

- Socrates first asks if *all the things* ('all' in the plural, πάντα) is distinct from the *all* ('all' in the singular, πᾶν). By example he asks if the following are the same:

    $1 + 1 + 1 + 1 + 1 + 1$
    $3+3$
    $3 \cdot 2$
    $4 + 2$
    $3 + 2 + 1$

Theaetetus responds that they are all the *same*, *six*. Therefore, in each articulation, they have spoken of the *all*, the *six*, says, Socrates. Therefore, when speaking of them all (all things), they are speaking an all.

Theaetetus states that they speak of *nothing else*.

204d

So. "Therefore, in those things in which the quantity **is one of number (τοῖς ὅσα ἐξ ἀριθμοῦ), we address either the all or all things [as the same].**"

- This hint seems to fall flat on the ears of our young mathematician. One of the most common intellectual errors is to take one's own field of knowledge as a common measure for all other fields. The primary element of arithmetic is the unit. Every single number is composed of a multitude of units and is *nothing but the multitude of those units*. These units are absolutely uniform and however they are combined, they remain the same. It does not matter *which* unit one places first or last. This is why one does not ask of the number six which of its units is the first or middle. Their ordering is indifferent. As pure units, we actually cannot even meaningfully conceive of a unique ordering!

204d-204e

So. "...the number of the plethron (30 meters) and the plethron are the same. Are they not?...and the stade?...and the army, and all such things are similar? For *all the number* is *all the thing* in each of these?...And is the number of each of these anything other than the parts?"

- Socrates gives three examples of the way in which the *all* and *all things* are the same. He does this by treating number as the measure of each thing. He lists the plethron, the stade, and the army. There is a steady shift in these examples from the abstract to the concrete.²⁷⁷ We can attend to this shift by asking what ambiguity might occur in the following:

- Is a certain distance nothing but the quantity of that distance?
- Is a race-course nothing but a certain arithmetic quantity?
- Is an army nothing but a *number* of army?

A distance is precisely a quantitative measure, but an army is not merely a quantity. It has organization and purpose. We will have a chance to recur to this at 207a. It seems Socrates is examining precisely what we find reflected in a logos, either an *all* or *whole*. If a logos is an account of a thing, of its elements or parts, does it merely *enumerate*? There may be more than one kind of enumeration—the way of the *all* and a way of the *whole*.

- Theaetetus assents to this argument. And from this Socrates makes the following conclusions:
    - The number of each thing is the parts of each thing
    - Everything that has parts is from (made of/exists/is) its parts

---

²⁷⁷ See Sachs note 60, p.118. Mollin Williamson notes a similar change in the *Meno* during the geometric inquiry with the slave boy. Socrates shifts between the use of the abstract quantitative term πόσοι and the more substantial or concrete πούς. He also contrasts the quantitative ποσάπους with the qualitative ποῖος. The power of the double square in *Meno* is never quantified numerically. It is *pointed out* but never *enumerated*. The boy is able to say precisely *what sort* of line it is (the diameter or *through-measure*), what we would call the 'diagonal'. See Williams p.352-363.

- - The all must be all of the parts, if indeed the all-number is the all
  - Therefore, the whole does not consist of parts (or else it would simply be an all—all the parts)

This last conclusion is the most crucial. It arises from what immediately preceded and also their agreement to distinguish an all and a whole. In what ways might this conclusion be objectional? One might review their agreement to unequivocally equate arithmetic units with parts.

So. <u>"But is a part the very thing it is, other than as [a part] of a **whole**?"</u>
- This is a most precise statement. It should return us to question of parts, elements, wholes, and all's. Perhaps it is not Theaetetus the *mathematician* who will ultimately clarify what is at stake here, but rather the philosopher—the person. Recall that a unit is just as much a unit when part of a whole as when not. Even in Euclid, parts are that which properly measure a whole! Parts are parts precisely in relation to a whole.

204e-205
The. <u>"Indeed, of the all"</u>
- Theaetetus is doing *manly battle* here. We might recall how he was described at the opening of the dialogue. He attempts to preserve his thesis (that the whole and the all differ) by attempting to associate parts with the all rather than the whole. He does this because he wishes to preserve the claim that somehow the syllable is not merely parts, but rather a single look. He is wrestling with the one and many, with parts and wholes, with various forms of opposition or

contrariety which need to be properly ordered. It is always a temptation to prematurely reject a part of the whole which seems contrary to another part. We can recall that it belongs to the wise to order.

So. "...is not whenever nothing is absent, is not that very thing the all?...And is not the **whole** this very thing, that from which not even one thing at all has deserted?"

- Keeping with the military theme, Socrates suggests that the all and the whole must be the same since neither of them lack anything. Nothing has defected from the whole. Wholeness is a kind of perfection.

We might note that even after a battle, when an army has suffered losses one can still speak of the whole army in a way that one might not speak of a whole car if it was missing a wheel or engine (or the whole of seven if it was missing two). A whole is not a numeric heap!

The. "It seems to me now that there is nothing **different** between the all and the **whole**." (δοκεῖ μοι νῦν οὐδὲν **διαφέρειν** πᾶν τε καὶ **ὅλον**.)

- As in the discussion of wisdom and knowledge, Theaetetus does not divide.

So. "If the syllable is not the letters, isn't it necessary that it does not have the letters as parts of itself, or being them [constituted of the letters], to be intelligible in the same way they are?"

- If a syllable is more than letters, it seems it should not have parts which are letters. If it is only its parts (the

Commentary

letters), than it seems it will be precisely intelligible or definable in the way its parts are.

We can point out that this is certainly not the real case with words. Words are not merely intelligible in the manner that letters are, unless we think of them merely from a material standpoint—the matter of which they are composed. A person reading does not merely learn what letters are on a page.

205c

So.   "**Altogether** then, Theaetetus, according to the logos now, the syllable must be some **one part-less idea**." (παντάπασι δή, ὦ Θεαίτητε, κατὰ τὸν νῦν λόγον **μία τις ἰδέα ἀμέριστος** συλλαβὴ ἂν εἴη.)

- This conclusion, ironically introduced (after their discussion of the all) by 'altogether', leads to the claim that there is equal intelligibility of syllables and letters. This whole section of the dialogue was introduced to account for the knowability of syllables. It was for this reason that the whole, the all, and parts were taken up. They asked how one could know a syllable if knowing it ultimately only amounted to knowing parts or elements which are themselves unknowable. They argued that perhaps the syllable had a unique look or form which made it intelligible in a distinct manner from its parts. But they were unable to maintain the distinction of an all and a whole or explain the relation of parts to a whole. Socrates now points out that if the syllable is itself an indivisible look, this will result in the syllable itself being *elemental* or *indivisible* and thus unknowable.

We are again left to ask whether the indivisible is truly unintelligible. We are further along here because we have been presented with a new sort of 'indivisibility'—a whole.

In fact, it may be that all intelligibility actually depends on knowing something indivisible, some whole.[278] This is just what Klein argued about numbers, mathematics, and forms. We are called to wonder here whether we can have knowledge of anything that is one! At the same time, what would it be to have knowledge that is not one or of that which is not one *at all*? The ambiguity of 'element' and 'whole' stand firm. Knowledge must somehow reckon with the one **and** many, but not indifferently. There must be something which orders or unites that which we know. There must be something which are knowledge is about. There in fact must be something first. They will momentarily explore what comes first with regard to letters and syllables.

- Socrates takes this occasion (205c) to state that because these things have been found not to be composite but rather, simple, we cannot apply the terms 'to be' or 'this' to them.[279] It should not be ignored that

---

[278] Cf. Klein (1992) ch.6. In the *Metaphysics*, Aristotle repeatedly states that unity and being are convertible. He remarks that unity is meant in precisely in the number of ways that being is, that there are as many forms of unity as being. From this, we might reflect on the fact that whenever we grasp that something is, we grasp some form of unity.

[279] Substance (ousia) is characterized by being 'a this', 'seperable', one, and true in Aristotle's *Metaphysics*. Preeminent being is characterized by Aristotle as separable (τὸ χωριστὸν) and a this (καὶ τὸ τόδε). It is hard to imagine Socrates really intends to deny this. Nevertheless, there is no limited being that is utterly simple and utterly independent.

Socrates is not only denying the knowability but the being of that which is one. He is dividing unity and being from one another!

205d-206b

In rehearsing their argument, Socrates states rather ambiguously that if syllables are simply many letters, than the letters and syllables are in the same way (or similarly) intelligible and expressible (ὁμοίως αἵ τε συλλαβαὶ **γνωσταὶ καὶ ῥηταὶ** καὶ τὰ στοιχεῖα)—since the parts are the same as the whole. This is because the whole is nothing but parts and equal to the *all* (205a). He chooses 'ῥηταὶ' here instead of logos, perhaps to distance the act of speaking from its rationality.

But if the syllable is without parts and one, then the letters and syllables are both irrational and unintelligible.

For this reason, they must conclude that the distinction between letter and syllable does not hold. Either letter and syllable are intelligible and speakable in the same way (in the manner of the whole and all), or they are unintelligible and unspeakable in the manner of what is elemental and has not parts.

Reversal—letters as the most knowable

Having rejected the argument that the syllable is unintelligible while the letter is not, Socrates now proposes the opposite, that the letter is *more knowable* than the syllable. He does this by reminding Theaetetus that the letters are what we all first learn. The letters are more readily learned and it is only by distinguishing between them that we know how to read. Similarly, in music we must learn to distinguish notes and connect them to their strings. In this manner, he returns the discussion of elements to the broader field of education, memory, learning, and intelligibility. This also recalls the question of whether the liberal arts are a study of the elements, and if so, in what sense. Are the liberal arts the beginning or the end of all study?

From these examples, Socrates argues that the elements are indeed exceedingly more knowable, manifest or brilliant, and more important for becoming perfect in each area of learning (206b). This is of course true in some respect. They will now take it as a joke if someone asserts the elements are less intelligible than the compounds or syllables.

Let us not lose sight of something obscured by this line of reasoning. It is true that the elements or letters are first in the order of learning, but letters are not the most intelligible thing in the context reading and writing. Unless, by most intelligible one merely means the *easiest or first thing learned*. We might also note that children normally learn to speak before they engage in the 'scientific' study or analysis of letters.

There is something higher, some whole and end which is more perfect than those elements or parts. In music, the end is not knowing which notes belong to which strings. The end of music is not notes; it is song. Neither letters nor syllables mark the end of grammar. That which is first to us is not always first simply in intelligibility or being (*Physics* I.1). This was hinted at earlier when Socrates asked Theaetetus about perceiving a language which one does not speak (163c).

In the *Cratylus*, Socrates argues that it is neither letters nor the syllables which are the smallest parts of speech. He argues there that the very smallest part of a logos is, instead, a name (385c). In the *Theaetetus* also, he has suggested something like this, that it is names rather than syllables that are the fundamental parts of speech and reasoning (202b). It is the intertwining of names rather than parts of words that results in logos. But names inmixed, without judgment or reasoning are not yet knowledge.

On Elements, Parts, Wholes, and the All

Let's explore a few of the implications of this reading. All along we have been considering a manifold and analogical topic: knowledge. We have been considering what it is to know, what it is *that* we know, and therefore, the sorts of things that exist. The question of knowledge cannot remain isolated from the mystery of being (or from the mystery of our own being—our psychological powers). Being is not an abstraction that terminates in a concept. Instead, it concerns all the numerous kinds of beings there are, as well as their real conditions of existence—their causes, principles, parts, and elements.

Contrary to the Cartesian turn, it was long thought that being (rather than thinking) held first place in knowledge. "Will one happen upon truth who has not happened upon being" (186c)? The presocratic philosophers, following this train of thought, argued that various fundamental elements accounted for the kinds of beings we encounter. The universe was thought to be composed of those elements. The presocratic philosophers even tried to account for the soul by means of these elements. Some said the soul was made of water, while other said it was made of air. The atomists posited the soul was made of particles of fire and described knowledge as caused by reflective fire-flakes. Plato himself takes up a complex and playful attempt to describe the beginning of all things, In the *Timaeus*, he gives a mythic account (a *likely story*) which includes a geometric-molecular analysis (an early chemical-molecular mythology) of the four elements.

But not everything is composed of material elements. In the *Phaedo*, Plato argues that the soul is spiritual or *most like spirit*—that which is uncompounded, invisible, and divine. Aristotle, following him, shows that a soul cannot be a body or composed of elements but is instead that which causes a body to be a *living body*. The soul is the organizing formal cause of the complex unity of an organic being, a creature constituted by diverse organs (each with distinct ends and operations) which serve to perfect and preserve the life of that being. One cannot explain unity and organization (especially not that of a living creature) by pointing only to a material cause. This is because the non-accidental organization of matter itself demands an explanation (why it is organized this way rather than another). To point to DNA or to some other material *part* would merely back the question up a step (*what causes the organization of DNA?*). The mystery of matter presents itself because we never encounter mere or pure matter without also experiencing the effects of organization and activity.

It is a testament to Plato's method that though he clearly recognizes the problem of materialism, he does not overstep himself and attempt anything like a deductive or systematic theory of forms. A reticence to do anything like this is reflected in all his work. This is especially manifest in the *Theaetetus* where such a system would be so serviceable. Instead, the forms are rather an implicit question in this dialogue. Nascent philosophic inquiry needs a proper entry point, not a full-blown metaphysic.

We have done much if we admit that the world is indeed full of *kinds*—beings which have specific types of organization (or unity) which exhibit various powers, ends, and ways of existing.[280] Plato accounts for this diversity and regularity by the forms (εἶδος). An eidos or form is simply a way of describing the *look* or shape of a thing, the visible or intelligible pattern it presents.[281] The etymology of eidos express that of 'seeing'.

---

[280] Redpath, "The One and the Many."

[281] The Latin 'video' (to see) is related to eidos, which is thought to have lost a digamma or 'w' sound (*weidos*). In meaning it is expressed both by the Latin species (look or see) and forma (shape, visible look).

This is why *morphe* (μορφή) or shape is often a synonym for form in Aristotle—expressed characteristic or shape of a thing, an appearance which presents itself as a *kind* of *look*. It is after all in these appearances that being first discloses itself to us, that what is first makes itself manifest through self-disclosure.[282]

When a doctor identifies someone with chickenpox, she brings to bear, not just what she sees, but a knowledge of something she intelligibly grasps in that pattern, a pattern which the thing seen con*forms* to. In such a case, that pattern includes spots, itching, and fever. Something like this happens when we know what a wagon is, what justice is, or what a human being is.

An account of the forms, therefore, does not begin in mysticism, but in a need to reckon with the world as it is: ever changing, yet stable and intelligibly, causally organized. The ontological status of the forms, whether they exist on their own or only in the very patterns of things, is a different question. First and foremost, Plato recognized that we need a way of giving a causal account of the world as we experience it. There must truly be some *formal* (shaping or organizational) cause which makes each thing what it is, which accounts for the unique constitution of various kinds of beings. Modern science, in this light, merely follows Plato's lead.

Plato, and other thinkers who follow him, say much more about the forms and their mode of existence. But the basic admission (that of formal unity) is the entryway into all western science and philosophy (perhaps all human knowledge). Whether these patterns or looks are separable, eternal, multiple, or one, we need not clarify here. We do not need to determine the *mode* of their existence. Act III has set the stage for

---

[282] Borrowed from a reframing of Husserl by Randall Colton. Randall Colton, "Modern and Contemporary Philosophy," 2017.

us to consider forms and definitions—what it is we know when we know. We are pressed to consider both what we know and what *is* from multiple perspectives: that of elements, composites, wholes, and even mathematics.

It is by formal organization that we make sense of the world, that the potentially infinite and unlimited world becomes limited.[283] Through form alone are the many reduced to unity.[284] But this implies that what we *see* when we look is not just multitude, a bunch of parts, elements, or discrete sense data. We experience wholes which are not just "heaps" as Aristotle says.[285] Their organization is not something we merely imagine. We could no more construct them *ex post facto* than could a man who started from letters (elements) alone arrive at words and rational speech!

This means that science (philosophy) must attend to parts and wholes, to the fact that we continually encounter complex kinds of unity. Therefore, we have to attend to the ways in which parts and wholes are related. We also have to determine which is the cause of which—whether parts or wholes are prior, and in what sense. As when we discovered that being and truth are prior to error in Act II, here we must clarify the true order between parts and wholes.

Our reading suggests that we encounter *unified wholes* (parts coordinated with regard to some unity of end or nature). There-fore, we can argue that parts and wholes are intimately related. There is not contrary opposition between them, even if they are known differently. We need not be

---

[283] Both Aristotle and Thomas argue that form limits matter. Such an analysis goes all the way back to the 6th century BC when Anaximander posited the fundamental principles or elements of being to be the limited (πέρας) and unlimited (ἄπειρον). The limited and unlimited have been a consistent theme in the dialogue.

[284] Redpath, "The One and the Many."

[285] Aristotle, *Metaphysics*, 8 (1045a8)

caught between the horns of the dilemma—parts *vs.* wholes; letters *vs.* syllables.

This is why the following questions are so fundamental to (and characteristic of) science:

- What makes up the unity of an animal? Is it the atomic parts, the organs, or the body and soul?
- What does the 'rational animal' (human) include? Does it include body? Soul? Does it include accidents? If it does not, does it exclude them?[286]

Theaetetus introduces us to these sorts of problems from a playful distance, through the analogy of syllables and elements. It suggests some fruitful avenues of inquiry. For instance, the distinction between *part* and *element* is philosophically pregnant. As stated above, 'part' has a different implication than 'element'; it implies a necessary relationship to a whole which an element only distantly or distinctly suggests (204a). A part is properly a part by being a *partaker* of a kind of whole. An element, on the other hand, has a less intrinsic relation to the whole—more easily associated with an *all*.[287] An element, depending how used, might express a certain indifference to the whole.

The part of one animal, a leg (a part which may belong to other animals), is a part which only exists as part of an animal. One never finds a leg other than in animals. A table has legs only metaphorically. An element on the other hand does not have so definite a relationship to things. One may find nitrogen in dirt, in a plant, and in the leg of an animal. Further, that

---

[286] It is through these sorts of considerations that philosophers clarify categories or terms such as accident and essence; form and material; property, part, element, and cause, genus and species.

[287] Regarded from the cosmic perspective, we might revisit this distinction with wonder.

very atom of nitrogen may or may not remain where it is, even while that specific animal's life continues. Because of this, there is a reason we might logically divide a person into body and soul, but not as readily into nitrogen, calcium, oxygen, and hydrogen.

If we treat parts and elements indifferently, we are likely to fail to understand the nature of things: the real formalities and finalities we encounter. No sound biologist, psychologist, theologian or philosopher would do this. What this might suggest is that biologists and those who study the hard sciences sometimes veer off hastily into philosopher when they speak reductively and describe a flora and fauna as nothing but chemistry or physics. Peter Kreeft refers to this as the "nothing buttery" fallacy.[288] Etienne Gilson presents a powerful critique of this sort of reductionism in his work *From Aristotle to Darwin and Back Again* (esp. p.133-134).[289]

The part/element distinction allows us to treat the things of the world as the truly present themselves, not simply as indistinguishable and independent arithmetic units. The things of the world present themselves in great diversity. But this is a diversity not only of mere arrangement, of various kinds of heaps. As the example of nitrogen hints, there is a diversity of being as such—of modes of existence. Our consideration of elements, parts, and wholes suggests that there are things whose unity (and thus existence) is actually more or less perfect, things which exist or *are* more than other things. Somethings exists only in relation to wholes, whether the universe as a whole or as parts to an independent substance. This is why quantum particles are so indefinite—they remain

---

[288] Kreeft and Dougherty, *Socratic Logic*, 109.

[289] Etienne Gilson, *From Aristotle to Darwin and Back Again: A Journey in Final Causality, Species, and Evolution* (San Francisco: Ignatius Press, 2009).

indeterminate without higher or more perfect substances acting upon them and actualizing them.

The more perfect substances, those things which more properly deserve the name *being* are more definite in their nature and less free, as compared to Nitrogen, because their existence is less arbitrary, less instrumental, and more perfectly directed to an end (to the realization of some kind of organizational unity).[290] Perfection does not lend itself to being haphazard (*Metaphysics* 12.10, 1075a11-24).

For this reason, we cannot be lazy in our thinking. We have to attend to the real and meaningful patterns of things, to consider carefully the relationship and distinction between elements, parts, and wholes. A human being may have a body that is materially constituted by atoms, but that body is more than just atoms.[291] If we attend to beings in their true and hierarchical unity, we will be sure to know the world better. This does mean we will have to attend to the various modes in which a thing can exist, to the variety of ways in which something can said to be one. This simply means we will be sensitive to the analogy of being.

A chart may be helpful in thinking about various modes of being and unity, such as elements, parts, mixture vs. composition, an all, a whole or unity. Neither the rows nor columns are meant to be conceptually equivalent, though some parallelism should suggest itself. The point is to compare and contrast various modes of division and of unity. Not all of these divisions are as precise or meaningful as others. Not all the forms of unity are of the same mode or grade.

---

[290] Redpath, "The One and the Many."

[291] At the end of the day, some unities are more governing, some less so. There is a reason that being and unity are transcendentals—that a thing is one precisely *insofar* as it exists or has being.

Ways of *Part*itioning: Parts; Wholes; Elements; Syllables?

a. Sandwich	b. Cake	c. Water	d.* Human	e.* Human	f.* Human	g.* Human	h.* Human	i.* Human	j.* Human	k. Tree
Eggs	Eggs	Hydrogen	Arms	Body	Hydrogen	Electrons	Rational	Blood	First 12" of the body	Trunk
Bacon	Sugar	Oxygen	Legs	Soul	Oxygen	Neutrons	animal	Bones	2nd 12"	Leaves
Cheese	Flour		Torso		Carbon	Protons		Heart	3rd 12"	Roots
bread	Milk		Head		Nitrogen			Wax	4th 12"	
	Butter							Ears	5th 12"	
	Baking Soda							Cells	6th 12"	
								Air		

*You can substitute 'organic body' or 'animal' for d-g & i-k

Here are relevant questions concerning the table:
1. In what way do these various elements or parts exist in the whole? Compare *a* and *b*. We cannot say that eggs are in an egg sandwich in the same way that they are in a cake. Is *c* more like *a* or *b*?

2. In what way are these parts or elements separable from the whole? Consider each example.

3. Which parts properly the divide or measure the whole? Which divide it randomly according to some extrinsic consideration or accidental measure? For instance, we can divide a person by body and soul or by groupings of 12 inches.

4. Which should properly be called parts? Which, elements? It depends on the subject or whole!

5. Which treats the subject as a *whole*? Which treat the subject as an *all*? Are some subjects more truly wholes?

6. Do all the elements exist in the whole *actually* or do some exist *potentially* or *somewhat altered qua potency or act*?

In meditating on these questions, we consider the problem of the one and many from various perspectives:
- whether a whole and an all are the same
- Part/syllables vs. elements
- essential vs. accidental parts
- actual vs. potential parts
- the variety of substances which exist

- Whether there are natural wholes
- Whether a whole is more intelligible by its parts (or parts by a whole)
  - And what *kind* of parts would make the whole most intelligible—form and matter are strong candidates
- Whether an atomic (elemental) description is ultimately the most definitive. Again, it may depend on the subject or 'whole'.
  - This means determining whether everything is ultimately the same thing or same 'stuff', distinguished only by atomic quantity or composition.
- Is everything fundamentally quantitative (number)?

The Third Act of the Mind: Reasoning (Syllogism)

"As judging is more complex than simple apprehension, reasoning is more complex than judging. As judging moves from one act of simple apprehension (the subject) to another (the predicate), reasoning moves from two or more judgments...to another." -*Socrates Logic*, Peter Kreeft[292]

When we speak, we generally combine words together. Words themselves are usually a combination of letters (though not always). The etymology of λόγος (and its verbal form λέγω) suggest just this, that reason and speech are intimately related to an act of *selecting, arranging, gathering,* or *ordering* a complex whole. Plato frequently recurs to the image of weaving when describing reason. These connotations reflect the character of what is called the *third act of the mind* and most characteristic of human cognition: *rea-soning*, whose product is the *syllogism*. What this suggests is that reason gather what is many and unifies it through logos.

While logos is often used to express apprehension or judgment (the first and second acts of the mind), it is most characteristically displayed in discursive mental activity, an act of knowing one thing *through* another.[293] "It is characteristic of

---

[292] Kreeft and Dougherty, *Socratic Logic*, 28.

[293] Kreeft states, "The larger, older meaning of 'rational' includes wisdom, intuition, understanding of the nature of essence of a thing (the 'first act of the mind'), self-knowledge, moral conscience (awareness of good and evil), and the appreciation of beauty, as well as reasoning and rational calculation (the 'third act of the mind'). Even in this larger, ancient sense of 'reason', human reason has weakness as well as power. Compared with angels (pure spirits), we

reason to move from one thing to another."²⁹⁴ Reason operates by moving from a know to an unknown, discovering something new by means of something already grasped or understood in some respect. Discursive reason *reasons* then by seeing how one thing is somehow connected with or already *within* another. Reason can do this because it reflects on beings which are somehow complex, which have features or parts which are, in a sense, woven together with, contained within, or that relate to other things.

It is through reason that something known in one sense can come to be known in another. Thus, reason is intimately concerned with learning. Through logos and syllogism, we attend to causes and effects, means and ends, parts and wholes, past and present, and the relations of things. This discursive and collating work is emblematic of human thought and human life.²⁹⁵

Reasoning, as such, begins with what is known, however imperfectly. Treating the known as a principle or premise, that which is unknown is made manifest. What comes first to our reason is prior logically then, but not necessarily in being. Our reasoning moves in this manner from what is unclear in itself, but known by us, to what is clear simply (Physics I.1).

The product of this kind of reasoning is a syllogism. When the premises are not explicit, the expressed argument is called an enthymeme, rather than a syllogism. Syllogism (or its scientific form, demonstration) arrives at a conclusion by means

---

are like slowly crawling insects: we must gather all our data from our five senses, and we must usually proceed slowly, step-by-step, deducing or inducing one thing from another." Ibid., 186.

²⁹⁴ St. Thomas Aquinas and Mauer, "Commentary on Boethius's De Trinitate." See footnote 49.

²⁹⁵ Thomas, *Summa Theologica*, Complete English ed. (Christian Classics, 1981), pt. III. q.11, a3.

of premises. Every logos is not equal; therefore, not all syllogistic reasoning is scientific (or demonstrative).

The mark of scientific reasoning is that it begins with what is not merely opinion but with what is known to be truly first and causal. Only from such premises can a conclusion be known as necessary and known scientifically. To know a thing scientifically is to know t in its cause, by what is essential or essentially related to a thing (per se). It is only when something is so grasped that one is said to have knowledge unequivocally. Only then is a syllogism is said to be demonstrative. There is a meaningful difference then between a merely valid chain of reasoning and a demonstrative syllogism. This is the difference between knowing *a fact* and knowing *why*. Science, as Aristotle says, is the search for the *why* (Physics II.3). Science is a relational habit which sees into the why or nature of things. We can grasp the intentional causal character of science by comparing two syllogisms:

> All the animals in this field are human.
> John is one of the animals in this field.
> John is human.

This reasoning is formally correct. The argument is true and does not violate any rules of logic. But it fails to be demonstrative or scientific in the strict sense because it does not prove its conclusion through an essence or a necessary cause. It is *accidental* that all the animals in a field happen to be human. The conclusion that John is human is therefore not a result of knowing anything about the nature of animals. The conclusion is merely the result of observation and a circumstantial accident. It produces not scientific knowledge, only information. We can compare the previous syllogism to this one:

> All animals are that which have composite bodies.
> All that have composite bodies can suffer decomposition (mortality).

All animals can suffer decomposition (mortality).

Here the middle term (composite) links animal and decomposition. We not only know that animals *can* die, but one of the reasons *why* they can die. We know the material cause or potency for decomposition. Through this kind of reasoning, we move beyond facts and discover the causes of things. The mark of good reasoning then is not mere logic validity, but insight into the nature of things, into what they are and why.

Let us take one last example, adapted from Aristotle's *Posterior Analytics* I.4, which will be helpful in our upcoming and final reading. Let us imagine that we have proved that the interior angles of all isosceles triangles are equal to two right angles. We would certainly be correct. Further, it would not be the case (as in the field full of humans) that such a property or conclusion would be sheerly accidental. But this would still not be demonstrative because we would not have proved the property of its proper subject. Because of that, we would not have insight into a *why*. This is because there is a prior cause or genus which has been ignored. It is not the isosceles per se which causes this property; it is triangularity. It is by virtue of being a triangle that such a shape's three interior angles equal two right angles. We would need to know then that this feature is *common* to all triangles and not only to isosceles triangles. As we are about to see in the next reading, it matters how and why a thing is common or shared. It matters what properties are unique or specific to various kinds of beings. Therefore, in the case of these interior angles, a truly scientific proof would have to focus on triangles per se (generically) and not only a species of triangle.

We can notice something about the scientific process here. It is possible for a person to first discover a property belonging to a species and only later learn that it belongs to a genus. It is possible to discover a general (generic) cause or relation later. In fact, this is perhaps the ordinary course of experience and scientific discovery. This is precisely how reason coordinates or collates know-ledge, by moving from what is first to us, to what is first simply, and back again.

This means it is possible to mistakenly ascribe what belongs to a particular (or to a species) to what belonging to a species (or genus). It is possible to mistake what is accidental for what is necessary or what is generic for what is specific. Thus, scientific inquiry is by no means easy. There is a reason mathematics is one of the first sciences taught. Mathematics uses reason, but because its objects are purely formal, confusion of accidents and principles is less substantial. Therefore, mathematics can be learned when relatively young and is an appropriate starting place for a philosophical or liberal arts education. On the other hand, natural science, philosophy, ethics all require experience and careful distinction between a multitude of principles.

This serves to remind us that we begin with what is less clear and confused and only painstakingly move toward that which is clearer in itself: to causes, sources, and elements (Physics I.1). This is both the glory and the humility of reason: that it belongs to man to order, but that we learn to do so only slowly, through very imperfect beginnings. Man is a creature who stands in the midst of things, whose life and existence is complex. Yet, it is only by bringing unity to multitude that we experience happiness or attain to any rightful understanding of the world. We must continually order ourselves, as well as a vast multitude of things, by various principles. This is because we are neither just body or intellect; we have work *here and now*, but we are also ordained to that which is everlasting; we are called to love One who is above all others, but we are also called to love one another.

We therefore begin our lives in need of orientation, and we are continually in need of reorientation, of rediscovering the true order of things. It is a gracious thing that we need not begin from scratch. It is only through logos that this is ever accomplished. This is because the being has the character of a word. The world is itself constituted or woven together by a hidden thread, by Logos. We have a power or capacity to grasp this only because we are formed in the image of the One who constitutes all things, who weaves the world together through his Word.

It is therefore through word that we make sense of the world and ourselves. Nevertheless, it is not only the spoken word that speaks forth the being of things, even if speech holds a certain preeminence. Rather, we know the world through all the richness of our lived experience which is itself part of the woven tapestry of the Word. We must not forget that our reckoning with things is not through abstraction or the spoken word only. Our grasp of being is through a cognitionally informed encounter with being at every level of existence. Such encounters are not apart from 'speech'—they are in some respect the sources of our poetry. We might even characterize this as an intuitive or immediate encounter with logos, expressed in the nature of all things (Psalm 19:1-6). What we experience, day after day, night after night, is that all beings are all self-communicative—communicative of their constitutive formalities or logoi, but also communicative of their Source. We too are part of this communication of God's glory. It is our glory, as the bearers of God's image, to learn to receive, rejoice in, and even direct what might be described as a cosmic liturgy. This cosmic-priestly office is precisely what we find the expressed in Psalm 148. The Psalmist *gathers* together through the command of word all the heavens and earth, sun and moon, angels and men, young and old, water and fire, and directs them to the worship of God.

The whole world is capable of signification; thus, Heraclitus instructs us to listen to the logos.[296] Nevertheless, it is uniquely man who *reads* this order, who knows signs as signs—who reads the complex tapestry of things. Reason is our preeminent and characteristic mode of receiving and expressing the truth. Speech is, again, a fitting medium for our reflection because it is itself a reflection of reality (*Phaedo* 99d-e).[297]

Socrates attends in Act III to the analogical features of being and speech. Just as things themselves are in some way complex, in some way woven together, so too are our words, our very speeches and thoughts which reflect the being of things. The theme of weaving is especially prominent in the *Sophist* (259e) and the *Phaedo*.[298] Plato tapestry attempts to unite not only terms, but logos and myth (story), the forms and those things which they constitute, as well as the forms themselves. Plato expressly relies on a correlation between speech and reality. We too rely on this analogy or correlation throughout our daily life, from moment to moment. Philosophy and theology merely bring this correlation to our attention by exploring its Source. It is no small wonder that logos can be explored through logos, that it can even search after its first Cause.

We can conclude with two points. First, an inquiry into knowledge has led us to inquire into speech (logos). It has led us to something at the heart of human life, to something akin to the underlying structure and cause of reality (*Meno* 81d).

---

[296] Fragment 50. Heraclitus and Robinson, Fragments, 37.

[297] The forms are described both by Plato and Aristotle as logos, as intelligible organizing principles which make things what they are. Cf. Psalm 19:1; Gen. 1:11, 2:19

[298] See Brann, Kalkavage (p.3-5, 17-18) on weaving in the *Phaedo* and also Mouzala on the *Sophist* 2019

We are thus partakers of logos, but not unequivocally its source. Logos leads us beyond itself. Second, if we are to reason well, that is, if we are to come to know this world better, we will have to attend carefully to logos. We will have to somehow learn to measure the good from the bad, the likely from the true. But this means we must somehow attain to a measure by which to judge logos, even while we search for such a measure *in* or by means of logos.

What a tangle! One thing reason shows is that we lack sufficient reason! Again, the question of wisdom raises its head (145d). Only a preeminent Logos could ultimately provide us with a comprehensive measure of all things. Knowledge of our limits is partly why Socrates claimed ignorance. But his deep awareness of those limits also made him ready to leave this life. He hoped to move beyond the limits of human reason (our little share of wisdom here) and gaze into a Light in which all things are made light—that which causes things both to be and to intelligible. Whether vainly or not, he hoped to look upon the face of God and live (*Phaedo* 63b; *Republic* 506b-518d).

Ninth Reading

206b-210d   Kinds of logos, Critique, & End
             Three kinds of logos; The way of difference;
             Example; A regress to opinion;
             Recapitulation

Focus Questions:
1. What are the three kinds of logos Socrates enumerates and how do they differ?
2. Why is knowledge of *difference* so important?
3. Is all knowledge based on knowing *difference*?
4. How is difference related not just to speech but to the very being of things? If we return to the idea of *nature* or to contraries intimated in the first readings (Theaetetus's character), how does nature's multitude depend on difference?
5. In reflecting on the example of Hesiod's wagon, is there more than one way of defining: giving a logos *according to parts*?
6. Why is the third and final definition in *Theaetetus* (opinion + logos) rejected by our interlocutors?
7. Has the dialogue been a failure?

Theaetetus and Socrates are not yet ready to give up on the great hope awoken by this *logos of a logos*. They do not want to give up on the claim that the **most perfect** knowledge comes (τὴν τελεωτάτην ἐπιστήμην γεγονένα) through possessing a true opinion with an account. It is remarkable that Socrates qualifies the *kind* of knowledge that comes with a logos. It suggests that there are other kinds. It suggests that knowledge is brought to perfection through logos!

Let's pause for a moment and ask what it might be for them to give a thorough account of logos. What would such an account need to comprehend? It would certainly require going beyond examples of knowledge, Theaetetus very first attempt. One might even need a knowledge that in some respect encompass all knowledge. This has been the problem of *Theaetetus* all along. We can see another reason why wisdom was mentioned early on. The very fact that we can inquire into such things suggests that we may already possess a rudimentary wisdom, but not a comprehensive form of that intellectual virtue.

In our prior reading, they rejected the statement that the elements are less knowable than the syllables (the composite *all's* or *wholes*), in part, because our experience of learning contradicts this. The elements or letters are the first thing we learn as children and therefore seem *more* intelligible than they wholes. *Physics* I.1 suggests this may be somewhat more complicated. Do we really learn letters first? We need to distinguish between the order of learning and the order of being. We might also need to distinguish various kinds of knowledge or experience.

Three kinds of logos;

In order to give this another go, Socrates suggest that a logos may signify one of three things.

- The expression of thought in speech
- To say what a thing is through its elements
- The power to say how a thing differs from another thing

An account or logos might simply mean making one's **thinking** (διάνοιαν) manifest through the voice with words and names (206d).[299] Socrates says that, in such a case, it would be

---

[299] Cf. Aristotle, *On Interpretation* 16a1-10

Commentary

just as if one formed an image of one's opinion in a mirror of flowing water.[300]

There is unmistakable similarity to this first description of logos and Socrates account of his own second sailing in the *Phaedo*. A 'second-sailing' refers to the hard-going work of rowing when, for whatever reason, one is unable to use the wind and sails. In *Phaedo* 99d-e, Socrates states that he had wished when young to inquire into being by looking directly at things but was nearly blinded. He was forced to pursue being as in a reflection through speech (logos)! Because perception alone is insufficient and misleading (blinding), just as we saw in Act I of *Theaetetus*, philosophy must have recourse to the demanding work of reason. It must look into things as reflected in logos. This mirror of flowing speech evokes two Heraclitean principles: flux and logos.

Theaetetus agrees that someone who does this *is said to speak*.

This first depiction of speech is reminiscent of perception and apprehension, insofar as those acts are in some manner a reflection of what we experience.[301] In those apprehensions and in the speeches which reflect them, we do not necessarily find scientific knowledge. But perhaps within such experiences and speeches, we find the first sources or potentialities of science. Reflection, both conceptual and verbal, express what we might in a limited sense call knowledge, though not that most perfect kind of knowing (206c).

However, if merely **showing** (ἐνδείξασθαι) what one thinks is to express knowledge, it will turn out that everyone who speaks is a knower and all speech will, in fact, be

---

[300] Logos here is primarily a kind of φημί, a bringing to light of one's thought, not apart from reason, but focusing on the speech-act or communication itself.

[301] Cf. *On Interpretation* 16a.

knowledge. This would be a disappointing return to the problems of the perception thesis in Act I.

The second kind of logos which Socrates now presents is a **power (δυνατὸν)** to answer what a thing is through its elements (206e-207a). This is the kind of logos we first began to consider in Act III, though it is being stated afresh, with a few significant distinctions.

Theaetetus requests an example and Socrates reminds him that it is the elements that demonstrate one's knowledge of a thing, rather than the syllables. He says that while Hesiod claimed a wagon is a hundred pieces of wood, it would be enough for him to say that a wagon is 'wheels, axle, box, poles, crossbar'.[302]

Though they do not examine this, the two logoi of a wagon, Hesiod's and Socrates' are significantly different. The distinction between parts and elements could not be more clearly marked. The distinction even seems to hint at a division between form and matter. The two definitions are not equal.

Socrates suggests that Hesiod might think his own description laughable, just as if one could list the letters in a name and think oneself a grammarian. He claims that one must instead give an account which enumerates all the elements of a thing, otherwise it is only opinion. The meaning of element is extremely ambiguous here. The one who spells a name correctly has listed the material elements. Socrates, however, if we take his example of the wagon parts or names, is using element to mean something like *formal principle*.

Someone who can spell a word correctly has only opinion, he says, if they do not know something else. What would this be? What kind of knowledge of letters is needed? Socrates suggests that they need to know the art (or science) of grammar.

---

[302] Hesiod, author of *Works of Days*, was a farmer and knowledgeable of such things.

Commentary

He now states this in a provocative new way. He says that one does not truly have knowledge until one has the **power** (δυνάμενον) of logos by which to go through the **very being** (τὴν οὐσίαν) of each thing by means of or through those hundred pieces. Such a person recites from beginning to end the **whole** (ὅλον) by means of or through (διὰ) the elements.

In Act I, Theaetetus had agreed that one could never arrive at knowledge without first knowing the **being** (οὐσίαν) and truth of a thing (186c). Being is now here correlated with the *whole*. Further, one is said to be able to give an account of the being or whole through a logos of the elements. By means of this logos, such a person is said to possess an **art and knowledge about the being of the wagon** (τεχνικόν τε καὶ ἐπιστήμονα περὶ ἁμάξης οὐσίας), not merely a true opinion.

In this light, Hesiod's hundred pieces of wood seem radically different than Socrates's axle, wheel, etc. One definition is merely an arithmetic enumeration, what amounts to a heap that is indifferent to the whole. The other recites the whole by means of or *through* the elements. The whole (the wagon) is *interwoven* throughout the parts by means of a unifying the account. Thus while 100 pieces of wood is merely a account of *matter* and is no more or less an account of a wagon than anything else made of wood, Socrates account is *specific* to the whole. This is the knowledge of a thing's being (οὐσίας). We could again reflect on their discussion of number and the number of the army (204d-e). It may be that not every enumeration is equal.

Socrates then asks Theaetetus if he accepts this, that to go through a thing by each of its elements is a logos, but to do so through the syllables or anything bigger is irrational (207d). Our lack of clarity about elements and syllables muddies the water here. After all, Hesiod's 100 pieces of wood seems much more like material elements, while Socrates' parts actually seem more like syllables.

Socrates continually describes this kind of account as a *way*, an *order*, or *road through* parts to a whole. We can recall that the logos has been characterized as something that weaves things together. To weave implies the relation of parts and wholes; it implies order.

Socrates next evaluates this kind of logos by looking into the sort of knowledge it would be (207d). He asks if a man who thinks that 'theta' belongs to '**The**aetetus" but that 'tau' and 'eta' belong to '**The**odorus' should be considered a knower (207e). Such a man only accidently spells the first syllable of Theaetetus's name correctly. We know this because he misspells the *same* syllable in Theodorus's name. This again draws our attention to a distinction between knowing particulars and knowing a principle or rule. There is a difference between perceptual knowing (or memory) and scientific/artful knowing. The knowledge of one is virtually accidental.

Is a scientific logos chiefly concerned with *elemental* matter or with some *elemental* principle? On the one hand, the person who errs can yet go through the whole (Theaetetus) by its letters (elements). On the other hand, there is a different way of knowing possessed by the grammarian and it is this second mode which Socrates is interested in here.

Theaetetus concludes that the one who errs in spelling 'Theodorus', who is **having such a condition** is not **yet** a knower (οὕτως ἔχοντα μήπω εἰδέναι 208a). His 'not yet' suggests that this person is, nevertheless, in a good position to become an epistemic knower.

This person is said to be without knowledge, even while he possesses a true opinion with a logos (true opinion about Theaetetus' name) (208b). If this is so, right opinion with a logos cannot **yet** (οὔπω) be called knowledge. Socrates again qualifies the conclusion, and Theaetetus agrees. They have not *yet* shown what sort of logos would amount to having knowledge. Recurring to a theme of Act II, we might state that

Commentary

it might not only be the kind of logos that matters here, but the mode of holding (hexis) such a logos which would most perfectly constitute knowledge. Theaetetus' statement above hints at such a hexis (οὕτως ἔχοντα μήπω εἰδέναι 208a).

The hope of defining knowledge seems about to fade away (208b-c). Still, one **form** (εἶδος) remains of the three. (It is no accident he characterizes their definitions by eidos here.) The final form, says Socrates, is that which *most people would give*. I admit, I am skeptical that most people would ever give such a precise definition of logos. This *logos of logos* does not seem obvious, but rather something very *specific*, something proper to science and philosophy—to knowers.

The way of difference;
208d

The third kind of logos is the ability to say how a thing differs. It is also described as a form of *having*. It is:

> "**to have** a **sign** by which to say how a thing **differs from all other things**" (ὅπερ ἂν οἱ πολλοὶ εἴποιεν, τὸ ἔχειν τι σημεῖον εἰπεῖν ᾧ τῶν ἁπάντων διαφέρει τὸ ἐρωτηθέν).

σημεῖον: A sign or semeion (σημεῖον) is a mark by which something is identified.[303] As sign may be the mark, trace, or the track of a thing.[304] The Liddell & Scott Greek-English Lexicon gives a number of examples:

---

[303] Plato refers to Electra's recognition of her twin bother Orestes in the *Libation Bearers*. She knows him partly by the sign of his footprint. He clearly has this in mind with the wax block (193c, see also Sachs p.99 n.48).

[304] Liddell et al., *A Greek-English Lexicon*.

a tomb; constellations; a signal (such as for battle); a standard or flag; a landmark; a boundary or limit; a device upon a shield; a watchword; birthmark; token; proof; instance; example; symptom; critical mark; a mathematical point (Euclid).[305]

These uses of 'sēmeîon' shows considerable overlap with ὅρος, which also means a *boundary* or a *definition*.[306] They both overlap with Plato's descriptions of the forms, those looks or limits by which things are known. A form, as the shape, limit, or the look of a thing, would *signify* the distinctive mode of a things being. It would be that intelligible *difference* by which a thing stands out and exists as what it is. Such a form would be first indicated by perceptual *differences*.[307] A sign or pattern would be that by which a thing is known. It would be closely related or associated with *what* a thing is (its *distinctive* nature). A sign would communicate them the sort of thing which stands before us: the way a fisherman distinguishes one fish from another; a birder distinguishes birds; or most of us with less expertise distinguish cats from dogs.

It is here in Act III that we finally consider more carefully what characterizes the inner content of knowledge (episteme)—we consider what *distinguishes* it from thought more generally. In Act II, it is made clear that a knower should be able to identify that which he knows (i.e., the Aviary). But here we examine the sign *by which* we are said to know a thing. Just as the ring-necked dove is distinguished from a pigeon by its ring, Socrates suggests knowledge generically operates by intelligible signs, by what are sometimes called *specific differences*. Knowledge of this sort of difference even distinguishes episteme as itself a *specific* form of knowledge.

---

[305] Ibid.
[306] Euclid's text begins with horoi (definitions).
[307] See the treatment of sensation in *Phaedo* 74b-75b

διαφέρει: To explore difference, we can say a bit more abouts signs. A sign signifies to us the *presence* of some specific thing—it is an awareness of that thing as *that*. It could be a sensible signal or an interior impression (an idea), perhaps even a locational *difference*, but there must be some characteristic which differentiates one thing from another. Otherwise, we could hardly be aware of a thing as such. For instance, we regularly differentiate the letter 'x' from the letter 'y', cats from dogs, day from night, happy from sad, healthy from sick, good from evil, and bicycles from unicycles. In each case, there is something which alerts us to the *specific* charac-ter of what we are attending to.[308] The line of the x crosses through it; night is usually dark or darker; unicycles have only one wheel. When this happens, when we grasp a sign which alerts us to difference, if indeed the sign by which we *pick that thing out from all others* is that which uniquely constitutes the thing, we are attending to what in philosophy and logic is called a *specific difference* (διαφέρει).[309]

---

[308] Species is sometimes more precisely used as distinct from form to refer to the mental concept or logical character of a thing. Thus when I know what a soul is, the form I know is an idea-species, a concept. There is not in my intellect an actual human soul which I am knowing. Whereas the actual human being has a soul or form which makes him a man. He does not have a species or concept that makes him what he is, but a soul (a form in the unrestricted sense).

[309] A specific difference is not something *added* to a form. Rather it names the aspect of form which sets it apart within a genus. Thus no animal could exists if it were *unspecified* or merely *animal*. A thing is not a genus. But each specific animal is not a species added to a genus. Rather, it is what it is by being a specified expression of a generic possible mode of being. Man is a rational animal, not rational + animal. Rational is man's specific difference, but man's species is not

A sign can also be communicated in speech when we signify anything (either interiorly or to others). This speech act, however, depends on becoming aware of things as distinct from other things. We only have a logos of one thing because it is distinct from and we can articulative its distinction from other things. It must be able to stand apart from other things in our thought and speech. If all things were the same, if all was one, we could not speak. There would be no need to and, further, such a word would be beyond our limited power of reason (logos).

Thus the fact that we speak reveals that we are in touch with a diversity of things and in touch with them in light of their diversity. Nevertheless, this whole dialogue has shown that discovery of their precise logos is by no means easy or automatic. It is sometimes at the very limit of human power. Despite such difficulties, throughout the dialogue, Plato and Theaetetus (and we along with them) have made and understood countless *distinctions*. We have divided, judged, and differentiated, and we have done so with a knowledge of difference—whether scientific or otherwise. We recognize the difference between square and oblong, perception and opinion, between good and evil. If we tried, we might even come to give a *specific* account (a logos) of some of these things.

This is simply to say that we operate implicitly by a recognition of differences which are by no means haphazard. The work of making these differences plain and dividing things rightly however is the hard work of philosophy, Socrates' *second sailing*. We are capable of dividing things by genus, species, property, and accident, but we are not always clear which division we have made or should make. This shows that we are simultaneously knowers and not-knowers.

'rational' because rational by itself is neither a form nor a species. A species always belongs to a genus, while difference by itself is what logicians refer to as *note*.

Commentary

Just because we apprehend a thing does not mean are able (or yet able) to give a formal or specific logos of it. But if the form of a thing causes it to be what it is, causes it to stand out in the word in some distinctive fashion, then it communicates to us something of its formal or specific nature. Our experience of things is therefore an experience of things which express their unique sources and causes. Through experiences something of the being of things is *signified* to us. To know *about* a thing is in then an excellent beginning to science. We can recall Theaetetus examples of know-ledge at the beginning of the dialogue. Where would we begin without such examples?

What we apprehend implicitly reveals the kinds of things we apprehend. Experience by itself might not be a comprehensive grasp of being but it presents us with material for thought. The diversity or our experience (of this 'material') is precisely a diversity of *significations* of specific kinds of being. Therefore, the formal natures of things are available to us through their effects.

An example of *difference* used by medieval philosophers was *risibility* (the property of or capacity for laughter). They considered such a property to be a *sign* of intelligence. There could be no other causes of laughter as such other than some form of intelligence. This of course means distinguishing laughter from comparable noises. Similarly, all our distinctions are based on such signs.

This reminds us that we work from effects to causes, from signs to what they signify.[310] We do not see essences directly.

---

[310] Plato would argue that the particular things we sense, remind us to analyze the forms we already know. Aristotle argues that we must apprehend such forms before we can know them. For Aristotle, the actual cat is the cause of us knowing what a cat is. Real cats,

Knowledge in its most proper sense is therefore not perception. Perception communicates signs or differences to us. But we apprehend these specific realities only confusedly. Each real whole we apprehend (*that dog there*) is more than an essence. Only through abstraction (a kind of division) and reasoning do we discern accident from property, and property from essence. Thus 'furry-barker' might be a good beginning, but not a resting place if we wish to define dog. We are often capable of deeper knowledge than such accidents.

But again, we do not look directly at essences. We see real beings of all different kinds and from such experiences, we come to distinguish them according to what those differences signify. We thereby abstract and approximate essential differences. We have real apprehension of essence even when our division or analysis remain imperfect, even when we have not 'looked' into or plumbed the depths of every being. All this implies certain limitations.

It is fitting to reflect on limitation at the end of a dialogue concerning knowledge. Limitation is reflected in the idea of difference. It also has implications related to our scientific aspirations: it simultaneously suggests something about human greatness and our need for humility. As St. Thomas said in the Prologue to his *Commentary on the Apostle's Creed*:

> But our manner of knowing is so weak that no philosopher could perfectly investigate the nature of even one little fly. We even read that a certain philosopher spent thirty years in solitude in order to know the nature of the bee.

Some things are indeed closer to us than others. We may be more ready to define justice than gravity, or a human than

---

for him, are not just signs which remind us to recollect. Rather, they communicate or signify their nature to us through their sensible effects.

a squirrel. In some cases, we seem to approach a most perfect kind of knowledge (episteme), while in others, it seems we can hardly distinguish accidents from properties.

This should not be discouraging. We truly apprehend something of the *what* (the form) of all that we encounter, insofar as they in some manner signify themselves sensibly.[311] In a remarkable manner, to simply name a thing is already to set it apart from other beings, both from things which are, and from those things which are not. Thus, all our names express that we do truly grasp the reality of things with more or less precision. We take hold of a thing in a name and somehow set it apart as *different* from other things. We know that *that* thing is not some other thing.

In light of this distinction, following Aristotle, St. Thomas divides knowing *that* a thing is from knowing *what* a thing is. "We know a thing in two ways: in one way when we know that it is, and in another way when we know what it is."[312] He thus affirms that not all our knowledge is episteme. On the other hand, he also states:

> It should be noticed, however, that we cannot know that a thing is without knowing in some way what it is, either perfectly or at least confusedly. As the Philosopher says, we know things defined [the whole] before we know the parts of their definition. For if a person knows that man exists and wants to find out what man is by definition, he must know the meaning of the term "man." And this is possible only if he somehow forms a concept of what he knows to exist, even though he does not know its

---

[311] To apprehend justice is not merely a sense experience but includes sense experience informed by rational knowledge of good and evil. We do not apprehend justice without experiencing it as enacted bodily, but justice is not a sensation per se.

[312] *De Trinitate* q.6 article 3 reply

definition. That is to say, he forms a concept of man by knowing a proximate or remote genus and accidental characteristics which reveal him externally. For our knowledge of definitions, like that of demonstrations, must begin with some previous knowledge.[313]

Thomas insists that there is difference between knowing *that* a thing is (its existence or being) and knowing *what* a thing is (its essence); nevertheless, he simultaneously argues that knowledge of a thing can never entirely include some knowledge of what it is.[314]

Socrates here in our dialogue is describing a preeminent characteristic of knowledge. One is thought to know when one can define it. The discussion implies that Socrates has an *essential definition* in mind, one that would include the specific difference pertaining to knowledge. Such a definition must state both a thing's genus and species. What is common and unique. This truly is a comprehensive way of knowing![315] But again, this is not to say that such knowing is easy to come by. Nor does this mean we can know all things in this manner. In

---

[313] *De Trinitate* q.6 article 3 reply

[314] Thus in the argument from which the previous quotation comes, St. Thomas states that we do not and cannot have scientific knowledge of God. Further, we do not know Him (his very Being or essence) in this life. Nevertheless, we can know that God exists and we can know something of God in accordance with three modes: negation (he is *not* like *this*: a creature, bodily, limited, spatial, ignorant, etc.); cause (creatures exist *because* of God); exemplar (all perfections such as wisdom, strength, goodness are from One who is the perfection of Wisdom, Strength, Goodness, not generically the same, but as source). Because God's existence is simple, we do not know a *little* of him, but know of him by way of judging him as exemplar, cause, and also by negation.

[315] Such preeminence would be meaningless without a scientific habit and intentionality, the personal grasp of truth.

fact, there are at least two fundamental requirements to know a thing epistemically—to give a thing this *kind* of definition. The first is that we must be capable of engaging it, capable of becoming familiar with it. The second, presupposed by the first, is that such an object would be a certain *kind of thing*!

We only define essentially by stating a difference, how something is species of a genus (proper or remote).[316] Nor is there an essence of anything that is not a species of a genus—that is not a *kind* of thing.[317] This is not just the rules of some intellectual game; this accurately expresses the facultative limits of our mental powers, as well as the ontological conditions by which a thing has a definition and exists as a limited being. This makes sense if one recalls that a definition expresses the limit eidos or boundary of a being. We will never give a proper *definition* to an unbounded or unlimited being.[318] Such a being could not have a definition and we could not know that being *epistemically*. Therefore, God, very Being (I am that I am), has no definition.[319] God is, as John F. Wippel

---

[316] All definitions imply genus and species in some respect, but not always strictly or properly. My cat could loosely be said to be in the *genus* of 'things in my house'. We have therefore no proper concept or definition of being. We know it through an act of judgment.

[317] Aristotle, *Metaphsyics* 7. This is why we cannot properly define the ultimate genera, those highest predicaments or categories (genus, quality, quantity, place, time, position, relation, having, passion, action).

[318] Aristotle states in *Metaphysics* 4.2 that "right from the start being and unity have genera," which is a way of saying that the beings which we encounter are always beings of various kinds and known as such.

[319] Thus we know God through effects (the creation and revelation) and not by apprehension or episteme in the strict sense. We form judgements about God based on evidence. Faith forms

says, "uncontracted Being."[320] God's existence is not contracted to some limited form or mode of being. He is being simply.

We can form no 'concept' of a nature or being that is wholly uncircumscribed. While we can judge that God exists, we do not judge him to exists by possessing a knowledge of his nature. We know on that he must be because there must be a cause being, but who is nevertheless not a creature and not limited. Our knowledge of God is therefore negative and positive. But if we recall what Thomas has argued, that to know *that* a being exists is to know in *some manner* what that being is, we can say that we are not without signs of the divine nature (Romans 1:20). God whom we know as cause of all things, who is yet *not* limited like the creature, must yet be the source of all perfections, the exemplar of all being. We can therefore ascribe to him all good things, for he is Goodness itself, even while we must deny that we know his goodness in itself.

Every definition (good or bad) expresses something as a species of a genus. If I think of a color, I think of some *specific shade*. If I think of color itself, I think of some *kind* of visual

---

judgements about God which surpass that which our limited evidence alone can supply. Faith is aided by and considers evidence, but forms conclusions through an act of the will strengthened by grace. Faith results in and is also caused by the love of One whom we do not see, by an apprehension that he is Good.. This is why Thomas teaches, contra Anselm or Descartes, that we do not possess a concept of perfection (of God), but instead by an act of judgment reason from the creature to the creator (Romans 1). If the intellect were in no way darkened, this act of judgment might be nearly immediate and certain for all mature people. Such a judgment can be based on enthymeme rather than an explicit syllogism.

[320] John F. Wippel, *The Metaphysical Thought of Thomas Aquinas: From Finite Being to Uncreated Being*, Monographs of the Society for Medieval and Renaissance Philosophy no. 1 (Washington, D.C: Catholic University of America Press, 2000), 212, 232.

quality. The cup I drink from is a *sort* of *container*. Hunger is a kind of feeling. Is clay a kind of earth (147c)? Socrates' initial pattern (clay is earth mixed with fluid) seems like an example of this sort of definition. We can understand that definition in two ways. Clay might merely be a heap of two elements (a sort of mixture or composition), or it might be considered a certain *kind of* earth (moist earth). It depends whether clay remains fundamentally two *elements* or when mixed together becomes a *syllable* or *word* with some one new form.

We can ask the same thing about our current definition of knowledge: Is an opinion with a logos a *species* of opinion? Similarly, this depends whether a logos joined to an opinion merely mixes with it, or when combined *specifies* and transforms opinion into something new.[321] To define these things well, to understand them, it seems we need to know how to divide them. To do this, we have to know something about genus and species. We also need to attend carefully to the things themselves and the ways in which they are one. A ham sandwich has a very different sort of unity then the original pig from which the ham comes.

The act of division has all along implied a vague idea of genus and species. Division also implies that we are concerned with modal or circumscribed being—things which are limited or created. This is why division is a fundamental methodology of all science and has its expression in so many other areas of life. The Tree of Porphyry, logical division, categorization (such as that encountered in the *Sophist*), the classification of animals, the organization of names in a phonebook, all reflect this mental act of grasping difference, differences which

---

[321] Whether we consider opinion or earth, we must discern whether the underlying matter is fundamentally changed by the specific difference (logos or moisture).

belong only to and the diversity of limited beings. The famous 'featherless biped' of Socrates is based on this principle.

We see this in more radical ways, such as in the promise of divine judgment or division (Psalm 1). God will one day separate the just and unjust. God is the true judge who divides according to Truth. He is in fact the cause of division for he is the cause of limited being. This is why judgment ultimately belongs to him and to his comprehensive Word (Hebrews 4:12; Matt. 25).

τῶν ἁπάντων

From all other things: This phrase is provocative. It may mean we have to distinguish:

- One kind from another (cats from dogs)
- One kind from all other kinds (cats from all animals, material substances, or beings)
    - Implicitly (by at least knowing this *one* being is *specifically*)
    - Explicitly (by knowing every single being specifically)[322]
- One particular from another (Theaetetus from Theodorus)
- One particular from *all* those which are same kind (Theaetetus from all humans)

First, if to know a thing or encounter it is engage with that which is a species of a genus, then definitionally, to truly know a thing seems to imply knowing *both* that which is common and that which is specific about them! Of course, to know the genus would again thrust one upon knowing that which is *relatively* specific, insofar as I distinguish one genus from

---

[322] Contextually, it is unlikely Socrates intends this last sense. We might note, that in designating something an animal, one has already marked it off from all non-animals.

another. In other words, a genus is both something common as well as a kind of distinction/ A problem of regress is lurking in the shadows here and will come to the fore momentarily.[323]

Second, there is the problem of turning knowledge into something merely negative. Distinction is not merely negation: 'x' is *not* all these things. This is because we distinguish by positive signs even while those signs signify by being distinctive from others. They stand out as particular because they are indeed a certain mode of being which is constituted by contrary oppositions, such as distinctive colors, shapes, acts, sizes, etc.[324]

Ferdinand de Saussure expressed this analogically in his *Course in General Linguistics*. He argues that a word, considered within a system of other spoken words, is 'dependent' and 'differential'.[325] It stands out by being different from other words. But considered as a unit, the word itself has 'signification' and is 'independent'.[326] For instance, when I distinguish living from dead, I do not merely think *not dead*, but have certain properties in mind. When I distinguish the mind from an inert rock, I do not mean, *not like rocks*. When I think of yellow, I do not think of all the colors it is *not*. Some concepts may in indeed be relative, but the act of knowing (or defining) is not merely the knowledge of negation or contrary opposition. We know things positively even as we know them as distinct from other things. If they were not limited, they could neither be

---

[323] Aristotle's categories or predicaments were considered the ultimate genera or modes of being under which creatures fall. Therefore, they could not be strictly or essentially defined. They stand at the limits of ontological analysis.

[324] Redpath, "The One and the Many."

[325] Ferdinand de Saussure, *Course in General Linguistics* (Open Court, 1986), 65–70, 11–120.

[326] Saussure, *Course in General Linguistics*.

known nor distinguished. If we could not distinguish something, we would not know it as a specific kind of thing.[327]

Example;
Such a logos (a logos of difference) would be something like saying that the sun is the **brightest** (λαμπρότατόν) of the heavenly things that goes around the earth (208d).

The sun is thus *one of many things* in the heavens going about the earth. In knowing the sun, we know something common then, but we also have a sign by which to distinguish it from others—it is the *brightest* of those heavenly things.

Our account of logos seems to be pitting the common (genus) against the specific difference. Is this logical? If one did not know the sun was the brightest, would one not know the sun? It is hard to imagine someone not knowing this, at least implicitly. Again, we need to keep in mind the distinction between other kinds of knowing (here characterized as opinion) and episteme. This is because opinion and apprehension sometimes potentially contain what episteme actually makes explicit. Similarly, a genus potentially contains its species (and vice versa, albeit in a different manner).

As long as one fixes upon that which is common and not that which distinguishes a thing, Socrates argues, one will have an opinion (not knowledge) and the logos one has will

---

[327] The Paramedian problem is again rearing its head. What does it mean to distinguish one being from another *being*? After all, everything we know is a being in some respect. We are first aware of the things we know, precisely insofar as they *are*. However, this is not apart from their being *in a certain way*. While being is in one sense our first 'concept' or experience, it is not a proper concept. We know it by judgement of our experience of modal being. See *Metaphysics* III.3-5 on why being and unity are not properly the genera of all things.

remain about *all those things* but not about *it*. We might wish Socrates was more explicit. Does he mean that the logos or knowledge is about *other things* but not *at all* about it, or rather that the logos not about it *only*? Surely, one who truly grasps that which is common has some knowledge of a thing, for instance its genus (or a property). Wouldn't a logos of any kind whatsoever have to expresses some *difference* or division?

Socrates concludes that when one has right opinion about any being and adds a difference to distinguish it from other things, one will have become a knower (208e). Without this, one has only opinion.

A Regress to opinion;
He then states that on closer examination there is a problem. Their definition is like a shaded sketch that looked good from a distance, but not up close. The image would be *generically like* but not specifically, or perhaps such an image is expressive only of accidents. The term Socrates uses (σκιαγραφήματος) may refer either to a *dream image* or to a *shaded painting*, perhaps a landscape. He certainly means that their account does not seem to hold up to logical scrutiny; it exhibits some of the same problems as did their other definitions of knowledge.

He gives an example. If Socrates only has an account of something about Theaetetus which Theaetetus has in common with all other men, than he has opinion about Theaetetus (209a). But once he adds a difference which distinguishes Theaetetus from all others, he then has knowledge. But how in the world then could his previous opinion be *about* Theaetetus (208b)? According to their argument, that opinion would be no more about him than anyone else.

To think that Theaetetus has a nose, eyes and a mouth could not make one think of Theaetetus any more than of Theodorus.

Is Socrates correct? Does this 'opinion' really fail to distinguish Theaetetus *at all*? For instance, he might know that Theaetetus is a human being, or at least an animal.

Socrates states that Theaetetus will not be known until a memorial of his snub-nose and other traits have been imprinted upon his memory (208c; cf. 143e-a). Only then will that memorial recall Theaetetus to his mind if he should meet him again. We can recall that Socrates was in fact first acquainted with Theaetetus through just this common similarity. Socrates first distinguished Theaetetus by means of his likeness to himself. Did Socrates not yet know Theaetetus there?

If Socrates is correct, then even a right opinion, to be right, requires a difference by which to distinguish its object from other objects. Thus opinion will suffer an infinite regress (it will not be *of thing*) unless we can show that something is already known in manner without resorting to yet another difference. Knowledge cannot be reduced to difference or sheer negation.[328] Or perhaps our first *kinds* of knowledge already implicitly present us both with that which is common and that which is specific. Parmenides might want to remind us that all being is one. He may in *some respect*, be correct but more needs to be said or distinguished. It is, after all, Parmenides who denied the possibility of distinction and negation.

---

[328] There are limits upon difference. Aristotle's categories of being reflect some of these limits. For instance, one cannot infinitely ascend from one quality to another without arriving at substance. Also, one substance does not infinitely inhere in higher substances. Substance is *being per se*, while quality is *being per accidens*. In saying this, the generic limits of our analysis can be quasi-expressed by the terms 'this' and 'this sort'.

Socrates told us that he holds him and his teaching in a certain awe or reverence.

The logos of difference seems therefore to have failed.

In a remarkable moment, Socrates states: to tell a person who has an opinion of something that he must yet acquire an opinion of a difference (if he is to opine about that thing) is like giving a blind man directions (209e). This might mean that the blind would yet need further directions. Or it might suggest that to seek to acquire what one *already has* is indeed like losing one's sight! One who has lost their sight is precisely one who *has* seen or known something. Even our opinions may not be entirely empty of knowledge and difference. Though, it may be that there is yet a real *difference* between opinion and knowledge.

If having a difference is to know a thing, then to tell someone with an opinion to acquire a difference is to enjoin them to acquire knowledge. But if to have an opinion already requires having a difference, then knowledge is nothing but acquiring an opinion about an opinion! In this light, the definition of knowledge as true opinion with a logos appears to be empty.

Recapitulation;

They therefore dismiss the dream of defining knowledge as true opinion with a logos. Socrates then enumerates their major conclusions (210a). Neither perception, nor true opinion, nor true opinion with a logos is knowledge. Theaetetus believes that he has brought forth more offspring with Socrates than he could have on his own (210b). Their conversation has in this respect been fruitful, even though every offspring has been declared a wind-egg.

Socrates concludes that although they did not find what knowledge is, Theaetetus will at least, in the future, be pregnant with better thoughts if he pursues this question again.

One might wonder if such offspring would be *altogether* different. Socrates says their conversation will also help Theaetetus be less harsh, gentler, and moderate. He will not suppose himself to know what he does not know (210c). In doing this, Socrates has accomplished the limits of his maieutic art. He knows no other, even among great and wonderful men, who can accomplish more.

Finally, he declares that he must be off to answer a lawsuit against him, a lawsuit which will ultimately result in his execution. However, he will return the next day, before his trial, and resume their conversation. This is, in fact, what is recorded in the *Sophist*.

Works Cited

Aristotle, and Joe Sachs. *Nicomachean Ethics.* Newbury, Mass: Focus Pub./R. Pullins, 2002.

Austin, John L., and Geoffrey James Warnock. *Sense and Sensibilia.* Repr. London: Oxford Univ. Press, 2010.

Burnet, John, and James Hastings. "Socrates." *Encyclopaedia of Religion and Ethics.* New York: Charles Scribner's Sons, 1908.

Caldecott, Stratford. *Beauty for Truth's Sake: On the Re-Enchantment of Education.* Grand Rapids, Mich.: Brazos Press, 2017.

Calvin, Jean. *Institutes of the Christian Religion.* Edited by John Thomas McNeill. The library of Christian classics. Louisville, Ky. London: Westminster John Knox Press, 20.

Chesterton, G. K., George William Rutler, and George J. Marlin. *The Collected Works of G. K. Chesterton. Vol. 2: St. Francis of Assisi.* San Francisco: Ignatius Press, 1986.

"Cleue - Middle English Compendium." Accessed March 17, 2021. https://quod.lib.umich.edu/m/middle-english-dictionary/dictionary/MED8009/track?counter=1&search_id=5606458.

Colton, Randall. "Modern and Contemporary Philosophy," 2017.

———. "Philosophical Anthropology." Course Notes. Holy Apostles College and Seminary, Cromwell, CT, spring 2019.

Coppens, S.J., Charles. *A Brief Text-Book of Logic and Mental Philosophy.* Schwarz, Kirwin, Fauss, 1891.

Cranney, Carl. "Opposites in Plato and Aristotle," 2005.

Deely, John. *Introducing Semiotic: Its History and Doctrine.* Advances in semiotics. Bloomington: Indiana University Press, 1982.

Friedlander, Paul. *Plato: An Introduction*. Princeton University Press, 2016.

Gallagher, Kenneth. *The Philosophy of Knowledge*. New York: Sheed and Ward, 1964.

Gilson, Etienne. *From Aristotle to Darwin and Back Again: A Journey in Final Causality, Species, and Evolution*. San Francisco: Ignatius Press, 2009.

Hancock, Curtis, and Eduardo Bernot. "The True, the False, the Lie, and the Fake." Course Notes. Holy Apostles College and Seminary, Cromwell, CT, spring 2021.

Heraclitus, and Thomas M. Robinson. *Fragments*. Toronto: University of Toronto Press, 1991.

Hopkins, Gerard Manley. *Poems and Prose of Gerard Manley Hopkins*. Repr. Penguin Classics. Harmondsworth: Penguin Books, 2000.

James, William. *The Will to Believe*, n.d. https://www.gutenberg.org/files/26659/26659-h/26659-h.htm.

John Paul II. *Love and Responsibility*. Boston: Pauline Books & Media, 2013.

———. "Redemptoris Missio," December 7, 1990. Vatican Archive. http://www.vatican.va/content/john-paul-ii/en/encyclicals/documents/hf_jp-ii_enc_07121990_redemptoris-missio.html.

Kierkegaard, Soren. *Provocations: Spiritual Writings of Kierkegaard*. Plough Publishing House, 2014.

Klein, Jacob. *A Commentary on Plato's Meno*, 2012.

———. *Greek Mathematical Thought and the Origin of Algebra*. New York: Dover Publications, 1992.

Klein, Jacob, Robert B. Williamson, and Elliott Zuckerman. *Lectures and Essays*. Annapolis, Md: St. John's College Press, 1985.

Knasas, John. "Gilson vs. Maritain: The Start of Thomistic Metaphysics,." *Communis* 43, no. 3 (1990): 169–183.

Kreeft, Peter, and Trent Dougherty. *Socratic Logic: A Logic Text Using Socratic Method, Platonic Questions & Aristotelian Principles.* Ed. 3.1. South Bend, Ind: St. Augustine's Press, 2010.

Kuhn, Thomas S. *The Structure of Scientific Revolutions.* 3rd ed. Chicago, IL: University of Chicago Press, 1996.

Lewis, C. S. *The Problem of Pain.* San Francisco: HarperSanFrancisco, 2001.

Liddell, Henry George, Robert Scott, Henry Stuart Jones, and Roderick McKenzie. *A Greek-English Lexicon.* Clarendon Press ; Oxford University Press, 1996.

MacDonald, George, Arthur Hughes, and Ursula K Le Guin. *The Princess and the Goblin*, 2016.

MacIntyre, Alasdair C. *Three Rival Versions of Moral Enquiry.* Reprint. Notre Dame, Ind: Univ. of Notre Dame Press, 2006.

McInerny, D.Q. *Philosophical Psychology.* Fraternity Publications, 1999.

Merzbach, Uta, and Carl Boyer. *History of Mathematics.* Third. John Wiley & Sons, Inc., 2011.

Mollin, Alfred. *An Introduction to Ancient Greek.* 4th edition. Lanham, MD: Hamilton Books, 2018.

Percy, Walker. *The Message in the Bottle: How Queer Man Is, How Queer Language Is, and What One Has to Do with the Other.* New York: Picador USA : Distributed by St. Martin's Press, 2000.

Pieper, Josef. *Faith, Hope, Love.* San Francisco: Ignatius Press, 1997.

———. *In Defense of Philosophy.* San Francisco: Ignatius Press, 1992.

———. *Leisure: The Basis of Culture; The Philosophical Act.* San Francisco: Ignatius Press, 2009.

———. *The Four Cardinal Virtues: Prudence, Justice, Fortitude, Temperance*. Notre Dame, Ind.: University of Notre Dame Press, 2011.

———. *The Silence of St. Thomas: Three Essays*. South Bend, Ind: St. Augustine's Press, 1999.

Plato, George Anastaplo, and Laurence Berns. *Plato's Meno*. The Focus philosophical library. Newburyport, MA: Focus Pub./R. Pullins Co, 2004.

Plato, Eva T. H. Brann, Peter Kalkavage, and Eric Salem. *Plato's Phaedo*. Focus philosophical library. Newburyport, MA: Focus Publishing /R. Pullins Company, 1998.

Plato, and Francis Macdonald Cornford. *Plato's Cosmology: The Timaeus of Plato*, 2014.

Plato, and Peter Kalkavage. *Timaeus*. Second edition. Indianapolis: Focus, 2016.

Plato, and Joe Sachs. *Plato's Theaetetus*. The focus philosophical library. Newburyport, MA: Focus Pub./R. Pullins Co, 2004.

Plato, and Paul Shorey. *Plato in Twelve Volumes, Vols. 5 & 6*. Reprinted. The Loeb classical library 123. Cambridge, Mass.: Harvard Univ. Press, 2006.

Pólya, George. *How to Solve It*. Princeton University Press, 2004.

Pope Paul VI. "Gaudium et Spes," December 7, 1965. Vatican Archive. https://www.vatican.va/archive/hist_councils/ii_vatican_council/documents/vat-ii_const_19651207_gaudium-et-spes_en.html.

Redpath, Peter. "The One and the Many." Course Notes. Holy Apostles College and Seminary, Cromwell, CT, fall 2019.

Reichmann, James B. *Philosophy of the Human Person*. Chicago, Ill: Loyola University Press, 1985.

Saussure, Ferdinand de. *Course in General Linguistics*. Open Court, 1986.

Searle, John R. *Seeing Things as They Are: A Theory of Perception*. Oxford ; New York: Oxford University Press, 2015.

Sertillanges, A.D. *The Intellectual Life: Its Spirit, Conditions, Methods*. Washington, D.C.: The Catholic University of America Press, 1998.

St. Thomas Aquinas. "Commentary on Aristotle's De Caelo," n.d. https://isidore.co/aquinas/DeCoelo.htm.

———. "De Veritate," n.d. https://aquinas.cc/la/la/~QDeVer.

St. Thomas Aquinas, and Armand Mauer. "Commentary on Boethius's De Trinitate." Toronto: Pontifical Institute of Mediaeval Studies, 1953, n.d. https://aquinas.cc/la/en/~DeTrin.

Thomas. *Summa Theologica*. Complete English ed. Christian Classics, 1981.

Tolkien, J. R. R. *The Fellowship of the Ring*. The Lord of the rings pt. 1. Boston: Mariner Books/Houghton Mifflin Harcourt, 2012.

Tredennick, Hugh. *Aristotle: in twenty-three volumes. 2: Posterior analytics. Topica*. Reprinted. The Loeb classical library 391. Cambridge, Mass: Harvard Univ. Press [u.a.], 2004.

Umphrey, Steward. *Is Knowledge True Opinion with a Logos?* Cassette Tape. Annapolis, Md, 1986.

Walker, D. P. "Kepler's Celestial Music." *Journal of the Warburg and Courtauld Institutes* 30 (1967): 228–250.

Weil, Simone. *Gravity and Grace*. Lincoln: University of Nebraska Press, 1997.

Wallace, William, and Rev. Griffithes Wheeler Thatcher. (1911). Avicenna. In *Encyclopedia Britannica* (11th ed., Vol. 3, p. 62-3).

Wippel, John F. *The Metaphysical Thought of Thomas Aquinas: From Finite Being to Uncreated Being*. Monographs of the Society for Medieval and Renaissance Philosophy no. 1.

Washington, D.C: Catholic University of America Press, 2000.

Wittgenstein, Ludwig, G. E. M. Anscombe, and G. H. von Wright. *On Certainty*. Oxford: Blackwell, 1969.

www.ingramcontent.com/pod-product-compliance
Lightning Source LLC
Chambersburg PA
CBHW060831190426
43197CB00039B/2551